Just Policing, Not War

An Alternative Response to World Violence

Gerald W. Schlabach, editor

with

Drew Christiansen, S.J.

Ivan Kauffman

John Paul Lederach

Reina C. Neufeldt

Margaret R. Pfeil

Glen H. Stassen

Tobias Winright

Foreword by
Jim Wallis

A Michael Glazier Book

LITURGICAL PRESS
Collegeville, Minnesota

www.litpress.org

A Michael Glazier Book published by Liturgical Press

Excerpts from Second Vatican Council documents are from *Vatican Council II: The Basic Sixteen Documents.* A Completely Revised Translation in Inclusive Language. Edited by Austin Flannery, O.P. Northport, NY: Costello Publishing Company, 1996. Used with permission.

A version of Glen Stassen's chapter first appeared in the *Journal of the Society of Christian Ethics* 24, no. 2 (Fall/Winter 2004): 171–91, entitled "Just Peacemaking as Hermeneutical Key: The Need for International Cooperation in Preventing Terrorism." Permission to reprint material from that article is gratefully acknowledged.

Earlier versions of Gerald Schlabach's chapters appeared as "Just Policing: How War Could Cease to be a Church-Dividing Issue," in *Just Policing: Mennonite-Catholic Theological Colloquium 2002,* ed. Ivan J. Kauffman, Bridgefolk Series, no. 2 (Kitchener, Ontario: Pandora Press, 2004), 19–75; and in the *Journal of Ecumenical Studies* 41, no. 3–4 (Summer-Fall 2004): 409–30 (copyright © by the Journal of Ecumenical Studies). Permission from Pandora Press and the *Journal of Ecumenical Studies* to reprint this material is gratefully acknowledged.

Cover design by David Manahan, O.S.B. Photo courtesy of iStockphoto, © Oystein Litleskare.

1   2   3   4   5   6   7   8   9

Library of Congress Cataloging-in-Publication Data

Schlabach, Gerald.
  Just policing, not war : an alternative response to world violence / Gerald W. Schlabach . . . [et al.].
      p. cm.
  Includes bibliographical references and index.
    ISBN-13: 978-0-8146-5221-3
  1. Peace—Religious aspects—Christianity.   2. War—Religious aspects—Christianity.   3. Pacifism—Religious aspects—Christianity.
  4. Just war doctrine.   5. Christianity and international affairs.   I. Title.
    BT736.4.S335 2007
    261.8'73—dc22   2007001371

Dedicated, with gratitude,
to the peacemaking legacies of
John Howard Yoder
and
John Paul II

All these factors force us to undertake a completely fresh appraisal of war.

Second Vatican Council, *Gaudium et Spes*, §80

Defining effective international government in this way is of course setting an idealistic goal; but it is less idealistic than the idea that military action could be truly an instrument of justice.

John Howard Yoder, *The Christian Witness to the State*, 47

Contents

This introductory chapter clarifies the nature of the just policing proposal. Christians from across the longstanding divide between pacifism and just war thought already find themselves converging and cooperating around a shared recognition that justice and peace are interdependent. Still, important questions remain. The proposal here is not for premature compromise, therefore, but for mutually challenging attention to the place of policing in each tradition, and the ways that policing differs from warfare. In order to demonstrate both the potential and the urgency of taking up this challenge, the chapter surveys the larger developments in modern warfare, Christian reflection, and related peacemaking initiatives that have made the current proposal possible.

Historic pacifism has failed to overcome the popular view that it entails an unwillingness to act decisively in the face of evil and thus means "passive-ism." Secular anti-war movements have largely remained just that—negative. The difficulty for both, Kauffman argues, is that they are clearer about what they are against than what they are for. Meanwhile, warfare by its very nature negates and destroys, even when it does so for justifiable reasons. Paradoxically, however, warfare is what most people think of as "doing something" active, positive, and just in the face of evil. Thankfully, with the development of Gandhian nonviolence, the success of active nonviolence in the face of brutal regimes around the world, and its under-noted embrace by Pope John Paul II, we no longer need to choose between just war and pacifism.

In the 1990s Stassen and some twenty other scholars representing both just war and pacifist traditions helped develop the tools of just peacemaking theory. Applying these tools, Stassen argues on the basis of recent case studies that there are alternatives to warmaking as an anti-terrorism strategy that are more not less realistic. In making this case, Stassen further develops Kauffman's argument that anti-war movements can only mobilize wide public support when they offer concrete proposals rather than simply saying no to war (as in the case of pacifism) or even specific wars (as in the case of just war).

PART II

Just Policing:
The Proposal

Schlabach argues that Christians might be able to move beyond their centuries-old impasse over warfare if representatives of the just war and pacifist traditions honestly acknowledged their respective neglect of the ethics of policing. Just war thinkers need to acknowledge ways in which warfare and policing differ. Pacifists need to recognize the implications of their calls for greater respect for international law. Joint examination of policing may thus point us towards conditions for the possibility of agreement concerning war. Along the way, the chapter locates the "just policing" proposal in relationship to denominational affirmations of both just war and active nonviolence, as well as the just peacemaking initiative by Christian ethicists of various traditions who identified shared normative practices that would render war increasingly obsolete.

Chapter 5
Practicing for Just Policing

Using the model of "community policing," Schlabach demonstrates ways that Christians affiliated with just war and pacifist traditions can collaborate to create practices that make less violent—or even nonviolent—policing possible. By way of illustration, he encourages Mennonites to continue developing alternatives to the retributive criminal justice system and conducting pilot projects for civilian-based defense. Likewise, he encourages Catholics to transform the just war tradition into just policing (and *just* just policing) by creating institutions that reflect more fully the tradition's presumption against violence. Finally, the theological category of vocation is used to reassure skeptics (particularly pacifists) that ecclesiological convergence need not mean capitulation.

PART III
And *Just* Policing:
Elaborations

Chapter 6
Whose Justice? Which Relationality?

Pfeil critiques the Turner Johnson/Weigel school of just war thinking that sees the obligation to preserve justice rather than a presumption against violence as most basic to the just war theory. Pfeil presses their assumptions about what constitutes justice and order in the first place. To demonstrate that Weigel's and Johnson's conception of justice is not self-evident she samples the indigenous peacemaking practices of a non-European culture. She then contrasts their position with a restorative account of justice designed to contribute to a tradition and culture of peace. While retribution involves the infliction of pain to vindicate justice, a restorative account allows the hermeneutic of peace to elicit transformative means of addressing the harm done. Biblical *shalom* thus becomes the horizon for the work of justice.

Chapter 7
Community Policing as a Paradigm for International Relations

Building on his work to collate just war criteria with the ethics of domestic policing, Winright provides additional background on different models of policing, especially the concept and practice of "community policing." He thus tests Schlabach's suggestion that it provides a promising paradigm for extension into the international sphere. In contrast to "crime fighter models" of policing, the community policing or "social peacekeeper" model holds potential for being extended into the international system without making violent use of force the very *raison d'être* of policing. Winright closes by assessing the prospects for this actually happening.

Chapter 8
Just Policing and International Order: Is it Possible?

Neufeldt brings the concept of just policing into dialogue with the fundamentals of international relations. Her chapter focuses on the theories that underpin and affect how politicians and bureaucrats think about the state system and their range of options for international order or just policing. She begins by examining central assumptions of just policing that are important concepts in international relations debates—notions of community, order, and the common good. She then views the concept of just policing through a series of theoretically-driven lenses. The first two lenses are the more traditional lenses of liberal internationalism and realism. The second two lenses are products of newer technologies and have a greater emphasis on the dynamics of change—globalization and constructivism. The final section of the paper imagines the newer technologies of change in action, in order to help visualize just policing in practice. The chapter ends with questions for a future research agenda on viable just policing at the international level.

PART IV

Conclusions:
The Nearing Horizon

Based on his experience as both a leading theorist and practitioner of international conflict transformation and peacebuilding, Lederach focuses on practical ways in which just policing is already available to peacebuilders and local partners. "Doables" are the small steps available in situations of seemingly intractable armed conflict. Identifying such doables is especially important to peace activists with strong convictions against the use of violence, but may also encourage those from the just war tradition who are wondering how best to move towards a just policing model. Asking what strategies are available, accessible, and acceptable, Lederach explores community policing in post-conflict zones, nonviolent peacemaking, and the establishment of community peace zones. A growing trend toward focusing on *human* security rather than *national* security provides a basis for continuing collaboration in ways that both just war and pacifist practitioners can affirm.

Benefiting from his vantage point as a member of the International Catholic-Mennonite Dialogue and editor-in-chief of the U.S. Jesuit weekly *America*, Christiansen argues for the increasing salience of the just policing proposal in international politics and in ecumenical dialogue. He argues for just policing in light of the growing political plausibility of international mechanisms for conflict resolution and transformation. He also notes convergences, on several fronts, between Catholics and Mennonites as to the nature and mission of the church and its relation to the world. With each point, Christiansen poses questions for both Catholics and Mennonites as to how they might further narrow the distance between them and suggests what would be required of each church to implement just policing as a church-uniting strategy.

Foreword

Jim Wallis

In the twenty-first-century world, many threats to peace are proving far graver than conventional wars between states: ethnic conflicts, states that violate the rights of their citizens to the point of genocide, and terrorist violence. Increasingly, this reality challenges the traditional Christian doctrines of pacifism and just war. Having debated the ethics of war for decades, Christians who seek effective means to combat terrorism sense that their traditional pacifist and just war positions both have limitations. A pacifism that refuses to recognize the reality of evil and stands above responding to the terrible violence of terrorism and genocide is not morally acceptable. And a pacifism that simply objects to war, but has no alternative answers to the real threats of violence—whether sponsored by international networks of terror or by states—isn't very helpful. Nor is classical just-war doctrine particularly relevant; it simply isn't enough to offer endless academic scrutiny of criteria for fighting war, especially when the arguments usually end up justifying wars, rather than actually preventing any. Just-war thinking has few answers to new forms of violence that are not as vulnerable to traditional war-fighting methods.

Recent examples are illustrative.

Following the attacks of September 11, 2001, the U.S. administration immediately turned to war against Afghanistan as its response. While Afghanistan's Taliban regime was certainly providing an operating base for al Qaeda, the solution to defeating the *tactic* of terrorism is not primarily military. Drying up the financial resources of terrorists, coordinating international intelligence, and relying on international law and institutions reinforced by a multinational policing force would have been far more effective. As we now see six years later, the battle against the Taliban continues and terror networks have simply spread around the world.

In Iraq, Saddam Hussein was indeed a brutal dictator, but war was not the answer. The establishment of an international tribunal (or the International Criminal Court) could have indicted Hussein and others of his regime, sought their capture, and put them on trial. A preemptive war of choice, fought against overwhelming world opinion and without the support of the United Nations Security Council has led instead to the current disaster in Iraq. Almost universally, Iraqis now view the United States as an occupier rather than liberator, while levels of violence and terrorism continue to grow.

Darfur raises another set of questions. In the face of a genocide that has killed as many as 400,000 people, the U.N. Security Council has demanded that the government of Sudan accept a peacekeeping force that can protect the people. Yet the government flatly refuses, and the United Nations appears unable to respond.

The common thread is that a new world order must be based on multilateral rather than unilateral action, international law rather than military power, and the deliberations of the community of nations rather than the sole decisions of the world's largest superpower. The dangers that terrorists and dictators pose certainly require opposition. It is a mistake to underestimate the threats they present to world peace. Resisting them requires a commitment to real multilateral action—an effective international court of justice, perhaps the development and funding of sizable multinational peacekeeping forces prepared to intervene to protect human rights, a broad-based commitment to selective but consistent economic sanctions, and a strong preference for genuinely international solutions. This will not be easy. It will mean strengthening international institutions and the rule of law that the United States often resists, perhaps in order to preserve its superpower position.

It also means a commitment to exploring alternatives other than war to resolve international conflicts.

Specifically, the creation of a much stronger international court could be central to resolving many of these conflicts. War criminals could be indicted for their crimes, and international warrants issued for their arrest. Bringing the full weight of international opinion to bear against criminal behavior would be much more effective if there were legal and institutional mechanisms to do so. The international community could then isolate the perpetrators and undermine their power without attacking their people.

To back up such judgments with more than symbolism, it would be necessary to create an international police force with adequate backing, sufficient funding, and extensive training in conflict resolution. Such a force should be genuinely international, using personnel from the regions where conflicts occur as well as those from other countries. Lightly armed—or unarmed, as Gandhi suggested—this force would bring the physical presence that the resolution of conflict usually requires, but without the military provocation that can easily escalate a crisis. If the full and legal weight of world opinion were behind such a force, petty dictators would have to think twice about attacking it.

Clearly, however, those of us committed to nonviolence must also examine the moral question of the potential use of lethal force by police action. As far back as 1972, theologian and ethicist John Howard Yoder wrote about a difference between the unrestrained violence of war and the potential for lethal force in policing. Since then, various conferences and publications have taken up this discussion. Gerald Schlabach now brings together in this volume a series of helpful essays that deepen the conversation.

In his introduction, Schlabach reviews the changing nature of war that led the Second Vatican Council to say that "these factors force us to undertake a completely fresh appraisal of war." He then raises the key question that the remaining essays in the book address: "Is policing different enough from war that something *more* like policing (humanitarian military intervention) could possibly constitute a practice for abolishing war?"

In the first section of the book, "Things that Make for Peace," Ivan Kauffman presents a short history of the church's response to war through the centuries, and the dilemma they faced after 9/11 as the Bush administration proceeded to launch a war against Afghanistan. Unable to strongly condemn the war because of the need for justice, but also unable to support it without violating basic moral beliefs, the majority of Christians accepted it as a necessary evil. The moral crisis that ensued, he suggests, is leading to a new understanding of peacebuilding in which just policing could play a central role.

Glen Stassen then recounts the development of just peacemaking theory, with a combination of initiatives that can both prevent conflicts from beginning and end them after they have begun. He offers a number of useful examples in which practitioners have employed these initiatives and made a difference.

Schlabach, in the book's two central chapters, initiates the fundamental discussion. He examines policing and the just war tradition, with a detailed moral examination of the significant ethical differences between war and policing. He also examines policing and the pacifist tradition, suggesting that the question here may be a vocational one rather than a matter of core principles. Finally, he reviews the convergence of the developments in nonviolent action and the framework of community policing, offering suggestions specifically for Mennonites and Catholics that could continue those trends.

The remainder of the book consists of responses and dialogue around these proposals from Mennonite and Catholic scholars. Margaret Pfeil engages an intra-Catholic debate over whether retributive justice or restorative justice provides the proper grounding for just war thinking. Tobias Winright explores more deeply the emergence of community policing as a paradigm for international relations in a model of "social peacekeeping." Reina Neufeldt discusses the concept of just policing in relation to fundamental theories of international relations—internationalism, realism, globalization, and constructivism. John Paul Lederach brings his experience as an international conflict mediator, noting trends toward policing in post-accord settings, nonviolent peacekeeping, and community peace zones. Drew Christiansen describes the changes that have occurred in both Catholic and Mennonite understandings of the church, and the further changes that each tradition would need to make in order to accept the concept of just policing.

One standard response to those who question war because of their principles is to affirm their moral integrity but then dismiss them under the assumption that war remains both necessary and unavoidable as a response to real evil. Alternatives to war may garner admiration for their principles, but assumed wanting in their effectiveness. Seldom does war receive comparable scrutiny to evaluate its actual effectiveness in responding and resolving the reality of evil. The utter failure of the war in Iraq, as a response to evil, could help us change such thinking.

It is time to put aside the assumption that war is the most effective response to real evil. It is time to subject the methodology of war to the same scrutiny that its alternatives have received. In the case of Iraq, the option of war has arguably made everything it portended to solve even worse. And the consequences are now visible for all to see. Other alternatives might have produced a far preferable result. They include a preference for international rather than preemptive solutions, the use of international law more than military force, a many-faceted response of carrots and sticks, and a robust peacekeeping force with the authority and capacity to enforce the demands of the international community—yes, including the use of force, but very targeted instead of indiscriminate. In the Christian tradition war has always been suspect at the point of moral principle. It is only fair to demand that the methodology of war also submit to vigorous examination of whether it is really even effective, and that other methods receive consideration and development

In that important discussion, this book could play a critical role. It is time to explore an alternative to war—not just because modern warfare fails to meet ethical standards, but also because it is failing to resolve the genuine threats of real evil in our time. We must find a better way.

Jim Wallis is author of *God's Politics* and president of Sojourners/Call to Renewal.

Acknowledgments

As an agenda for Christians divided over appropriate means of peace-making in a violent world, just policing resides at the confluence of multiple disciplines and conversations. Christian ethics, ecumenism, journalistic assessment of "the signs of the times," policy analysis, peace and conflict studies, international relations, and political science have all flowed into the concept of just policing—along with attention to emerging trends in community policing and restorative justice. As author of three core chapters in this volume and editor for the entire project, I am grateful above all to the friends and colleagues who have brought expertise from their own fields to the task of exploring, testing, and filling out the concept of just policing. Drew Christiansen S.J., Ivan Kauffman, John Paul Lederach, Reina Neufeldt, Margaret Pfeil, Glen Stassen, and Tobias Winright do not all concur with every one of my own arguments concerning warfare and policing. But that leaves me all the more grateful for their contributions here, and for their concurrence that just policing is a concept and a conversation worth pursuing.

In the form that I first proposed it, at least, the concept and the agenda of just policing emerged against the background of two major historic conversations. One of these is well known. It is no accident the broad outline of my argument—that pacifist and just war traditions must each come clean on the place of policing in their ethical systems, but must do so in conversation with each other—came to me in a rush one Sunday morning at Eucharist in the fall of 2001. Much else was rushing and focusing the minds of many in the weeks and months following September 11.

Yet another less frantic conversation of historic proportions had quietly been taking place for three years, and it provided the occasion for an initial paper on just policing. The first-ever international dialogue between the Pontifical Council for Promoting Christian Unity (PCPCU) and the Mennonite World Conference (MWC) had begun in 1998. Though I have never been a participant in this dialogue, and am acquainted with only a few of its delegates, Ivan Kauffman and I were following its progress closely and had convened a colloquium of Mennonite and Catholic scholars to provide unofficial background papers that might be useful to the delegations. I thus wish to thank the scholars in the colloquium who first responded to my paper: Joseph Capizzi, J. Denny Weaver, and Stanley Hauerwas. Likewise, I wish to thank the leaders of the international dialogue who were receptive toward our outside input: co-chairs Helmut Harder and Bishop Joseph Martino, as well as Larry Miller of the MWC and Monsignor John Radano of the PCPCU.

Two groups of friends and colleagues have taken special interest in this project as it has continued to develop. Bridgefolk is a grassroots movement for dialogue and unity between Mennonites and Roman Catholics that I have helped lead since its inception in 1999; it is with special affection that I acknowledge the friendship and support of Bridgefolk Board members over these years: co-Chairs Marlene Kropf and Abbot John Klassen O.S.B., Sheri Hostetler, Susan Kennel Harrison, Father Rene McGraw O.S.B., Weldon Nisly, Father William Skudlarek O.S.B., Regina Wilson, and (again, significantly!) Ivan Kauffman.

Since 2001 I have also had the privilege of serving on the Peace Committee that advises the international program of Mennonite Central Committee. As a setting that brings together academics, practitioners, and church representatives, the MCC Peace Committee is a particularly fruitful venue for a Christian ethicist who might otherwise attend mainly to scholarly debates. Though I have not asked and would not expect a group of historic peace church representatives to endorse just policing whole cloth, MCC and its Peace Committee have provided a set of resources and conversations that have greatly enriched this work. Of special note are my fellow team members in the MCC Peace Theology Project, which conducted a series of consultations in 2003 and 2004, resulting in the book *At Peace and Unafraid: Public Order, Security, and the Wisdom of the Cross* (Herald Press, 2006): Duane Friesen, Lydia Harder, and Pamela Leach, along with MCC staff members Robert and Judy Zimmerman Herr.

Finally, two of my former professors at the University of Notre Dame deserve special mention. Todd Whitmore was not able to contribute a chapter to this volume, but indirectly was a major contributor. An extended conversation he and I had over lunch a couple years after I graduated may mark the chronological start of the just policing project.

I hope that he will yet find opportunity to lay out his own proposals for the kind of institutions and practices that the Catholic Church needs if it is to receive just war teaching in fact and not just in theory.

And looming behind all of this is the presence of the late John Howard Yoder. The many references and footnotes to Yoder in my chapters only begin to indicate my debt to him, not only with regard to the question of policing but in his theology of Christian pacifism and his analysis of the just war tradition. I cannot attribute every idea I might owe to Yoder, not only because my reading of his work spans thirty years, but because I learned his analysis of the just war tradition less from his writing than from a doctoral seminar on that topic at Notre Dame. If I could hand Yoder a copy of this book, it would be with the expectation that I would shortly receive one of his characteristically trenchant multi-page critiques. Nonetheless, it is my most fervent hope that he would recognize here an outworking of hints and suggestions he left us, done with something of the care and rigor he taught us, located in a context of "believers church" discernment and ecumenical collaboration, which he showed us can converge.

Gerald W. Schlabach

INTRODUCTION

Chapter 1

Just Policing and the Reevaluation of War in a Less Divided Church

Gerald W. Schlabach

If the best intentions of the just war theorists were operational, they could only allow for just policing, not warfare at all. If Christian pacifists can in any way support, participate, or at least not object to operations with recourse to limited but potentially lethal force, that will only be true for just policing. Just policing—and *just* just policing.

That, in a nutshell, is the twofold thesis of the "just policing" proposal. What it calls for is not a grand convergence right now—or a mere compromise ever—between just-war and pacifist traditions. Rather, what it proposes is an agenda for mutual, mutually challenging, and self-critical conversation that explores the conditions for the possibility of further convergence. It notes that in the long-standing Christian debate between pacifist and just war positions, the moral status of policing has received surprisingly little attention. And it holds out hope that joint attention to this unmapped territory might open up a new horizon in which the possibility of agreement concerning war might come into view. Just as importantly, it calls forth greater faithfulness and coherence on both sides—whether or not further convergence becomes possible.

In other words, the concept of just policing *suggests* that Christians divided over war *might* be able to converge sufficiently that war would cease to divide them. But it *insists* that both sides *must* come clean about their respective views on policing.

3

"All of These Factors . . ."

At the beginning of the twentieth century, only five percent of war casualties were civilians. By World War II, sixty-five percent of casualties were civilians. As the turn of the twenty-first century approached, according to a United Nations report, ninety percent of casualties in war were civilians, and of these, roughly half were children.[1]

Perhaps the horror of war in the modern era has numbed us to the horror of war in the modern era. Or perhaps we suffer from a deeper complacency. As the influential American Protestant theologian Reinhold Niebuhr once remarked: "Contemporary history is filled with manifestations of man's hysterias and furies; with evidences of his dæmonic capacity and inclination to break the harmonies of nature and defy the prudent canons of rational restraint. Yet no cumulation of contradictory evidence seems to disturb modern man's good opinion of himself."[2]

If Niebuhr's assessment of modern self-complacency in the face of human horrors is all too apt, it is not uniformly so. When Roman Catholic bishops gathered from around the world in the early 1960s for the Second Vatican Council, modern war did disturb them deeply. True, in promising that the church's role was to accompany humanity on its journey as a generous friend rather than a stubborn adversary, the bishops put forward a fresh and markedly hopeful opinion of the modern world.[3] Yet honest friendship, as well as solidarity "especially [with] those who are poor or afflicted,"[4] also required a frank naming of modern griefs, anxieties, and violence. Christian love of neighbor carried an "inescapable duty to make ourselves the neighbor" to the weak and defenseless, which in turn required the council to name "all offenses against life itself" as nothing less than "criminal." Prefiguring Catholic moral concerns that would grow prominent in coming decades, the council identified abortion and euthanasia as examples—but also named genocide, torture, "subhuman living conditions, arbitrary imprisonment, deportation, slavery, prostitution," and "murder."[5]

When warfare fails to meet the "prudent canons" needed to qualify as just war, it really can bear no other name than a "type of murder." But war should be infamous rather than numbing in other ways besides. Throughout human history even putatively just wars have carried with them many of the *other* "infamies" on the council's list too, such as torture, arbitrary imprisonment, enslavement, and prostitution. War has often left in its wake "subhuman living conditions"—even for the victors and for those they claim to protect.

Longtime *New York Times* war correspondent Chris Hedges has poignantly described the devastating effects of war even on its victors and heroes. War is an addiction, he insisted in a 2002 book with a title tinged in darkly subtle irony, *War is a Force that Gives Us Meaning*. Hedges has seen its narcotic effect at work in warriors, correspondents, and civilian populations alike. However well a war may have been justified for the protection of a people and its culture, "in warfare the state seeks to destroy its own [authentic] culture" in order to forge a war culture with an ironclad cohesion capable of destroying the enemy's culture.[6] Mythmakers of all sorts peddle its mystique of heroism, camaraderie, and the opportunity to rise above ourselves.

But war's reality leaves actual warriors deeply scarred. However graphic the media portrayals of warfare may be, they still leave out the throat-gripping reality of fear. Outside of actual battle, all portrayals are sterile and safe. "We do not smell rotting flesh, hear the cries of agony, or see before us blood and entrails seeping out of bodies. We view from a distance the rush, the excitement, but feel none of the awful gut-wrenching anxiety and humiliation that come with mortal battle."[7] Though society now has a name for the effect of long-haunting memories from war, post-traumatic stress syndrome, such clinical language can become one more mechanism for shielding ourselves from war's reality. With modern weapons in "the universe of total war," wrote Hedges, soldiers "can kill hundreds or thousands of people in seconds . . . [and] only have time to reflect later." But "by then these soldiers often have been discarded, left as broken men in a civilian society that does not understand them and does not want to understand them."[8]

To subject oneself to such scarring of body and mind—perhaps this simply reflects how heroic is the self-sacrifice of warriors who give themselves in the defense of others. Perhaps a growing recognition of the complex and lasting psychological scars that war inflicts even on its victors can demonstrate just how much they have been sacrificing all along. Perhaps. Many families tell of aging veterans who have lived lives of pained silence, never speaking their experiences except reluctantly, when prompted, if at all. Family members and fellow citizens naturally desire to honor their soldiers, assuring both themselves and those they honor that their warriors' sacrifice has meaning. To countenance the possibility that the horror of war had no larger meaning or just purpose can seem even more horrible than war itself. In rituals private and public, therefore, the protected cultivate a gratitude that takes on a life of its own, quite apart from the gains and losses of the wars fought in their name, for their protection.

Here, however, we face another problem: The very distinction between protector and protected has been eroding at least since the French Revolution. If the percentage of civilian casualties in war has risen from five to ninety percent in the last century, that is but a cold statistical marker for this grim reality. Consider the following phenomena, and note what they all have in common:

- Mass armies: When French revolutionaries invented the citizens' army and Napoleon showed its power by marching across Europe in record time, they also created the expectation that any civilian, at least all males in the prime of life, were potential combatants. If war had once been the affair of gentlemen and nobles or aspirants to their class this has not been the case for two centuries. Military conscription has been one result. And in many wars, the targeting of all males except the oldest and youngest has been another result.

- Industrial mobilization: To be sure, modern militaries may now depend less on mass conscription than they once did, but they depend on technology all the more. The need to design, produce, and pay for military technology turns entire industries—no, entire economies—into military machines. Legally, manufacturers and workers may be noncombatants. But strategically, they become decisive targets.

- Threat of nuclear annihilation: In the ultimate example and symbol of modern warfare, these first two phenomena converge. The destructive potential of scientific and industrial warfare reaches an absolute. Discriminatory targeting that would distinguish between combatant and noncombatant all but disappears. The likelihood of nuclear escalation in fact puts the entire planet at risk. Actual weapon deployment may require only a handful of soldiers, aviators, or sailors, but that is because entire academic, economic, and industrial sectors have prepared the high-tech weapon. The inherent purpose of such weapons is at worst to incinerate and at best to terrorize entire populations.

- Guerrilla warfare: None of this means, of course, that all war in the modern world is high tech. Nations and insurgents who are too poor for high-tech weaponry can still acquire conventional and cast-off second-hand weaponry that richer nations put up for sale. To compensate for their disadvantages, guerrilla movements have sought to marshal and blend into the very populations they have claimed to liberate and hoped to rule.

- Low-intensity warfare: Recognizing the power of guerrilla warfare, even nations and militaries with the greatest available firepower have found that their most effective counter-measure is often to engage in their own guerrilla-style, low-level warfare. Generally such efforts can only be successful when coupled with another tactic from the guerrilla's playbook, projects aimed at "winning the hearts and minds" of the civilian population.

- Terrorism: Since September 11, 2001, many have claimed that the threat from non-state terrorist networks represents a qualitatively new phenomenon. If there is any truth to that claim it is overwrought. Terrorist networks simply recombine elements of the above in the context of a borderless globalized culture: They blend into some populations like guerrillas; they savvily appropriate the technologies of industrialized societies against them; they terrorize entire populations with biological, chemical, and suicide devices that some call "the poor man's nuclear weapons." Above all, they hope to extend their causes not by vanquishing the governing apparatus of any state but by imploding the psychological confidence, cohesion, and support within society that make the policies and very existence of a governing state possible.

- And on and on: In the early twenty-first century, military and civilian functions are becoming intermeshed in still other ways. In the U.S. war in Iraq, military functions have been "privatized" in unprecedented fashion through subcontracts for support services and security details. On the other hand, post-Cold War militaries of many nations find a new *raison d'être* as they lead or assist in the delivery of humanitarian aid in the wake of natural disasters.

By now the common thread running through these otherwise disparate phenomena should be clear. National leaders, armies, guerrillas, and terrorists alike all compete not so much against each other on the field of battle as they do for the power that resides in civil society. It is the middle sector of social organization that lies between the individual or the family and the state that has become the decisive arena of struggle. At great risk to civilian populations and cultures, militaries have entered this arena. But in doing so, they have acknowledged in backhanded ways that real and decisive power is social and political, not violent.

The blurring of distinctions between combatants and noncombatants can certainly pose a serious dilemma for all who seek to curtail militaristic policies or propose alternatives to war. The basic distinction between combatants and noncombatants is the cornerstone of all international law concerning warfare. Under their breath, antiwar activists might consider "The Law of War" an oxymoron, yet every time they call for respect of human rights in zones of conflict, or appeal to Geneva Conventions to make their case, they are relying on its principles and precedents. Likewise, the work of non-governmental relief organizations such as the International Red Cross and Red Crescent, Doctors Without Borders, or leading church agencies often depends on their ability to aid noncombatants on all sides without drawing charges from any side that they are aiding and abetting that side's enemies.

The dilemma is this: Some of these same groups are seeking to articulate an understanding of security that would rely far less (if at all) on military strategies; when they do so they themselves identify civil society as the decisive arena in which to contest social arrangements and political power. A document, *Vulnerability and Security,* by the Church of Norway's Commission on International Affairs urges us, for example, to conceive of security as pertaining to far more than sovereign states; the commission proposes "human security" as a broader but more accurate concept in light of the most pressing contemporary threats to life and well-being we actually face. While a well-run state structure contributes to human security, so too do all non-state efforts to enhance environmental and economic conditions.[9] Similarly, a study commissioned by the Peace Committee of Mennonite Central Committee sought to move beyond the "national security bubble" to a more inclusive conception of security based in the resourcefulness of societies themselves. As the study noted, however, this makes "especially important" the work of "non-governmental voluntary organizations and citizens' groups that bring together people from a wide variety of . . . backgrounds who seek to address the common good."[10]

So those who oppose militarism have an unmovable stake in maintaining distinctions between combatants and noncombatants. And yet the more convincingly they argue that civil society is its own source of security, the more incentive they provide for militaries to merge into civilian sectors after all in order to coordinate their efforts. Are we then at an impasse?

". . . these factors force us
to undertake a completely fresh appraisal of war."

When the Second Vatican Council explicitly turned to survey the issue of war and the prospects for peace in the modern world, its assessment of the "state of humanity" was anything but cheery and optimistic. In fact, it was nothing short of "deplorable."

> Even though recent wars have wrought immense material and moral havoc on the world, the devastation of battle still rages in some parts of the world. Indeed, now that every kind of weapon produced by modern science is used in war, the savagery of war threatens to lead the combatants to barbarities far surpassing those of former ages. Moreover, the complexity of the modern world and the network of relations between countries means that covert wars can be prolonged by new, insidious and subversive methods. In many cases terrorist methods are regarded as a new way of waging war. . . . The most infamous [of all crimes against humanity] is the rationalised and methodical extermination of an entire race, nation, or ethnic minority. . . .[11]

The bishops were hardly prepared to disavow the right of nations to defend themselves, though they did voice a new level of official ecclesial respect for Christian pacifists who renounced such rights for themselves. War that "[seeks] to conquer another nation" is clearly illicit, however. And so too are wars that surpass "lawful self-defense" simply because modern weaponry has become so indiscriminate.[12]

Clearly the bishops were alluding to nuclear armaments, but that was not all. The opening of the Second Vatican Council had coincided with the Cuban missile crisis, in which the United States and the Soviet Union came as close as they ever did to decimating the planet with nuclear weapons. Yet saturation bombing of entire cities during World War II had already demonstrated the indiscriminate character of modern warfare, even before the advent of the atomic age.[13] Pointedly, the bishops did not limit their exceedingly grave assessment of modern warfare to nuclear arms, even as they wrote:

> The proliferation of scientific weapons has immeasurably magnified the horror and wickedness of war. Warfare conducted with such weapons can inflict immense and indiscriminate havoc which goes far beyond the bounds of legitimate defense. Indeed, if the kind of weapons now stocked in the arsenals of the great powers were to be employed to the fullest, the result would be the almost complete reciprocal slaughter of one side by the other, not to speak of the widespread devastation that would follow

in the world and the deadly after-affects resulting from the use of such weapons.[14]

Thus the bishops gathered in solemn council from around the globe joined with recent popes Pius XII, John XXIII, and Paul VI in condemning total war: "Every act of war directed to the indiscriminate destruction of whole cities or vast areas with their inhabitants is a crime against God and humanity, which merits firm and unequivocal condemnation."[15]

But if war is wrong, what is right?[16] For all its historic prominence in Catholic deliberation over the ethics of war, the just war theory had never been promulgated as an official *doctrine* or dogma in the Catholic Church, and if ever there was a moment to do so, the Second Vatican Council was it. Insofar as just war principles simply reflect a mode of reasoning, reason itself does not require promulgation nor can it be rescinded. Nonetheless, a system of thought can certainly benefit from explicit endorsement. Although the bishops inevitably employed many just war principles in the key Vatican II section on war, and although they stated that "as long as the danger of war persists" governments have a "right to lawful self-defense," the bishops held back from endorsing just war reasoning as the church's preferred approach to war, much less as doctrine.

No, instead of either endorsing *or* renouncing, the bishops made a lateral move. They were, after all, pastors of a worldwide community that had just recommitted itself to accompanying all people in solidarity and friendship. As such they first needed alternatives that would provide the security to vulnerable peoples that military action has long claimed it could guarantee, but was evidently failing to do.

". . . a completely fresh appraisal of war."

When the Catholic Church speaks at its highest levels, as it did in the Second Vatican Council, it hardly ever makes pronouncements unless they represent settled understandings that have formed through a long and careful deliberative process. It is all the more striking, therefore, that on the matter of war the Second Vatican Council departed from longstanding practice and deeply Catholic sensibilities in order to *launch* a church-wide process of discernment instead. After surveying the growing violence and potential for catastrophe wrought by modern warfare, the bishops famously declared: "All these factors force us to undertake a completely fresh appraisal of war."[17]

That re-evaluation has not only continued in the forty years since; if anything it has grown more poignant. Catholics, and indeed all Christians for whom Vatican II was a historic watershed and source of hope, can be grateful for the courage by which the bishops opened up the question of peace and war for creativity and discernment. This implies that all of us throughout the whole "people of God" are responsible to discover and develop alternatives to war. But with every looming or protracted war, the unfinished business of re-evaluating war has divided Christian communities in painful debates.

Emblematic of the challenge that the Vatican council articulated not just for Catholics but for all Christians, and indeed the world community, is the plea that Pope Paul VI made on his first visit to the United Nations, and that Pope John Paul II made his own through frequent repetition. As John Paul II put it in no less weighty a document than his 1991 encyclical *Centesimus annus,*

> "Never again war!" No, never again war, which destroys the lives of in-nocent people, teaches how to kill, throws into upheaval even the lives of those who do the killing and leaves behind a trail of resentment and hatred, thus making it all the more difficult to find a just solution of the very problems which provoked the war.[18]

Thus, as John Paul also explained on various occasions, "war is a defeat for humanity."[19] Such a conviction has led to strenuous diplomatic efforts on the part of the Vatican to avoid particular wars, and even to pointed declarations that wars such as the U.S. invasion of Iraq would be unjust. Yet it has also prompted hasty clarifications that neither the pope nor the Holy See is "pacifist."[20]

From loyal Catholics to jaded journalists, the question thus arises: Just what are we to make of this? A nuanced theological explanation for the position of John Paul and other modern popes is certainly pos-sible. But Catholic teaching commends policy-makers and lay people for their active nonviolence, social justice activism, military service, or governmental leadership in the world alike, and they all have reason to feel puzzled.

That theological explanation? Because Catholicism does not under-stand human sin to have altogether destroyed human dignity and solidar-ity, human beings have the capacity to order their affairs without recourse to violence. *Hence: "Never again war!"* But because human sinfulness has joined with modern ideologies and technologies to produce some of the most systematic human rights abuses that the world has ever seen, the pope has not ruled out the need for humanitarian military interventions to halt egregious human rights abuses. *Hence: "The pope is not a pacifist."* Nonetheless, warfare as we know it exceeds the bounds of police action, killing innocent civilians, destroying social infrastructures, weakening international law, creating fresh resentments, and thus sowing the seeds of further conflict. *Hence: "War is always a defeat for humanity."*

Still, a nuanced theological explanation of this sort does not solve the practical problem. Until Christian leaders can propose or endorse politically viable alternatives to war, ordinary Christians and observers from outside the Christian community may be forgiven for wondering whether their church is trying to have it both ways on war. More to the point, they may be forgiven their puzzlement. For what are they to *do*?

Actually, virtually every Christian tradition is trying to have it both ways on war. This may be a sign of honest puzzlement, or it may be a sign of diplomatic fudging. But if nothing else, it is surely one sign of unfinished agenda.

Often, today, the two-track approach to war, peace, violence, and non-violence is quite explicit. The Catholic Church has long been custodian of the Christian tradition of just war deliberation, which began when Saints Ambrose and Augustine used arguments from Roman thinkers like Cicero in order to justify some wars while disciplining all wars. Since the Second Vatican Council, however, the Catholic Church has also given a new level of recognition to vocational pacifism, at least.[21] In the early 1980s, U.S. Catholic bishops writing on *The Challenge of Peace* explicitly paired the traditions of just war and pacifism or active nonviolence as legitimate Christian responses to war:

> Catholic teaching sees these two distinct moral responses as having a complementary relationship, in the sense that both seek to serve the common good. They differ in their perception of how the common good is to be defended most effectively, but both responses testify to the Christian conviction that peace must be pursued and rights defended within moral restraints and in the context of defining other basic human values.[22]

Three years later, Methodist bishops in the United States made a similar affirmation of both traditions in their statement *In Defense of Creation*, insofar as each serves "as a partial but vital testimony to the requirements of justice and peace."[23]

Even where not explicit, a two-track approach to warfare sometimes operates in subtle ways. Historic peace churches (Mennonite, Church of the Brethren, Society of Friends) certainly do not recognize the legitimacy of just war thinking with an easy reciprocity that would mirror statements by "mainstream" Christian traditions. Yet in their own way, peace churches have found that they too must "have it both ways" by acknowledging the need for someone, somewhere, to use potentially lethal violence to preserve order in a fallen world. In the formative years of the sixteenth-century Radical Reformation, the Schleitheim Confession of 1527 gave this recognition classical expression for Mennonites by speaking of "the sword" as "an ordering of God outside the perfection of Christ;" accordingly, "secular rulers" are "established to wield" the sword that "punishes and kills the wicked" but "guards and protects the good."[24] Though conservative rather than activist Mennonites are most likely to quote the Schleitheim Confession today, many of the very Mennonites who most sought to oppose the "war on terrorism" looming in September and October of 2001 found themselves reflecting the logic of Schleitheim nonetheless. How? In order to press their case for less violent responses, they called for alternative, international, judicial responses to terrorism that still would require some military or police force to apprehend the criminals.

Even when representatives of just war thought and pacifism have collaborated and discovered how much they already agree upon, the difficulty of having it both ways may remain and actually become more striking. A case in point is the "just peacemaking" initiative that gathered twenty-three Christian ethicists annually during much of the 1990s and articulated "ten practices for abolishing war."[25] The twenty-three scholars found much consensus by bracketing debates over theory or principles and instead identifying practices that are obligatory for all Christians. For those identified with just war teaching these are practices that Christians must seriously engage before resorting to warfare if any claim of "last resort" to military action is to be meaningful. For pacifists, these are practices that require positive engagement lest the "non" in "nonviolence" imply passivity at worst or mere protest at best.

With its focus on concrete practices, the just peacemaking approach offers a major precedent for the approach we are exploring in this book. Yet at one point their consensus proved particularly fragile. According to the introduction to *Just Peacemaking: Ten Practices for Abolishing War*, all participants agreed that among their "ten practices" they should include humanitarian military invention to halt egregious human rights abuses, yet not all were sure they could actually affirm it.[26] The problem, one suspects, was that for the pacifists in the just peacemaking initiative to affirm such a practice unambiguously would seem to have meant assent to a stringent, limited, and thus rectified just war approach—but a just war approach nonetheless.

To be sure, the just peacemaking initiative certainly moves us forward in at least three ways. First, by focusing on practices, the initiative reminds us of the path by which many Christians are already creating "conditions for the possibility" of convergence concerning war and peace, and how they should continue to do so. Second, attention to practices may further offer a way to deal constructively with remaining differences without underestimating or suppressing them. After all, if Christian practices cannot or should not be identical (insofar as every Christian community thrives on a diversity of gifts and callings, according to St. Paul), then we will need to pay close attention to what Christian communities must actually do in order to discern authentic vocations from God. And that may in turn allow us to reduce the differences in practice among currently divided Christians to vocational differences.

But third, even as the just peacemaking initiative has revealed its point of weakest consensus it has also marked out a continuing point of agenda: Is policing different enough from war that something *more* like policing (humanitarian military intervention) could possibly constitute a practice for abolishing war?

However fruitful, a point of agenda does not yet represent a clear path forward. To date, the just peacemaking initiative stands as one of the best efforts to transcend a centuries-old impasse between Christians working from pacifist and just war convictions. But when we get down to the toughest questions about how to practice love of neighbor and enemy alike amid tragic and violent situations, even Christians who think hardest about the challenge continue falling back into, and debating from, just war or pacifist categories. Meanwhile people around the world die violently.

Impasse as Cause for Hope

Sometimes, though, an impasse can give cause for great hope. Recall our first impasse, whereby peace activists and researchers argue that civil society is its own source of human security, but thereby invite militaries to merge into civilian sectors in dangerous ways that threaten to blur the crucial distinction between combatants and noncombatants. If we step back to survey "all of these factors" from an even wider historical angle, what we are dealing with at every juncture turns out to reflect an impasse in "the war system" itself, as international analyst Jonathan Schell calls it.[27] For if war is increasingly being waged within the civilian sphere, that is tragic evidence—but evidence nonetheless—of the very truth that Mahatma Gandhi helped the twentieth century to discover, and that the global movement for participatory democracy also reflects: *True power is social, not violent.*

As Schell has analyzed and retold the story of the twentieth century, four massive tectonic shifts have occurred.[28] (1) *Military might has rendered itself increasingly obsolete* as a tool for nations to promote their interests on the world stage. For centuries, but climaxing in the nineteenth and early twentieth centuries, nations were in an escalating race to "adapt or die," that is, to increase their military might before other nations beat them to it.[29] Always they dreamed of reaching a finish line in which absolute military power would guarantee their security absolutely. But when they actually achieved the absolute destructive capability of nuclear weaponry, it proved unusable. The "Great Powers" could then only confront one another indirectly through proxy wars and in the "realm of appearances" where world leaders publicly threatened but privately hesitated to use "the bomb."[30]

Meanwhile, around the edges of the international system, (2) *"people's war"* reflected the need of colonial populations and emerging nations to develop other forms of power. Waged in the name of a wide range of ideologies but always for self-determination, these movements could not compete with imperial nations in terms of sheer firepower. To be sure, the phenomenon of "people's war" has often been as locally bloody as nuclear war threatened globally to be. Yet even so, it pointed toward a way out of the impasse of the war system. A leader as ruthless and totalitarian as Chinese Communist Chairman Mao, for example, had to articulate the key strategic shift that people's war represents: In the decisive phase of a revolution, everything else is subordinated to politics—to winning the support of the population at large.[31] When one looks through the mythologized fog of violence, it turns out that nearly every revolution is won before it is "won," when the population withdraws consent from the *ancien régime* and shifts loyalties.[32]

Again providing evidence, albeit tragic evidence, people's wars thus mark a halfway point out of the impasse that war has become. Nuclear weaponry and the self-determination movements that often waged people's war were each paralyzing the war system and rendering it unable to serve as final arbitrator in global affairs.[33] Yet the genius of people's war was its rediscovery of social power—a.k.a. politics—in the very midst of battle; this has inadvertently raised the question of whether revolutions had to be violent at all.[34]

In showing that a revolution did not need violence, Mahatma Gandhi was also pointing toward a way through the impasse in the war system: For (3) *nonviolent revolution* "was proving the existence of a force that now could arbitrate" in global affairs.[35] Yes, the Gandhian alternative relies on *satyagraha* or the force of truth, as he preferred to name what others have unhappily called nonviolence. (The standard term "non-violence" is an unhappy one because the term only says what it is not, not what it is, and lends itself to rejection as merely passive.) And yes, Gandhian nonviolence insists that no truly liberating victory can come except through means that are morally consistent with the ends being sought. But as Schell insists, "Gandhi's politics was not a politics of the moral gesture. It rested on an interpretation of political power and was an exercise of power."[36] Gandhi was the first to found "a thoroughgoing program of action" upon the belief that political philosophers had been developing for centuries: that governments rest upon the consent of the people. "The central role of consent in all government meant that non-cooperation—the withdrawal of consent—was something more than a morally satisfying activity; it was a powerful weapon in the real world."[37] In the years since the independence movement in India, nonviolence has repeatedly demonstrated the power to face down terrorism and overthrow tyrannical regimes of all sorts, from Jim Crow segregation backed by KKK paramilitaries in the U.S. South, to military dictatorship in the Philippines and South America, to apartheid South Africa, to the Soviet Empire.

Gandhian precedents for the (4) *global movement of participatory democracy* that so dramatically altered Cold War international relations amid the 1989 Revolution in Central Europe have too often gone unnoticed. But in fact the two phenomena are mutually interdependent and reinforcing. Schell argues that the liberal democratic state represents the systematizing of nonviolence, for when successful "a country's constitution and its laws become a hugely ramified road map for the peaceful settlement of disputes, large and small."[38] Prior to 1989, of course, nearly everyone believed that a totalitarian regime so entrenched as the Soviet one was impervious both to nonviolent resistance and democratic transformation from within. Yet this "universal conviction" proved "stupendously wrong" precisely because it rested on faulty assumptions, beginning with the foundational belief that violent "force was the final arbiter in political affairs."[39] The weakness of the totalitarian Soviet regime, as well as the assumptions about power that the West widely shared with it, is evident in the way that Eastern European activists employed core Gandhian strategies though only dimly aware of their precedents. They set for themselves only modest, immediate goals that would create zones of freedom within the Soviet structure. And they simply did what playwright, activist, and future Czech President Václav Havel called "living the truth." But this was enough to bring down the empire and end the Cold War through a social rather than nuclear chain reaction. As Schell has put it: "It was the equivalent of a third world war except in one particular: it was not a war."[40]

So, humanity may have come a lot farther in the violent last century than we often think. Based on one of the most thorough compilations of data to date, the Human Security Centre at the University of British Columbia reported in 2005 that the number of wars, genocides, and human rights abuses had finally begun to decline dramatically in the fifteen years since the end of the Cold War.[41] If most people think otherwise, the researchers argued, that is because news media focus on dramatic exceptions like Rwanda or Iraq, while largely leaving unreported the hundred or so conflicts that have quietly ended since 1988. Also, while the outbreak of war is always pointed, the work of peacebuilding is usually diffuse. One source of the global decline in armed conflict is the unheralded work of United Nations diplomatic missions and peacekeeping operations, which draw little attention precisely because they succeed far more often than they fail. Likewise contributing are the cumulative efforts of international lending institutions, donor states, regional organizations, and thousands of non-governmental organizations. "Taken together," insists the Human Security Centre, "their effect has been profound."[42]

All of this makes the topic of just policing more rather than less timely. For one thing, despite its surprisingly optimistic assessment of global data, the Human Security Centre has rightly warned against complacency.[43] For another thing, even a less war-ridden planet must face the problem that nonviolent peace activists often wait far too long to anticipate, but that quickly presses upon societies and regions faced with the promise of a transition away from armed conflict: *What do you do if you actually win?*

It should stand as a warning that Gandhi's independent India quickly built its own military, became embroiled in decades-long stand-offs with neighboring Pakistan and China, thus fueled militarism, and is now a nuclear power. If nothing else, societies at peace continue to need domestic policing and should take care that their police avoid the brutality that comes with militaristic "crime-fighting" models. For even the sorts of de-militarized societies for which peace activists work would still need some kind of police function, though surely less violent and perhaps even nonviolent. As we will see, the very arguments that historic peace churches and antiwar activists have made since September 11, 2001 for responding to terrorism under a strengthened rule of international law—thus treating acts of terror as *crimes* against humanity rather than launching a *war* on terrorism—suggest a greater rather than lesser need for attention to policing. Implicitly, the goal of peace church activists and stringent just war policy makers alike becomes just policing—just policing, not war.

Just Policing as a Proposal,
a Conversation, but Still a Call

While just policing finds its place within this broad historical and global background, the reader may find it helpful to know that it first emerged as a proposal within a very particular context. What occasioned my first paper on just policing was, to be sure, the manifold debates among citizens and Christians following 9/11, but also one very specific dialogue. The first international dialogue between representatives of Mennonite World Conference and the Pontifical Council for Promoting Christian Unity was roughly midway through its initial five-year cycle at the time.[44] Though not a participant in the official dialogue, I had already moderated two rounds of unofficial dialogue by a group of a dozen or so scholars we called the Mennonite-Catholic Theological Colloquium; the MCTC had formed to provide background resources for the official delegations should they find our work helpful. Knowing that peace theology and practice would be the focus of a meeting of the international dialogue late in 2002, I wrote "Just Policing: How War Could Cease to be a Church-Dividing Issue" in order to launch a third round of the colloquium.[45]

In the intervening years the concept of just policing has gained far wider circulation,[46] and the pressing need for non- or less-violent ways of providing security in a jittery world has always loomed large in the hearts of my colleagues and myself. Still, the prospect that just policing suggests "how war could cease to be a church-dividing issue" has never been absent. While casting an eye to other conversations among other Christian traditions and, indeed, in the international community, the contributions and concerns of the Mennonite and Catholic faith communities inevitably receive special attention in this book.

Precisely here, though, a reassurance bears repeating. In the context of ecumenical relationships between just war and pacifist Christians, just policing is a proposal, yes, but not for some grand convergence right now. Nor does it propose a mere and premature compromise requiring that churches give up confessional beliefs that are integral to their identities. Rather, it proposes a conversation over the status of policing in Christian ethics and practice that will challenge both sides (or every side) to greater faithfulness. If further convergence on the ethics of violence becomes possible in the Christian community, what will prepare the way will be greater coherence and more consistent practice in every tradition.

The just policing conversation cannot move very far forward unless both sides embody their arguments through lived communal practices. Churches that have traditionally affirmed the possibility of just war have no chance of moving pacifists with their arguments unless they do a far better job of showing *in practice* that they can render their "exceptional" use of lethal violence truly exceptional, in effect turning just war just into policing. Churches that have traditionally affirmed the moral requirement of nonviolence even in the face of grave injustice have no chance of moving just war folks unless they do a far better job of showing *in practice* that they have ways to participate in governance that can be as effective as they claim to be faithful.

To these ends, and for the common good of neighbors around the globe, may we not only talk but work together. For potential victims of violence around the world, after all, Christians do not have to be fully united around issues of peace and war. For Christ's church simply to be less divided may be quite enough.

Notes

1. Graça Machel, *The Impact of War on Children*, a review of progress since the 1996 United Nations Report on the impact of armed conflict on children (New York: Palgrave, 2001), 1. Also see Save the Children, *Mothers & Children in War & Conflict*, State of the World's Mothers 2002 (Westport, CT: Save the Children USA, 2002), 8–9; United Nations Development Programme, *Millennium Development Goals: A Compact Among Nations to End Human Poverty*, Human Development Report 2003 (New York: UNDP, 2003), 45; Save the Children, *Protecting Children in Emergencies: Escalating Threats to Children Must be Addressed*, Policy Brief, vol. 1, no. 1 (Westport, CT: Save the Children USA, 2005), 1. These statistics are receiving scrutiny from a major new initiative housed in the Human Security Centre at the University of British Columbia in Canada. One source of contention, however, comes

from differing definitions of civilian casualties, depending on whether the data is limited to battlefield deaths and injuries, or expanded to include indirect deaths from disease or malnutrition that would not have occurred in the absence of war. See Human Security Centre, *Human Security Report 2005: War and Peace in the 21st Century* (New York: Oxford University Press, 2006), 2, 4–5, 17–21, 29–31. The Centre promises that the indirect costs of war will receive major attention in its 2006 report (7).

2. Reinhold Niebuhr, *Human Nature*, vol. 1 of *The Nature and Destiny of Man*, reprint, 1941, The Scribner Lyceum Editions Library (New York: Scribner's, 1964), 94.

3. See especially the opening pages of *Gaudium et spes [Pastoral constitution on the Church in the modern world]* (1965), which identify the church as a companion to "the people of our time" on their journey, sharing their "joys and hopes" in solidarity §1.

4. Ibid.

5. *Gaudium et spes*, §27. This section is also quoted at length in John Paul II, *Evangelium vitae [The gospel of life]*, encyclical letter (1995), §3. Also on the list of infamies were "degrading working conditions where people are treated as mere tools for profit."

6. Chris Hedges, *War is a Force That Gives Us Meaning* (New York: Public Affairs, 2002), 3, 62.

7. Ibid., 83–84.

8. Ibid., 86.

9. Commission on International Affairs in Church of Norway Council on Ecumenical and International Relations, *Vulnerability and Security: Current Challenges in Security Policy from an Ethical and Theological Perspective* (2002), http://www.kirken.no/english/engelsk.cfm?artid=5850.

10. Duane K. Friesen and Gerald W. Schlabach, ed., *At Peace and Unafraid: Public Order, Security and the Wisdom of the Cross* (Scottdale, PA: Herald Press, 2005), 60–61, 89–90, cf. 104–8. Quotations are from pp. 89 and 60, respectively.

11. *Gaudium et spes*, §79 The council's summary description of the state of humanity as "deplorable" vis-à-vis modern warfare also appears in this section.

12. Ibid., §§79–80.

13. Cf. John C. Ford, S.J., "The Morality of Obliteration Bombing," *Theological Studies* 5 (September 1944): 261–309. Published as it was while World War II was still raging, Ford's article had initially been a "voice crying in the wilderness," but became increasingly influential in the decades to follow.

14. *Gaudium et spes*, §80.

15. Ibid. A footnote specifies previous papal condemnations of total war: From Pius XII, an allocution on September 30, 1954 and a radio message of December 24, 1954; from John XXIII, his 1963 encyclical letter *Pacem in terris*; from Paul VI, a speech before the United Nations on October 4, 1965.

16. Title of Ivan Kauffman's chapter two in the present book.

17. *Gaudium et spes*, §80.

18. Pope John Paul II, *Centesimus Annus [On the Hundredth Anniversary of Rerum Novarum]*, encyclical letter (1991), §52. The pope continued: "Just as the time has finally come when in individual States a system of private vendetta and reprisal has given way to the rule of law, so too a similar step forward is now urgently needed in the international community. Furthermore, it must not be forgotten that at the root of war there are usually real and serious grievances: injustices suffered, legitimate aspirations frustrated, poverty, and the exploitation of multitudes of desperate people who see no real possibility of improving their lot by peaceful means." Available December 11, 2006. www.vatican.va/holy_father/john_paul_ii/encyclicals/documents/hf_jp-ii_enc_01051991_centesimus-annus_en.html.

19. E.g.: Message for the World Day of Peace, January 1, 2000; address to diplomatic corps, January 13, 2003.

20. ZENIT News Agency, "Pope Isn't a Pacifist, Says Vatican Spokesman," February 13, 2003; ZENIT News Agency, "Holy See Is Not Pacifist But Peace-Making, Says Cardinal Sodano," February 18, 2003.

21. "[W]e cannot but express our admiration for all who forgo the use of violence to vindicate their rights and have recourse to those other means of defence which are available to weaker parties, provided it can be done without detriment to the rights and duties of others and of the community." *Gaudium et spes*, §78.

22. United States Conference of Catholic Bishops (USCCB), *The Challenge of Peace: God's Promise and Our Response* (Washington DC: United States Catholic Conference, 1983), §74.

23. The United Methodist Council of Bishops, *In Defense of Creation: The Nuclear Crisis and a Just Peace*, Foundation Document (Nashville: Graded Press, 1986), 33, 88.

24. John Howard Yoder, ed. and trans., *The Schleitheim Confession*, introd. by Leonard Gross (Scottdale, PA: Herald Press, 1973), art. 6.

25. Glen Stassen, ed., *Just Peacemaking: Ten Practices for Abolishing War* (Cleveland: Pilgrim Press, 1998). More recently, see Stassen's refinements and responses to critics in "The Unity, Realism, and Obligatoriness of Just Peacemaking Theory," *Journal of the Society of Christian Ethics* 23, no. 1 (2003): 171–94.

26. The introduction closes with a page and a half of lingering differences and unfinished business. Only one sentence on those pages broaches a matter so fundamental that it might have meant crossing off one of the "ten practices" to make them nine: "We do not all agree with [the] affirmation of humanitarian [military] intervention" to halt egregious human rights abuses, "but we think it should be included." (Glen Stassen, *Just Peacemaking: Ten Practices for Abolishing War*, 26.) This refers to "practice" number eight, which called for strengthening the United Nations and other international peacekeeping forces—military ones—in order to halt genocide and other egregious human rights abuses. Cf. Michael Joseph Smith, "Strengthen the United Nations and International Efforts for Cooperation and Human Rights," in *Just Peacemaking: Ten Practices for Abolishing War*, ed. Glen Stassen (Pilgrim Press, 1998), 146–55. Lisa Sowle Cahill has also noted that the just peacemaking consensus is weakest around the ethical justification of coercion; see her "Just Peacemaking: Theory, Practice, and Prospects," *Journal of the Society of Christian Ethics* 23, no. 1 (2003): 195–96, 200–204.

27. Jonathan Schell, "No More Unto the Breach," two-part series, *Harper's*, March and April 2003, 33–46, 41–55; Jonathan Schell, *The Unconquerable World: Power, Nonviolence, and the Will of the People* (New York: Metropolitan Books, 2003).

28. Or as Schell put it: "Even the briefest review of the efforts of peacemakers from that time [August 1917] forward reveals that quiet but deep changes, both in the grand architecture of the world and in its molecular processes, have profoundly altered not only the shape of the global structures of violence but also the resources available for replacing them with something better." Schell, "No More Unto the Breach," I:36.

29. Schell, "No More Unto the Breach," I:42.

30. Ibid., I:38–40.

31. Ibid., I:42.

32. The Chinese case is by no means unique. In his longer work, Schell shows that in their critical phases, revolutions in Britain, the American colonies, France, and Russia all turned not on military force but on shifts in popular support that required revolutionaries to exercise restraint, even when their ideologies told them that military power would be decisive. Though only some revolutionaries would go on to concede the point, and few

would fully recognize its import, in every case the revolutions were won (through social mobilization) before they were "won" (through violent insurrection). See chapters five and six of Schell, *The Unconquerable World*.

33. Schell, "No More Unto the Breach," II:42.

34. Ibid., I:43.

35. Ibid., II:42.

36. Ibid., I:44.

37. Ibid.

38. Ibid., I:46.

39. Ibid., I:44.

40. Ibid., I:46.

41. Human Security Centre, *Human Security Report 2005*. For an overview, see pp. 1–11. The report is available online at http://www.humansecurityreport.info.

42. Human Security Centre, *Human Security Report 2005*, 9.

43. Ibid., 9–10.

44. The final report of the international dialogue is now available; see "Called Together to be Peacemakers: Report of the International Dialogue Between the Catholic Church and Mennonite World Conference, 1998–2003," *Information Service* 2003-II/III, no. 113 (2004): 111–48. The report is available online at www.bridgefolk.net/theology as well as at www.mwc-cmm.org/MWC/dialogue and www.prounione.urbe.it/dia-int/e_dialogues .html.

45. The initial version has been published with responses in Ivan J. Kauffman, ed., *Just Policing: Mennonite-Catholic Theological Colloquium 2002*, Bridgefolk Series, no. 2 (Kitchener, Ontario: Pandora Press, 2004). For a further refined version, see "Just Policing: How War Could Cease to be a Church-Dividing Issue," *Journal of Ecumenical Studies* 41, no. 3–4 (Summer–Fall 2004) 409–30. I have also provided certain comments and clarifications of special importance to historic peace churches in "Just Policing and the Christian Call to Nonviolence," in *At Peace and Unafraid: Public Order, Security and the Wisdom of the Cross*, eds. Duane K. Friesen and Gerald W. Schlabach (Scottdale, PA: Herald Press, 2005), 405–22.

46. See Gerald W. Schlabach, "Just Policing, Not War," *America* 189, no. 1 (July 7–14, 2003): 19–21; and the best-selling book by *Sojourners* editor Jim Wallis, *God's Politics: Why the Right Gets It Wrong and the Left Doesn't Get It* ([San Francisco]: HarperSanFrancisco, 2005), 165–68. A reference to just policing also appears in World Council of Churches, *Vulnerable Populations at Risk: Statement on the Responsibility to Protect*, approved by the 9th assembly, February 14–23, 2006, document no. PIC 02–2 (Porto Alegre, Brazil), §17.

PART I

Things that Make for Peace: Reconsiderations

Chapter 2

If War is Wrong, What is Right?
The New Paradigm

Ivan J. Kauffman

We have entered a new epoch in the church's history. It began in the ashes of World War II, after Christians had slaughtered each other by the millions in two wars that could have been avoided. It came to maturity in the forty years of cold war that followed, the war that could not be fought because the weapons available were too terrible to be used. And it gained its final shape at the hands of Mahatma Gandhi, who developed entirely new methods for combating injustice.

When Gandhian techniques brought an end to the cold war, Christians everywhere realized a new option existed and that their ethical argument was no longer between just wars and pacifism. For centuries the question had been, "What should Christians do when war breaks out?" But the Gandhian successes raised a fundamentally different question: "What are the alternatives to warfare? How do we prevent wars and end them once they have begun?"

These new questions do much more than simply restate the issues Christians have debated for centuries. They raise fundamentally new issues, and they require us to think in entirely new ways. They constitute a genuine paradigm shift.

The magnitude and reality of this historic shift in Christian thinking was clearly apparent in the statements church leaders issued in response to the attacks of September 11, 2001. Together they provide a revealing

snapshot of current Christian thinking on warfare, which one can summarize in this way:

- The just war theory no longer guides Christian thinking on the morality of warfare. It was notable for its absence in the churches' post-9/11
  statements. But despite this, the churches as a whole have not abandoned their belief that Christians bear responsibility for the order of
  society.
- The Christian churches as an international community are almost
  unanimously committed to peace. But despite this, few Christians
  would describe themselves as pacifists.
- Christians as an international group believe that practical alternatives to conventional military action exist. However, they can seldom
  describe these alternatives in politically viable terms.

These statements, and those that church leaders issued two years
later in voicing their virtually unanimous opposition to the U.S.-led
invasion of Iraq, mark a turning point in the churches' position toward
warfare. But despite their clarity and unanimity, government leaders
ignored them. Poll data indicated that lay Christians largely ignored
them as well.

The situation these events reveal is a genuine crisis, both political and
ecclesiological. Lacking clear moral guidance from their leaders, most
lay Christians, both as voters and as government officials, have reverted
to a pre-Christian doctrine of necessary war in some form. They appear
to have concluded that it is impossible to apply Christian ethics to the
often difficult decisions governments must make, and so they no longer
attempt to do so.

Only by offering a positive and practical alternative to warfare, and
offering it in politically viable terms, can that belief be changed.

Historical Perspectives

We can only appreciate the magnitude of the current shift by viewing
it in historical perspective. We cannot change the past; it is whatever it is.
But we can understand the past and learn from it. That is how we make
progress, not by rejecting history, but by interrogating it.

Jesus

To understand our history we must first understand Jesus' history. An immense amount of historical and biblical research has taken place in the past century that provides us with a much clearer picture of the political context of Jesus' ministry than the church has possessed since its early centuries. John Howard Yoder's *The Politics of Jesus* in particular has opened new perspectives on Jesus' ministry that continue to attract wide attention throughout the Christian community.

Unfortunately, we do not yet have an equivalently deep understanding of the five centuries of Yahwist and Judean history that preceded Jesus' life. This is the period that began with the return of Judean exiles in the late sixth century B.C.E., and continued through the Greek and Roman Empires. It ended with the construction of a grand new Jerusalem temple shortly before Jesus' birth.

This colonial period was a vivid contrast to the four centuries that had preceded it. Then, Jerusalem had been a thriving and independent city-state, founded by King David and governed by his descendents. In the centuries immediately prior to Jesus' birth there had been attempts to restore the Judean city-state to independence by military action, the third-century Maccabean revolt being the most significant. In Jesus' time guerrilla bands inspired by the Maccabeans were still active.

Jesus' attitude toward this historical legacy was complex, and has been difficult for subsequent Christians to understand. On the one hand Jesus accepted the fundamental assumption of his tradition, that Yahweh intended to create a new kingdom centered in Jerusalem. But he rejected what most of his contemporaries considered to be an equally basic part of that tradition, the assumption that the Yahwist kingdom would be governed as David's had been, by military power.

Jesus' decision to go to Jerusalem to confront the political establishment of his time was not accidental. It was a carefully considered action, one intended to inaugurate a new kingdom in which he and his followers would rule. But Jesus' decision to confront the political establishment of his time with nonviolent power was equally intentional. Jesus' actions at the end of his life completely redefined what it means to be a kingdom and what it means to be a king, and by his death and resurrection he supplied the power that has allowed that new vision to become an historical reality.

To spiritualize the concept of kingdom, as many Christians have done, completely distorts Jesus' message. Jesus clearly taught us to pray for a kingdom on earth, where Yahweh's will is done. But in the twenty centuries since Christ's birth his followers have tended either to believe that Christ's kingdom is like any other kingdom, and therefore must be governed like any other kingdom, or else to believe that Jesus' use of the word "kingdom" is simply a metaphor for something non-political and exclusively spiritual.

Christians through the centuries have tended to divide between those two aspects of Jesus' political witness. Pacifists have championed Jesus' nonviolence, but have for the most part ignored his sense of responsibility to inaugurate a new political order. Just war Christians have focused on Jesus' recognition of the need for a new political order, but have in effect sided with Jesus' executioners in assuming that political structures can only be created and maintained by means of religiously legitimated violence.

The Early Church

For a few weeks after the Resurrection, Jesus kept the infant Christian community alive by appearing to its members in his resurrected body. But with Pentecost those appearances ended, and the first generation Christians, who numbered at best in the thousands, were left with a truly daunting task. Jesus had commissioned them to communicate the almost incredible story of his life, death, and resurrection to a civilization whose values and practices were profoundly incompatible with that story.

It quickly became clear that Jesus' followers would meet the same opposition he had, and recognition of this reality fills pages of the New Testament. Nonetheless, the early Christians responded exactly as Jesus had—nonviolently. There is not a single incident known to us in which the early Christians responded to violence with counter-violence.

Their heroes were the martyrs, whose memories they revered and remembered in much the same way they remembered Jesus' life. The martyrs' influence in early church history was so great that it eventually became the cult of the saints that still exists.

Outside the church, meanwhile, the martyrs' witness had such great impact they earned the name "seed of the Church." Within only two hundred years, what began as a tiny sect had become a major international religious institution with its own organizational structures, liturgical practices, writings, and doctrines, as well as a growth rate that continued century after century. Persecution continued on a sporadic and local basis, but after each episode the church emerged stronger, and with more members.

The church's vitality was in marked contrast to the Roman Empire, which was crumbling under the huge and endless costs of maintaining an army to defend the empire against its numerous enemies, especially along its northern borders. By the end of the third century, Roman government had become chaotic, with military strongmen ousting one another on almost a yearly basis. One of them, Diocletian, finally established order and he determined to use his power to eradicate the church once and for all. His persecution was the most violent to date, but it also failed and left the church triumphant. Diocletian's successor, Constantine the Great, himself became a Christian and ended the Empire's persecution of the church.[1]

Constantine opened a new era in the church's political life. Christians no longer faced the challenge of surviving political hostility. Now their challenge was converting existing political structures into something compatible with Christian belief. The first battle had been an epic one that changed human history. This second would be no easier, nor its impact on human history any less.

Charlemagne

The centuries immediately following Constantine were characterized above all by Christian evangelism, and the success of this evangelism eventually resulted in the spread of Christianity throughout the Mediterranean and the area now called Europe. Early Christians believed it was their mission to convert all humans to Christianity, and as Christian evangelism continued to succeed in one culture after another, it became clear that the final result would be societies where everyone was Christian, and therefore everyone in authority was Christian.

But how were Christians to govern themselves? That question became very real when the western half of the old Roman Empire collapsed in the fifth century. This produced political chaos in Italy, southern France, the Rhine Valley, and England, all the places where Christianity had first taken root.

In the newly evangelized Frankish and Germanic territories, people were still in a tribal stage of political development. Here the church was dealing with ethnic groups that had lived on the periphery of the Roman Empire for centuries, enjoying many of its benefits but never experiencing the rule of law that made those benefits possible.[2]

In the Greek-speaking East, the area where the imperial capital was now located, Christians faced a different but no less difficult challenge.

Here deeply embedded traditions that had been in place for millennia virtually demanded a fusion of religious and political authority.

What made things even more difficult everywhere was that newly converted Christians often had only a rudimentary grasp of what it meant to be a Christian. Their immediate and understandable inclination was to view Christianity as simply another in the long line of polytheist religions they had always known, and not as a way of life.

From this powerful and intense interaction of political, cultural, and religious forces a new civilization emerged in the eighth and ninth centuries. The leader of this epochal development was Charlemagne, one of history's greatest political geniuses. Charlemagne came to power in a situation of almost unparalleled chaos, and by his death had bequeathed to subsequent generations the foundations on which European civilization rests to this day.

Charlemagne's civilization was based on a partnership between the warrior class, which he led, and the intellectual class that had emerged from the growing network of monasteries in Europe. Charlemagne incorporated the monks' intellectual skills into his government structures, thus making efficient and honest administration possible, and in turn the monks lent their considerable moral authority to Charlemagne's vision of an empire based on Christian belief—what would eventually be called Christendom.

This new political partnership was phenomenally successful. It eventually established a rule of law that greatly decreased political disorder throughout Europe, and it made education and spiritual development available to ordinary people, producing an unusually productive, inventive, and self-reliant citizenry.

But despite its great success, this partnership contained within itself a defect that plagues western civilization to this day. Charlemagnian governments could maintain order internally, essentially by adapting Roman political institutions to Celtic traditions, but they had no way to establish peace along their borders, just as the Romans had not been able to do.

So long as there was strong central power there was reasonable peace within Europe, but there was rarely someone of Charlemagne's abilities available to govern his empire and it increasingly disintegrated into a patchwork of competing warlords, each with his own castle—what subsequent historians would call feudalism.

Crusades

In the eleventh century, 250 years after Charlemagne, the great spiritual leader Bernard of Clairvaux advocated a solution to the problem of feudalism. It was to enlist Europe's numerous warriors into a single grand army dedicated to defeating the Muslim Empire that then occupied many formerly Christian territories, above all the area surrounding Jerusalem, which Christians regarded as "the Holy Land."

The Crusades were a failure militarily, but they initiated a process that eventually produced a system of more or less cohesive European nation states. The Crusades and the emerging nation states left their deepest and most permanent mark on European civilization by providing a theological validation for violence. The widely held argument was that if Christians allowed error to go unopposed, they were responsible for the damage it might do both to individuals and to society.

A more attractive rationale for "redemptive violence" can hardly be imagined, allowing the Crusaders to put on baptismal garments with a cross emblazoned on them and go off to kill people, thinking it a saintly act. In turn, the same theological arguments that supported the Crusades would later be used to support the Inquisition, in which religiously legitimated violence became part of the church's permanent structures.[3]

The Reformation

Today the theological rationale for the Crusades and Inquisition is widely regarded as a terrible error. But in the sixteenth century the Reformation gave it even greater legitimacy. The idea of national churches was central to sixteenth-century Protestantism, and it was only a short step from belief in legitimated violence to belief in the autonomous nation state, whose self-interests were the basis for all moral consideration.

As a result, both Catholic and Protestant Europe came to accept as a fixed principle that all conflicts could ultimately be resolved only through violence. This principle led in the sixteenth century to something that had never before taken place, at least not on a broad scale, the systematic persecution of Christians by other Christians.[4] In the seventeenth century the acceptance of this principle would produce a series of religious wars, both civil and international.

After two centuries of inter-religious warfare, Europe would turn to rationality as the way to international order. In the eighteenth century, diplomacy and negotiated treaties came to be the preferred alternative to warfare. But despite this development, the theological legitimation of warfare that had been developed to justify the Crusades retained its unquestioned validity. Resort to warfare thus became routine.

The Just War Theory

Beginning in the medieval period there had been a significant effort to subject warfare to the rule of law, and this effort gained force in the eighteenth and nineteenth centuries. Although the ultimate source of this legal theory had been the theological writings of St. Augustine, the just war theory of the Modern Era was essentially a legal rather than religious theory, developed primarily by legal theorists. This development was an important part of an effort to subject international conflict to rational control.

The just war theory never succeeded in achieving the goal of its authors, however. Instead it evolved into an autonomous intellectual theory that could be used to legitimate any military action that any sovereign state chose to undertake. Rather than limiting warfare to just cases fought by just means, it increasingly came to justify warfare under all circumstances.

That fact would have immense and profound impacts in the twentieth century, when the Western nations would devote large proportions of their political and economic resources to conducting warfare against one another.

The Post-War Era

Witnessing millions of Christians being killed by other Christians in World Wars I and II raised profound moral questions. But these wars would be followed by two equally significant meta-events,[5] which would intensify the crisis the Christian world now faces. These meta-events were the development of nuclear weapons, and the development of non-violent techniques for resisting political injustice. Both were fundamental changes, not merely an extension of previous trends, and together they would play the major role in bringing about the paradigm shift now taking place in the Christian community.[6]

The use of nuclear weapons by the United States in World War II impacted Christian attitudes toward warfare as nothing else in recent history has done. The just war theory, which had reigned virtually unchallenged for centuries, now came under increasingly skeptical scrutiny not only by Christian theologians and ethicists, but also by bishops and pastors and by lay Christians everywhere in the world.

Only three years after World War II ended the World Council of Churches declared, at its founding meeting in 1948, that war is a sin against God and humanity. Fifteen years later the world's Catholic bishops, convened at the Second Vatican Council by Pope John XXIII, called for "a completely fresh appraisal of war" in a groundbreaking document that removed the just war theory from the place of unquestioned authority it had long held.[7]

Forty years after World War II the Catholic bishops of the United States issued a pastoral letter in 1983 that questioned whether nuclear weapons could ever be used. "We are living in a global age with problems and conflicts on a global scale," they said. "Either we shall learn to resolve these problems together, or we shall destroy one another." [8]

A few years later the European churches—Protestant, Orthodox, and Catholic—issued a united statement confessing that the European churches "have caused wars and have failed to use all opportunities" to prevent them. "We have condoned and often too easily justified wars," the seven hundred leaders said. "We strongly affirm the importance of nonviolent political means as the appropriate way of seeking to bring about change in Europe," they said. "There are no situations in our countries or on our continent in which violence is required or justified."[9]

But despite the strong questioning of the just war tradition that took place after World War II, no significant new Christian pacifist movement developed. Many church leaders regretted their involvement in the pacifist movements of the 1930s, believing their efforts to prevent Western nations from going to war had the unintended consequence of strengthening the Nazi government. In their view, pacifists of the 1930s had encouraged Germany to invade the nations on its borders, under the assumption that Western democracies were so constrained by the pacifist movement they would not interfere. The acquiescence of Chamberlain's government to Hitler's invasion of Czechoslovakia in 1938 certainly supported that view.

Leading the reaction against pacifism was Reinhold Niebuhr. Niebuhr had himself been a pacifist before World War II, and he argued with a convert's fervor against what he had come to believe was its naive utopianism. In an essay entitled "Why the Christian Church Is Not Pacifist," he said of his former colleagues, "They merely assert that if only men loved one another, all the complex, and sometimes horrible, realities of the political order could be dispensed with." What they failed to see, he said, is that "their 'if' begs the most basic problem of human history." Since humans are by nature sinful, justice can be achieved only "by a certain amount of coercion on the one hand and resistance to coercion and tyranny on the other hand."[10]

Niebuhr's analysis produced what he acknowledged to be "a frank dualism in morals." In a book entitled *Moral Man and Immoral Society* he argued that Christians must distinguish between "what we expect of individuals and of groups." The highest ideal for Christians as individuals is unselfishness, but for nations the rules are different. "Society," he wrote, "must strive for justice even if it is forced to use means, such as self-assertion, resistance, coercion, and perhaps resentment, which cannot gain the moral sanction of the most sensitive moral spirit."[11]

With the advantage of hindsight it is now obvious that Niebuhr had completely missed the significance of what was happening in India during his lifetime. This was so despite all his intellectual power, his admirable realism about the reality of evil, and his appreciation for the differences between individual morality and political ethics. His contemporary Mohandas K. Gandhi was an equally profound thinker, but one who held a very different view of human nature and of political power. And he was leading a historic political movement for Indian independence that would call into question much of what Niebuhr had uncritically assumed to be axiomatic.

Niebuhr of course was not alone. In the 1950s and even into the 1960s virtually all Western observers regarded Gandhi's success as a political aberration, brought about by a unique combination: an oriental holy man, India's ancient culture, and the English people's unusually high moral standards. However, in the decades following Gandhi's death the world would witness a series of similar liberation movements, all based on Gandhian techniques and all successful.

First was the U.S. Civil Rights Movement, led by Martin Luther King, Jr., who had traveled to India to study Gandhi's techniques. This was followed in the 1980s by similar liberation movements in the Philippines, Korea, and Haiti, all achieved despite very powerful military opposition. And following all these victories was an even more amazing event, the victory of the Solidarity movement in Poland that in turn brought an end to the Soviet occupation of Eastern Europe. The next year the deeply entrenched apartheid regime in South Africa also fell, once again nonviolently.

This completely unexpected process culminated in the collapse of the Soviet Union itself in the early 1990s, and in the establishment of a democracy in Russia. All this happened virtually without military combat, using only techniques that Gandhi had developed. No precedent in human history exists for these events. The Christian churches strongly supported all these movements, and were often involved in their leadership.

We are still too close to these events to understand them. Indeed we often find it difficult to believe they actually happened (despite our having witnessed them) and we have only begun to chronicle their detailed history. Still, their existence is beyond question, and it is forcing us inescapably to a profound paradigm shift, a questioning of things that human beings have taken for granted for thousands of years. It is very difficult for us to imagine conducting our political affairs if these old assumptions are not true, but it is clear we must find a way to do so. This is equally true for persons who have held just war beliefs and those who have been pacifists.

9/11

Our increasing awareness that there is a third option is very different from the ability to apply it to specific cases, as the churches' leaders were to learn following the terrorist attacks of 9/11.

Within hours of the attacks church leaders in the United States began issuing statements, and they would continue to do so in a more or less steady flow for the next ten weeks. These statements came from every part of the world, and from every major Christian group, with the exception of the independent Evangelical churches, which lacked the institutional capacity to issue statements that represented an entire body of believers.[12]

As a group these statements provided something of a snapshot of the churches' current thinking in regard to warfare, and what this snapshot reveals is both hopeful and disturbing.[13]

It is symbolic of these statements that the ones issued by the Mennonite Central Committee and by the Episcopal Bishops of the United States are in many ways indistinguishable. Although Mennonites have historically rejected the just war theory's reliance on consequential arguments, one of their major 9/11 statements relies heavily on such predictions. "A military strike against Afghanistan risks massive human suffering," the Mennonite Central Committee statement said. "In an area of the world where almost half the population is below the age of fifteen years, this experience will shape attitudes and emotions for generations to come."[14]

The Episcopal bishops of the United States have traditionally rejected pacifist arguments based purely on theology, but their 9/11 statement is filled with them. "We come together also in the shadow of the cross," the bishops declare; the cross is the "unequivocal sign that suffering and death are never the end." They describe Jesus' death and resurrection as a "radical act of peace-making" that had as its goal "nothing less than the right ordering of all things," a world organized "according to God's passionate desire for justness," a world in which "the full flourishing of humankind and all creation" takes place. This project, in which all Christians participate "by virtue of our baptism," involves "reordering and transforming the patterns of our common life."[15]

Indeed virtually all the statements issued after 9/11 combine just war and pacifist arguments, often in the same paragraph, as some of the statements candidly acknowledge. But despite this melding of what had once been considered incompatible, none of the statements attempted to explain how it had become possible to combine pacifist beliefs and the just war theory into a single coherent viewpoint.

Despite this uncertain rationale, the statements do present a virtually unanimous opposition to U.S. government policy. Not a single statement by a major church body anywhere in the world offered blanket support for a military campaign against Afghanistan. Catholic and U.S. Lutheran leaders were willing to provide a reluctant and highly qualified acceptance of it as a regrettable but necessary evil, but they were alone even in this tenuous support. There was an historic consensus throughout the international church that a military response to the 9/11 attacks was mistaken and should be avoided.

In this regard the qualitative difference between U.S. leaders' statements and those from elsewhere in the international community is quite striking. When the bombing campaign began in Afghanistan, the presiding bishop of the Evangelical Lutheran Church in America wrote that although Christians are obligated to "act to prevent wars and seek alternatives to them," now that the war had begun his church understands that "under certain circumstances there may be no other way to offer protection to innocent people."

But the next day the general secretary of the Lutheran World Federation, of which the ELCA is a member, issued a statement that was harshly critical of the U.S. action. "The United States must, henceforth, play a new and different role" it said, becoming a "team player" that listens to other nations and works with them. The "globalized world" that is coming into being cannot simply be "a stage for free competition"; it must be based on a common search for "humankind's common future."[16]

Not only were other church leaders much more critical of U.S. government policy than their American colleagues, they also differed with them about the causes of the conflict.

Metropolitan Kirill, speaking for the Russian Orthodox Church, spoke for his colleagues throughout the Middle East and Asia when he said he feared the September 11 attacks were the beginning of a "civilization war." A new global civilization is being constructed, based entirely on "western liberal values" he said. "I wish all of us, including Americans, understood that it is impossible to build a mono-polar world," the Orthodox leader said. "Humanity can't live according to one standard, no matter what standard it is—western liberal, Islamic, Catholic or Orthodox." The terrorist attacks took place because people couldn't find any other way "to fight against the order imposed on them."[17]

Most Western leaders assumed that the conflict with Islam was caused by the disparity in economic standards, whereas Christian leaders in the Middle East and Asia believed that it was caused by the West's lack of respect for other cultures and civilizations.

The statements also reveal a widespread consensus that nonviolent alternatives to military action exist. The head of the Presbyterian Church (USA) urged that "every non-violent alternative be employed before there is a resort to the use of violence." The national leadership of the United Church of Christ called on the U.S. government to "use the even more massive non-violent power available to us to address those chronic conflicts that destabilize the world."

The Catholic bishops of Asia issued a statement that was explicitly Gandhian: "The Bishops of Asia have known for long years the brutal reality of violence and the depth of inhumanity it can reach," they said. Quoting Gandhi's observation that "An eye for an eye leaves everyone blind," they declared that he was speaking "in the spirit of the Sermon on the Mount" in saying this. "Hatred is not quenched by hatred, but by compassion and love," they added. "The Church is deeply committed to the summons of Jesus to peace-making," and joins with "all people of good will in . . . building a just, nonviolent, and peaceful world."[18]

Both the quantity and the quality of these statements is impressive. They reveal an historic consensus in the Christian community, one that has profound implications for the future. But suddenly they ended.

In the ten weeks following 9/11, more than seventy-five official statements by the leaders of major bodies were issued, on average more than one per day. But when the military invasion of Afghanistan succeeded in mid-November and newspaper and television reports began to suggest that the Afghan people as a whole were pleased to see the fundamentalist Taliban government defeated, along with the largely foreign al Qaeda military organization, the flow of church statements came to an abrupt halt. After November 18 there would be none.

Why? Why did the churches have so much to say while the war was going on, but nothing to say after the Afghan invasion was successful?

One obvious reason was that the negative consequences which virtually all church leaders had predicted turned out to be mistaken, at least in the short term. The bombing campaign had caused far fewer civilian casualties than critics had expected. The refugee crisis many experts had predicted did not occur. And rather than producing widespread hunger, as many critics had predicted, the U.S. military action allowed the U.N. Food Programme to move massive grain shipments into Afghanistan.

But this was only the beginning. How could the churches criticize a policy that appeared to have succeeded when they had nothing to offer as an alternative? The result was that the churches, along with all the opponents of the Afghanistan invasion, were left with the appearance of being sideline critics, or what was even worse, critics whose information was faulty and whose judgment was naive.

And there was a third factor: it had never been clear exactly what motivated the churches' opposition to the invasion of Afghanistan. Was it based on pacifism or the just war theory or something else? Pope John Paul instructed his press secretary to tell reporters, "The pope is not a pacifist. . . . If someone has done great harm to society, and there is a danger that if he remains free he may be able to do it again, you have the right to apply self-defense for the society which you lead, even though the means may be aggressive."

"The pope understands the difficulties of a political leader who has to respond to such issues," the press secretary said. But he added that if the pope is not a pacifist neither is he a militarist. "Some people in Europe would like to present the pope as a pacifist," he said, "and some people in America would like to see him as someone who wants to see the application of justice by any means. Both are wrong."[19]

That important statement surely left many, including numerous Catholics serving in the military, wondering what official Catholic teaching on warfare now was.

Two years later when an invasion of Iraq was being debated, it became clear the churches' post-9/11 experience had been far more than an embarrassment. Having discredited themselves by making predictions that were inaccurate, and by failing to present credible alternatives or even to offer a clear moral vision, church leaders found themselves being ignored in the great debate that led to the invasion of Iraq.

What was most alarming was that church leaders appeared to be ignored by their own members. Polls in this period indicated that the more frequently people attended church services, the more likely they were to support the Bush administration, presumably including its foreign policy. A Lutheran pastor from South Dakota said that after 9/11 there was "a chasm" between the churches' leaders and the people in the pew. "We need prophetic leadership that acknowledges the pain and anger but moves us in a new way," he said. The need for that leadership became clear following the Iraq invasion.

Increasingly it has become apparent that the American public, both Christian and non-Christian, has adopted a theory of necessary war that owes much more to Darwin than to Christ. A letter writer in the *New York Times* stated this with great candor shortly after 9/11: "The children who have lost parents suddenly and violently suffer equally, in America and Afghanistan," she wrote. "We, however, must now fight for our survival with total dedication. If we let ourselves get caught up in sympathy for the enemy, we will lose this war, and untold numbers of children throughout the world will suffer even more."[20]

No Christian leader would endorse such an argument, but what were the alternatives? Christian leaders from all denominations and traditions faced the same dilemma: they could not condemn the war because they recognized the need for justice, but neither could they support it without violating their most basic moral beliefs.

The Christian community wanted peace, but it had to permit war. It wanted to forgive its enemies, but it had to protect innocent people from further attacks. It was deeply aware that injustice—much of it caused by the West—provided an incentive for terrorism, but it could not excuse terrorism under any circumstances. It knew that U.S. military action would inflame the already strong anti-Western sentiments in the Islamic world, and it knew a war would put the tiny Christian communities there in grave danger, but it did not know what else to do. We wanted to follow the Sermon on the Mount, we wanted to be faithful to Jesus' teachings, but we did not know how.

And so in the end the vast majority of Western Christians accepted the U.S. military campaign in Afghanistan as a necessary evil, a violation of Christian ideals, but nevertheless necessary to prevent an even great evil.

Faced with the choice between passivity and violence we chose violence, although with extreme reluctance. We knew no other way.

Just Policing and the New Era

Ultimately the only convincing argument against the theory of necessary warfare is an action that by its success proves that warfare is not in fact necessary. Fortunately the Gandhian Revolution has provided us with that proof. Pope John Paul observed shortly after the fall of the Communist Empire, that although it had appeared the Soviet occupation of Eastern Europe "could only be overcome by another war" it was instead "overcome by the nonviolent commitment of people, who, while always refusing to yield to the force of power, succeeded time after time in finding effective ways of bearing witness to the truth."[21]

What we now know, based on incontrovertible evidence from conflicts in more than a dozen large nations on every continent, is that injustice of all kinds can successfully be resisted without employing politically legitimated violence.[22] Equally important, it has demonstrated that nonviolent techniques can replace unjust political structures with successful democracies.

The long debate between just war and pacifism is over, and the winner is neither St. Augustine nor St. Francis, neither John Howard Yoder nor Reinhold Niebuhr. It is Mohandas K. Gandhi and his followers: Martin Luther King, Jr. and the African-American churches; Benigno and Corazon Aquino; Lech Walesa and Cardinal Wojtyla; Nelson Mandela and Archbishop Tutu. To continue the moral debate as though their experiences did not exist, or were of only minor significance, would itself be immoral. It would be immoral not only because it would be dishonest, but even more because it would have the practical consequence of lending the theological community's de facto support to the theory of necessary evil.

The success of Gandhian techniques utterly transforms the ethical debate from one about philosophical and theological principles to one about political practices. The issue is no longer what is necessary, or what is right, or what is acceptable, but what is possible in actual human affairs.

The task of moral theology now is to listen to those Christians who have participated in successful Gandhian campaigns and to identify the reasons for their success, and then to describe these successful techniques in replicable terms, so that they can become the moral standards for other Christians in the future.

We must learn to think in entirely new ways, resolutely turning our backs on the old ways and committing ourselves courageously to an entirely different way of thinking. We must acknowledge the essential defect in the just war theory, which is its assumption that violence can somehow achieve justice. And we must with equal courage acknowledge the essential defect in pacifism, which is its assumption that justice can somehow be achieved simply by opposing violence.

In recent decades we have come to understand that peace is more—much, much more—than the absence of conflict and violence. Instead we have come to see that peace is the secondary result of something far more basic, something we have difficulty even conceptualizing, much less naming.

In the Hebrew Scriptures this basic reality is called *shalom,* but we have no word in our Greek and Latin-based languages that corresponds to that ancient Semitic word. The very concept of an integrated wholeness that this word represents is so alien to our analytical way of thinking that we can comprehend its meaning only with great difficulty, and then only imperfectly.

What has emerged in the Western theological community to fill this need is a consensus that peace must be made, and that peace can only be made by creating the conditions that do not require conflict. Pope Paul VI summarized this view with his oft-quoted words, "If you want peace work for justice." Pope John Paul II raised it to a new level of prominence by promoting the vision of a "Civilization of Love," which he advocated on numerous occasions since 1994, and made a cornerstone of his social teaching.[23]

In the United States this new understanding of peace has produced the concept of *peace building.* This phrase is in stark contrast to two older ones, *peacekeeping* and *peace advocacy,* the first favored by just war adherents and the second by pacifists.

The concept of peace building reflects a growing realization that peace cannot be kept if the conditions necessary for large-scale social and political harmony do not exist. Attempting to keep the peace where no real peace exists simply adds additional layers of violence to those that already exist. It is ultimately self-defeating, as the United States learned at great cost in Vietnam, and is re-learning in Iraq.

But neither can pacifists advocate peace when the conditions necessary for peace do not exist. To advocate peace in situations where injustice is taking place without some realistic action for dealing with that injustice is simply to ask those who are suffering to do so in silence so that others can have the benefits of peace.

Peace building requires personal involvement from everyone. We cannot say, "Let the army do it," nor can we claim the moral high ground by simply saying, "Let's protest what the army is doing." We must instead ask ourselves three very simple questions: "What is the problem causing this conflict?" "What is the solution to that problem?" and "What can we do to contribute to that solution?" Then we must act on the answers to those questions. If we do not we are part of the problem, which is largely caused by what human societies have failed to do.

Action is absolutely central to the paradigm shift that is taking place, for this new paradigm counters violence with nonviolent alternatives. It is as much a political theory as it is a theological one.

How do we begin to implement this new paradigm? This book is itself an encouraging and concrete step in that direction. That it is a collaboration between scholars from both just war and pacifist traditions is a real sign of hope.

The concept of just policing clearly places the focus on achieving justice in human society, rather than on simply reacting to war when it breaks out. It is inherently proactive. And it takes seriously the need to have a practical means to respond to injustice when it occurs, as inevitably it will in a world filled with inherited evil. But by combining the concepts of policing and justice, this new concept subjects policing itself to the very standards it tries to enforce.

Just policing's most hopeful potential as a concept is its ability to provide a common base on which Christians on both sides of the political spectrum can join forces. Just policing is something both liberals and conservatives can support. There will of course be vigorous debates over precisely what constitutes just policing, and how best to carry it out in specific cases, but that is as it should be. We will never have truly just policing on any level in society without the contributions of everyone involved. What is essential is that the need for policing and the need for it to be done justly both be acknowledged.

The new epoch that has opened before us is a major opportunity, one of the most important in all Christian history. Let us accept it as a gift, and move forward in humility and in strength.

Notes

1. The history of Constantine has been a major point of contention between those inclined to the pacifist and just war doctrines. Pacifist groups tend to regard his reign as the "fall of the Church" whereas supporters of the just war doctrine tend to regard it as "the triumph of the Church." The first view is summarized by Franklin Littell in *The Origins of Sectarian Protestantism: A Study of the Anabaptist View of the Church* (New York: Macmillan, 1964); and by Donald Durnbaugh in *The Believers' Church* (New York: Macmillan, 1968). Hermann Dörries, *Constantine the Great* (New York: Harper & Row, 1972) contains a history of the history of Constantine. Recent scholarship is summarized in Michael Grant, *Constantine the Great: The Man and His Times* (New York: Scribner's Maxwell Macmillan International, 1994).

2. Richard A. Fletcher, *The Barbarian Conversion: From Paganism to Christianity* (New York: H. Holt and Co., 1998).

3. These developments are richly documented by Frederick H. Russell in *The Just War in the Middle Ages*, Cambridge Studies in Medieval Life and Thought, 3rd Ser., vol. 8 (Cambridge; New York: Cambridge University Press, 1975). The neglect this important work of scholarship has been met with is difficult to understand. The information it contains is essential to understanding the crisis in Christian moral and political theology the church now faces.

4. Brad S. Gregory, *Salvation at Stake: Christian Martyrdom in Early Modern Europe*, Harvard Historical Studies, vol. 134 (Cambridge, MA: Harvard University Press, 1999).

5. The word *meta-event* is used to refer to events of large scale, wide impact, and long duration which shape the cultures in which they take place, in contrast to events of lesser magnitude that can be absorbed into that culture without requiring fundamental structural change.

6. Jonathan Schell documents this development in considerable detail in "No More Unto the Breach."

7. *Gaudium et spes*, §§33–39. The phrase quoted is from §80.

8. National Conference of Catholic Bishops (NCCB), *The Challenge of Peace*. The phrases quoted are from §244.

9. This document was issued by a conference that took place in Basel, Switzerland in May 1989. The seven hundred delegates present included more than forty Catholic bishops, as well as the European leadership of the World Council of Churches, and numerous Orthodox bishops. Every European nation except Albania was represented, including those under Soviet domination, even though the fall of Communism would not take place until later in the year.

10. Reinhold Niebuhr, *The Essential Reinhold Niebuhr: Selected Essays and Addresses*, ed. Robert McAfee Brown (New Haven: Yale University Press, 1986), 109.

11. Reinhold Niebuhr, *Reinhold Niebuhr: Theologian of Public Life*, ed. Larry L. Rasmussen (Minneapolis: Fortress Press, 1991), 69, 77.

12. For a less charitable explanation, see the analysis of University of Virginia religious studies professor Charles Marsh, "Wayward Christian Soldiers," *New York Times*, January 20, 2006. An Evangelical himself, Marsh nonetheless concludes by attributing Evangelical support for the recent U.S. wars to having "isolated ourselves from the shared faith of the global Church," while making a "Faustian bargain for access and power."

13. The documents cited below are available on the Internet, either at www.wfn.org, or at the issuing body's own website.

14. Mennonite Central Committee Executive Committee, September 22, 2001.

15. "On Waging Reconciliation." Statement of the Episcopal Bishops of the United States, September 26, 2001.

16. Rev. H. George Anderson, Presiding Bishop, Evangelical Lutheran Church in America, October 7, 2001; Dr. Ishmael Noko, General Secretary of the Lutheran World Federation, October 8, 2001.

17. Metropolitan Kirill of Smolensk and Kalingrad, chairman of the Dept. of External Church Relations of the Moscow Patriarchate, text of a television interview issued by the Russian Orthodox Church and reported by www.zenit.org, October 5, 2001.

18. Statement of the Federation of Asian Bishops Conferences, October 26, 2001.

19. Sharon LaFraniere, "Vatican Says Use of Force by U.S. Can be Justified," *Washington Post*, September 25, 2001.

20. *New York Times*, November 1, 2001.

21. John Paul II, *Centesimus Annus*, III, §23.

22. This is not to say that all violence can be avoided. In virtually every conflict where Gandhian techniques have been used a certain number of persons have suffered injury and other violations, and a few have died. But these casualties have been relatively few in number—miniscule in comparison to those that occur in warfare—and they have in nearly every case involved persons who voluntarily chose to undergo violence rather than inflict violence on others, so that instead of being casualties of war they became martyrs.

23. The *Compendium of the Social Doctrine of the Church*, compiled by the Pontifical Council for Justice and Peace at Pope John Paul's initiative and published by the Vatican in 2004, concludes with a section entitled "For a Civilization of Love." A comprehensive collection of statements on the vision of a "Civilization of Love" by both John Paul and his predecessor, Paul VI, is available at www.civilizationoflove.net.

Chapter 3

War on Terrorism?
A Realistic Look at Alternatives

Glen H. Stassen

In the early months of 2003 debates about war in Iraq rolled over and through churches and church members like a tidal wave. The deep need for teaching Christian ethical criteria about peace and war well in advance of a specific conflict was clearly evident. What was also clear is that this teaching needs to be concrete and deeply rooted in Christian formation if it is to survive the hot winds of secular ideologies.

But which ethics should the churches, their pastors, and their theologians teach? In order to include diverse church members in their discussions, many churches will teach both pacifism and just war theory—and rightly so. But the national debate in the United States in the lead-up to war in Iraq has demonstrated dramatically that this is not enough.

Yes, pacifism and just war theory are crucially important. Every church member and every student of Christian ethics should know both of them well. Christian communities should engage in a process of discernment to know which ethic accords with their deepest convictions about how God is at work in the world and is calling God's people to participate in that work. Christians should be receiving deep biblical, spiritual, and character formation so they care deeply about this discernment, and about the destruction of war and the need for peacemaking.

But pacifism and just war theory by themselves are inadequate. They need help in a major way. As usually taught, they are usually two-dimensional: war or no war. They need a third dimension, the peacemaking practices that give pacifists an alternative to passivity and that help just war Christians from needing to reach the last resort of war.

Before the Iraqi war, *Time* magazine columnist Andrew Sullivan argued that the war met just war criteria, while Christian ethicist Stanley Hauerwas countered by arguing decisively for nonviolence and pacifism.[1] Sullivan argued that there was no reasonable alternative for dealing with Saddam Hussein and his (alleged) weapons of mass destruction. Because Hauerwas did not respond to this claim that there was no reasonable alternative, and offered no other resort, many felt Sullivan had won the debate. To his credit, Hauerwas said "Nonviolence means finding alternatives to the notion that it is ultimately a matter of kill or be killed." But the only alternative he suggested was "asking the many Christians in Iraq what we can do to make their lives more bearable."

Likewise, at the annual meeting of the Society of Christian Ethics in January 2003, ethicist James Childress incisively examined the impending war in the light of just war theory, concluding firmly that this war would not be just. Respondents agreed, but asked, "What is the alternative?" Childress replied, "I don't know." He was doing just war theory; he was not responsible for suggesting constructive alternatives. Yet the sophistication of just war analysis had not, in the end, taken us much farther than the sloganeering on the streets. Placards nationwide read: "War is not the answer," prompting the impatient response, "Then what *is* the answer?"

I cite Hauerwas and Childress not because their work as Christian ethicists is inept, but because they are two of the best. I have known both since graduate school, count them as friends, and respect their work greatly. We share many loyalties, and have done numerous projects together. My point is not to criticize either them or the just war and pacifist paradigms they employ, so far as those models go. I am seeking to argue decisively that these two traditional paradigms need something further in order to strengthen what they do. It was that conviction that brought twenty-three of us together in the 1990s to create the just peacemaking theory. All were either pacifists (in some cases) or just war theorists (in most cases). We wanted to strengthen the two traditional paradigms and make them more convincing, not less. We wanted to give them additional ammunition persuasive enough to win national debates.

Public Sentiment, Moral Argument
and Just Peacemaking Alternatives to War

We need to be realistic. The public opinion polls during the buildup to the Iraqi war disclose a powerful reality that our ethics has been overlooking: simply arguing no to a war is bound to lose in the national debate. In January of 2003, polls consistently found fifty-six percent of the U.S. public supporting military action against Saddam Hussein's regime in Iraq. This was in spite of worldwide opposition to the war, unprecedented near-unanimity against the war among church leaders who issued statements, the largest pre-war demonstrations against a war in U.S. history, and failure to get support of more than two members besides the United States in the U.N. Security Council despite powerful U.S. financial and political pressure. Is there some realism here that should be learned?

Americans initially supported every war in the twentieth century, including the Vietnam War, which failed all eight criteria of just war theory, and which eighty percent of Americans ultimately came to view as a mistake. In his book, *War, Presidents, and Public Opinion*, political scientist John Mueller analyzed polling data about the Korean and the Vietnam Wars.[2] Mueller argued that moral arguments about the injustice of the Vietnam War had no discernible effect in the polls on support or opposition for the war, yet the data he marshaled argues otherwise.[3] One indication of public sense of injustice is the rate of military desertions. In World War II, which Americans widely judged to be a just war in the face of Hitler's thoroughly evil Nazi regime, desertions were few. During the Vietnam War the desertion rate was far higher. Mueller hypothesized that support for both wars steadily declined as a logarithm of the number of body bags of U.S. soldiers that came back. That was true of the Vietnam War, but clearly untrue of the Korean War. When the Chinese soldiers entered the Korean War and people suddenly realized it would be a long, hard war, support immediately dropped to forty percent. But by contrast with Vietnam, thereafter support held steady at forty percent throughout the several years of the war, regardless of the continuing flow of body bags. People saw the Korean War as just and the Vietnam War as unjust. The conclusion surely is that just war theory is important, especially as people assess a war when they see how it is being conducted.

Still, articulating a clear alternative to war fares better than antiwar protest alone in national debates. During the buildup to the war in Iraq, much of the peace movement focused on the alternative: "Let the inspections work." In February and March CBS News polls asked, "Should the United States take military action against Iraq fairly soon, or should the United States wait and give the United Nations weapons inspectors more time?" On three different occasions, by a ratio of almost two to one, respondents preferred the clear alternative of giving inspectors more time.[4] The war's opponents won this debate, especially as the U.N. inspection team reported that weapons of mass destruction were not being found, and that Iraq was cooperating with the inspectors' demands for immediate access anywhere, overflights, and destruction of those slightly over-range missiles. The White House had to shift its argument from the alleged threat of the elusive weapons of mass destruction to the dictatorship of Saddam Hussein and a promise to bring democracy with human rights to Iraq. President Bush thus committed himself verbally to the "nation-building" that he had previously opposed.[5]

A strategically important realism is speaking to us from these data: If the president advocates a war, and the question is simply whether or not to support the war, majorities will say yes. Posing the ethical question that way is almost a guaranteed way to lose the national debate. The reality is that an ethic that focuses on a constructive alternative has a much better chance to win the debate. Christians should not be surprised. The prophets of Israel did not just say no to war, but spelled out the changes, the repentance, the practices of justice and wisdom that were necessary in order to avoid the judgment and destruction of war.[6] Jesus did not just say no to anger and revengeful resistance, but commanded the transforming initiative of going to make peace with your brother or sister; and going the second mile (Matt 5:21-25, 38-42).[7]

Just peacemaking theory is designed to point to a set of constructive alternatives that are realistic. What makes these alternatives realistic is that each just peacemaking practice has demonstrated its effectiveness in preventing some wars in actual historical context. The theory presents ten practices that not only have the support of various theological and ethical schools of thought, but are already being implemented in various historical contexts.[8] Each has demonstrated empirically for political science that it has a preventive effect.

Although just peacemaking theory emerged in the 1990s, prior to the new historical context shaped by the events of September 11, 2001, it points toward foreign policies capable of responding effectively and realistically to the threat of terrorism. Their effectiveness is being demonstrated in actual practice, in recent and present history.[9]

Turkish and Russian Antiterrorism Compared

Turkey has wrestled with decades of terrorism by Muslim ethnic-minority Kurds seeking independence in southeastern Turkey, just as Russia has wrestled with terrorism by Muslim ethnic-minority Chechens also seeking independence in southern Russian. A comparison is instructive. Russia chose a scorched-earth military approach, attacking repeatedly with large force. The result has been enormous devastation, many deaths, and no end to terrorism. Fareed Zakaria, editor of *Newsweek International*, wrote in December 2003 that in the four previous months:

> seven Chechen suicide bombers, all but one of them women, have detonated explosives that have taken 165 lives, including their own. In the early 1990s, there were no Chechen suicide bombers, despite a growing, violent movement against Russian rule. Reporters who covered the Chechen war in the early 1990s mostly agree that there were very few "international Islamists"—Saudis, Afghans, Yemenis—present. They grew in numbers as a direct result of the "brutal, botched, and unnecessary" Russian military intervention of 1994–96.[10]

Turkey had an analogous and very serious problem with the Kurdish rebellion and terrorism led by the PKK (*Partiya Karkeren Kurdistan*). It had killed more than thirty thousand persons since its beginning in 1984. The Turkish army had been attacking them with widespread force, but in the mid-1990s, they developed a much more disciplined approach to avoid attacking civilians, and introduced health and education for the Kurdish area.[11]

One just peacemaking practice is *sustainable economic development*, and the key to that is community development—development of the civil society of local communities.[12] Kurdish areas have long been economically worse off than other regions of Turkey and neglected by the central government. But in a change of course promoting sustainable economic development, the government "initiated huge investments in the southeast, exemplified by the $32 billion Southeastern Anatolia Project, to improve the long-languishing region's economic prospects. Indeed, between 1983 and 1992 the southeast received twice as much investment per capita as any other region in Turkey."[13] The national government recognized the Kurdish language and community customs. It invested extensively in improving education, including for girls and women. Instead of trying to break down Kurdish tribal structures, as it had previously sought to do, the government recognized those structures and sought to enlist them in the struggle for economic development, community development, and political representation.[14]

Another just peacemaking practice has been to *advance human rights, democracy, and religious liberty.*[15] Kurds have actually gained more representation in the Turkish parliament than their proportion of the population. In part this has been a response to pressure from the European Union and Turkey's drive to be accepted as a member of the EU. The Kurds have favored Turkish membership in the EU as promising them improved democratization as well as economic development.[16] "Civil associations in Turkey are growing in strength and exerting increasingly effective pressure on the government. The election of Ahmet Necdet Sezer, a prominent democrat from the judicial establishment, to the country's presidency could also have a positive effect."[17]

The pressure, and the allure, of the EU suggests the importance of *working with emerging cooperative forces in the international system*, another practice of just peacemaking.[18] The international community was also important in arresting Ocalan, the leader of the terrorist organization. He had been living in Syria, safe from Turkey's military, but Syria expelled him as part of its effort to improve relations with Turkey and international pressure against terrorism. Ocalan sought refuge in Italy and other countries, but instead Italy arrested him.

Turkey then negotiated with Ocalan, and achieved his cooperation in ending the terrorism in exchange for forgoing the death penalty. Here is the just peacemaking practice of *cooperative conflict resolution.*[19] "In 1996 the journalist Franz Schurmann called the PKK 'the biggest guerrilla insurgency in the world.'" But by May 2000, the PKK had basically quit.[20]

The painful and tragic irony is that in late 2003 we saw two more days of terrorism in Turkey. But this was not Kurdish terrorism against the Turks. Apparently this was al Qaeda terrorism against Israel and the British-American "coalition of the willing." As President Bush and Prime Minister Tony Blair were meeting in London, November 20, 2003, terrorists attacked the London-based HSBC Bank and the British consulate. Twenty-six people were killed, including British Consul Roger Short. Five days previously, two Jewish synagogues in Istanbul were bombed, killing twenty-three people and wounding more than three hundred.[21]

It is a tragic symbol. It symbolizes that the anger in Turkey has been shifted from Kurdish anger against the government to terrorist anger against Israel and the alliance between the U.S. and Britain. It suggests what works and what does not work in combating terrorism.

Rewarding Terrorists?

The Turkish experience helps us respond to the common objection, "we must not reward terrorists." Turkey did not reward the PKK terrorists; the Turkish government pursued them in a carefully targeted way. They separated them from the people by energetic action for justice for the people. They convinced the Kurds that their future would be better with Turkey than with the ideology of the terrorists. They undermined the ability of the terrorists to recruit more support, and they enlisted international forces in arresting the leader of the PKK.

Terrorists thrive by identifying themselves with the just demands of the people. A policy that fears rewarding terrorists easily becomes a policy that avoids doing justice for people. If a region is being oppressed, and the terrorists identify with that oppression, doing justice for the people is not rewarding terrorists. Hence just peacemaking focuses our attention on justice, on sustainable economic development, and on human rights, democracy, and religious liberty. In this case, Turkey rewarded Ocalan not for his terrorist activity but for his cooperation by keeping him imprisoned rather than seeking the death penalty.

The belief that "we must not reward terrorists" derives in part from a behaviorist view of human nature that sees human action as a mechanistic response to stimuli, which policy makers can manipulate.[22] This view of human nature coincides with the lesson many take from the failed Munich Agreement of 1938, between British Prime Minister Neville Chamberlain and Germany's Adolf Hitler; that lesson is that aggressors must never be rewarded or in any way "appeased." This apparent lesson can lead to its own problems, however. One example is the Bush administration's policy toward North Korea that has gone so very badly. The administration entered office declaring its unwillingness to support any peacemaking with North Korea, and when South Korean president Kim Dae Jung visited him, president Bush publicly scorned Kim's peacemaking efforts, thereby undermining his peacemaking. The continuous monitoring of nuclear facilities, which former President Carter had worked out, discovered North Korea was cheating in a minor way. Instead of confronting North Korea in firm dialogue, the Bush administration took a punitive approach, cutting off the oil that was the agreed alternative to nuclear power, and threatened North Korea by lumping them with Iraq and Iran as "the axis of evil." Until 2007, Bush was unwilling to negotiate a non-aggression agreement in exchange for North Korean compliance with the demand to do without nuclear reactors, because that might seem to reward the North Korean government.

Social movements are far more complicated than mere behaviorist understandings assume, or than the Munich image suggests. People are not merely the rationalistic model of stimulus/response to be rewarded or punished; they perceive in complex ways and they have complex drives. One must ask what drives for justice, security, honor, and cultural recognition are involved, and what initiatives and what policies make sense and work effectively to prevent terrorism.

Rob de Wijk of the Royal Military Academy in Leiden makes an analogous point. Strategies of deterrence or coercion developed for interstate war do not work in terrorism

> because the coercers—the United States and its allies—must clearly indicate that the war is not against the Afghan people, but against terrorists and the regime supporting them. Thus there are no civilian populations (such as the Soviet people in the Cold War) to threaten in the effective use of coercion. Worse, excessive military force could split the fragile Islamic alliance that is cooperating with the United States in the war against terrorism. For that reason, humanitarian aid for the civilian population accompanied the initial attacks on Afghanistan in early October 2001.[23]

The point is to separate the terrorists from the people, and to do justice for the people so they separate from the terrorists. As Susan Thistlethwaite writes, "The spiral of violence will end only when justice is done. No amount of retaliatory violence will give us security in the age of terrorism."[24]

Biological Weapons

The biggest fear is chemical and biological weapons, and especially biological weapons. One can see this throughout the most recent literature on terrorism.[25] If terrorists use biological weapons, the diseases may be spreading for a week before the first outbreak of symptoms, and medical personnel are not likely to diagnose their source for another week or so. By then the disease may have spread to many cities. That is the obvious reason, explains Anthony Blinken, why the United States

> has a profound interest in preventing other countries from testing nuclear arms and stopping rogue regimes and terrorists from acquiring biological weapons. Despite their imperfections, the [Comprehensive Test Ban Treaty and Biological Weapons Convention] would advance these important goals. If the United States rejects the restraints these agreements impose or declines to negotiate improvements, how can it ask others to embrace them?[26]

Yet the Bush administration did precisely that. "In the summer of 2001, the United States shocked its peers when it rejected the protocol to the bioweapons treaty" that would have established verification procedures.[27] Without verification, the treaty had no teeth. And without the United States, the verifications do not go into force. The treaty had already been signed and ratified in 1975, but negotiations to establish legally binding verification did not begin until 1995. Verification would include annual declarations by nations describing their programs and the factories they could use to produce biological weapons, random visits to declared facilities, and short-notice inspections of facilities suspected of producing bioweapons. Clearly this would be useful in preventing many likely sources of bioweapons for terrorists.

> By mid-2001 a consensus text was emerging, and on July 23, 2001, the twenty-fourth negotiating session convened. Delegates expected their efforts would soon result in a final text. During the first three days, more than 50 nations spoke in favor of promptly completing the negotiations. Then U.S. Ambassador Donald Mahley brought the entire process to an end: "The United States has concluded that the current approach to a protocol to the Biological Weapons Convention is not, in our view, capable of strengthening confidence in compliance with the Biological Weapons Convention. . . . We will therefore be unable to support the current text, even with changes."

Later in 2001, "the United States tried at the last minute to terminate protocol negotiations completely, throwing the meeting into disorder and leaving no option but to suspend the conference until November 2002." This earned the U.S. great disappointment, criticism, and anger from the world community. Furthermore, it moved the other nations toward inspection-free development of biological weapons that can be placed into the hands of terrorists. It blocks an enforceable international law that mandates inspections where terrorists might be seeking to develop such weapons for their own use.

One just peacemaking practice is to *reduce offensive weapons and weapons trade.*[28] Surely this practice is the way of wisdom for bioweapons. In an age of terrorism, does the United States want to be in a world where it is responsible for blocking the very inspections for bioweapons that it demanded of Iraq and North Korea? Another practice already mentioned is to *work with emerging cooperative forces in the international system.* And still another is to *strengthen the United Nations and international efforts for cooperation and human rights.* Yet the Bush administration withdrew from the Comprehensive Test Ban Treaty designed to stop nations from developing nuclear weapons, from the Antiballistic Missile Treaty designed to keep outer space unweaponized, from the International Criminal Court, from the Kyoto Accords, from the fissile materials cutoff treaty designed to halt any further development of highly enriched uranium or plutonium for nuclear bombs, and from engagement in peacemaking in the Middle East and with North Korea. These decisions go in the opposite direction from just peacemaking practices. Surely it seems clear to us now after 9/11 that we need cooperation with international networks in supporting international treaties like the bioweapons treaty.

Apparently this reality sunk in for some in the Bush administration. When the conference met again in November 2002, the chairman proposed annual two-week study meetings, looking toward a possible reconsideration in 2006. This time the United States softened a bit, allowing the studies to go forward. We do not know what the United States will do, but just peacemaking suggests reducing bioweapons and working with the cooperative forces of the international community is more necessary than ever.

Israel and Palestine

The greatest source of anger for Arabs and Muslims in the Middle East is the ongoing occupation of Palestine by Israel, the increasing spread of Israeli settlements in Palestine, and the assassinations of terrorist leaders plus Palestinian citizens in their vicinity, with U.S. support. The Israelis are likewise angry at the terrorist violence. The history and the issues are enormously complicated.

I can only point to three just peacemaking practices that can make a difference. First, *nonviolent direct action* is a strategy for Palestinians to achieve international support instead of the widespread revulsion against their terrorism. The first Palestinian *intifada* was known as the popular *intifada*—people could and did participate widely, because no gun or explosive was needed. This relatively nonviolent *intifada* did garner growing international support and some flexibility from the Israeli people and government, as seen in the Oslo Accords. The second *intifada*, however, was carried out by elite groups rather than the people as a whole, because it relied on suicide terrorism. Terrorism is the random targeting of noncombatants for the purpose of striking fear in the population generally in hopes that they will revolt against the policies of their government. It is always immoral, regardless of the rightness or wrongness of its objectives, because its means are attacks against noncombatants. Surely by now we see clearly that Palestinian terrorism has driven Israeli voters to the right in support of Ariel Sharon's militaristic and hard-line opposition, has driven the political parties themselves farther to the right, and has weakened external support for Palestinian justice. (It has done similarly in the United States, shifting politics to the right.)

Robert Pape argues that leaders of suicide terrorist campaigns do have objectives and do make calculations about effectiveness.[29] To support this thesis, he states that five of ten Palestinian terrorist campaigns did appear to lead to modest concessions, although in only two cases were the concessions clearly the result of the terrorism. Two of the five were Israeli withdrawal from parts of occupied territory, which, as Pape concedes, Israel subsequently reoccupied in retaliation against further terrorism, and Israel has increased settlements several fold. One was the release of Sheikh Ahmed Yassin from prison, which was actually done not in response to terrorism but in order to obtain the release of "Israeli agents [who] were captured," and also "was the product of American and Jordanian pressure"; and Israel has since assassinated the Sheikh. Thus the terrorism has achieved little in lasting results except for greatly increased bitterness and hawkishness by Israel.[30] When we contrast this with the way nonviolent direct action successfully built up the internal pressures that toppled dictators in East Germany, Poland, Iran, the Philippines, and many other places, we can argue that active nonviolence provides justice and security more effectively than terrorism.

Second, the "Geneva Accords" of October 2003 were a dramatic example of *cooperative conflict resolution* engaging Israeli and Palestinian leaders who were prominent and respected leaders, though they did not speak for their governments. They met in Geneva and worked out borders and arrangements for a Palestinian state with integrity, a shared Jerusalem, and security for Israel. This was the practice of conflict resolution in a truly hopeful sense. Getting that plan into the public awareness sets a target, a reasonable solution that takes both sides' interests seriously, and is already pressuring the governments to move toward a resolution to the seemingly unending conflict.

In contrast, the Bush administration announced from its first days that it was disengaging from efforts to do conflict resolution in the Middle East. This left the Palestinians in a weak position as they faced a powerful Israeli government led by hard-line Prime Minister Ariel Sharon, and led to a huge increase in terrorism.

By any measure 2002 was an astonishing year for Israel in terms of suicide bombings. An average of five attacks a month were made, nearly double the number during the first fifteen months of the second intifada—and that number was itself more than ten times the monthly average since 1993. Indeed, according to a database maintained by the National Security Studies Center at Haifa University, there were nearly as many suicide attacks in Israel [in 2002] (fifty-nine) as there had been in the previous eight years combined (sixty-two)."[31]

Third, the just peacemaking approach would urge the administration to re-engage in practicing conflict resolution. And indeed, Tony Blair eventually persuaded president Bush to become engaged in the "Roadmap for Peace." The Roadmap corresponds to the just peacemaking practice of *independent initiatives*.[32] In this practice, the two sides do not wait for the slow process of negotiations that in cases of great distrust and threat may be impossible. Instead, one side takes initiatives of threat-reduction independent of the process of negotiations. The Palestinian Authority chose a prime minister who could act somewhat independently from Arafat, as Israel had demanded. And he persuaded the leading terrorist organizations to suspend terrorist acts for a three-month trial period. Israel freed most of Gaza from military occupation, freed a few prisoners, and loosened curfews and checkpoints in a few places. These are independent initiatives. However, Israel did not pull back any significant settlements, and it continued to assassinate Palestinian leaders whom it identified as terrorists. Nor did the Palestinian Authority disarm terrorist organizations. And the United States did not push forcefully for implementation of further initiatives. As a result, the Roadmap failed, at least for the time. In 2004 reports were that the Bush administration was again disengaging for the election year.

Perhaps I can propose an innovative independent initiative. The world knows that Israeli settlements in the Occupied West Bank constitute an immense obstacle to peace between Israel and Palestine. And the Palestinian terrorism is causing Israeli politics to shift to the right, becoming more rigid. Any realistic assessment must point out that Palestinian leaders cannot clamp down on terrorist organizations unless they see significant progress at pulling back settlements. Realism also must recognize that Ariel Sharon's political support depends in part on the settlers' movement; he is not pulling back settlements, and the Roadmap to peace is being undermined. Waiting for him to pull them back is waiting for an unlikely hope. The Israeli government subsidizes the settlers financially, and in turn the U.S. government subsidizes Israel at a rate of $3 billion per year.

An independent initiative that the U.S. government can take would be to use a portion of the $3 billion to buy settlers' homes at prices high enough to give them good incentive to move back, provided they use the money to buy homes in Israel, thus contributing the money to Israel's economy and saving the Israeli Defense Forces the cost of defending the settlements. According to polls, most settlers would be willing to move back to Israel if the financial incentives were reversed. Other settlers, seeing their neighbors leave, and not wanting to be left alone with Palestinian neighbors, would start leaving also. For the first time, Palestinians would see the trend toward reduction instead of expansion of settlements. Their leaders would then have something real to point toward as they persuaded the terrorist organizations once again to halt the terrorism.

Failing to make peace in the Middle East is quite sure to cause terrorism against the United States, and will be responsible for additional destruction in the near future. If the administration is serious about reducing the threat of terrorism, it will heed the warnings that failure to engage in strong support for conflict resolution and independent initiatives in the Middle East will cause violence against Israel and against its main supporter, the United States. Such failure causes angry recruits to terrorism.

Failed States as Havens for Terrorists

A *Washington Quarterly* reader, *The Battle for Hearts and Minds: Using Soft Power to Undermine Terrorist Networks*, pays special attention to "failed states." These are states that lack an effective government, so something like anarchy reigns. Examples of failed states are Afghanistan, Angola, Burundi, Congo, Liberia, Sierra Leone, and Sudan; a dozen others are candidates. Failed states create havens where terrorists can organize and train recruits, can establish weapons collections; and can engage in drug trade or other money-gathering endeavors. The obvious example was Afghanistan, where al Qaeda organized and trained.[33]

Military action is not sufficient here; these states need rehabilitation and democracy-building. A bipartisan consensus supports efforts at building democracies,[34] which is a practice of just peacemaking. The authors of *The Battle for Hearts and Minds* do not call this nation-building because that carries historical associations with failed efforts in Vietnam, and because president Bush campaigned for the presidency while denouncing nation-building:

> I would be very careful about using our troops as nation builders. I believe
> the role of the military is to fight and win war and, therefore, prevent war
> from happening in the first place. . . . Morale in today's military is too
> low. . . . I believe we're over-extended in too many places.[35]

Therefore, the new terms are now "postconflict reconstruction" or
"democracy-building."[36] Since President Bush's election, however, we
have seen the truth in what candidate Bush said. Not only is the military over-extended, it is, as he said, "over-extended in too many places."
The military is not trained for nation-building, and we are seeing that
Pentagon control of the rebuilding process in Iraq has not worked well.
Furthermore, morale indeed is low.

The Battle for Hearts and Minds has much wisdom about building democracy, and about why it should be led by civilians focused on rehabilitation of civil society, not elections and military security alone. It
requires strengthening the rule of law and respect for human rights,
developing genuine political processes, fostering the development of
civil society, promoting accountable public institutions, and developing
governmental capacity to deliver basic public goods. Thus far, say the
authors, there has been too much attention on building a police force
while overlooking other dimensions of democracy-building.[37] Karin von
Hippel is especially insightful in her study of Haiti, Bosnia, Kosovo, and
East Timor. She affirms what just peacemaking theory also notes: "The
promotion of democracy is based on the assumption that democracies
rarely go to war with each other, and therefore an increase in the number
of democratic states would imply a more peaceful and secure world."[38]
Democracies in turn produce far fewer terrorists because disgruntled
citizens have other means for seeking change, as an essay by Jennifer
Windsor explains.[39]

This is bipartisan consensus, and it affirms the just peacemaking practices of *advancing democracy and human rights*, and *fostering just and sustainable economic development* that depends on community development.
The problem that the book identifies is that present policy emphasizes
military action too much and community-development and civil-society
development too little. So much anti-terrorism money and attention goes
to strengthening the military forces in countries like Indonesia, the Philippines, Pakistan, and Israel, where military forces have often been the
enemy of human rights and democracy. Thus many see the United States
as the supporter of autocracy and the enemy of citizen movements.[40]
When the United States declared its military war against terrorism, In-

donesia canceled peace talks with the rebels in Aceh and instead made war against them; Israel increased its military attacks against Palestinian leaders; and Russia pursued its destructive war against Chechnya free of U.S. government criticism.

Recruiting Terrorists

For all the wisdom in *The Battle for Hearts and Minds*, it may have been over-influenced by the war in Afghanistan that had just occurred at the time of the writing. Other studies of the recruitment of terrorists point not so much to failed states such as Afghanistan as to autocratic states. The failed states are havens for terrorist organizations that come from other countries, and they do create the terrorism against their own people that comes with anarchy. But Afghanistan, Angola, and Burundi themselves have not been known for producing international terrorist recruits. It is authoritarian autocracies such as Saudi Arabia and Egypt that produce these recruits. Yet not all autocracies produce terrorist recruits either. Syria, Iran, and Iraq before the defeat of Saddam Hussein have not produced terrorists who attack the United States, because the United States government did not support those autocracies. Thus the people who chafed under those autocracies did not resent the United States. It is the U.S.-supported autocracies that produce terrorists against the United States. The conclusion would seem to be that the United States should be nudging these autocracies in the direction of human rights and democracy, a key just peacemaking practice.[41]

In *The Battle for Hearts and Minds*, Windsor's chapter describes "authoritarian political systems" in the Middle East that the United States government has supported. Almost every Arab country is less free than it was forty years ago. "In such societies, severe repression drives all politics underground, placing the moderate opposition at a disadvantage, and encouraging political extremism." Double-digit unemployment causes the educated but unemployed youth to grow increasingly angry and frustrated.[42] It is not the poorest states, but the autocratic states, that are the prime generators of international terrorists. Autocracy generates terrorists.[43]

Others too have pointed out that the poorest and least educated do not become international terrorists, but have wrongly concluded that economic development is not important for preventing terrorism. Michael Radu, for example, first shows that joblessness of educated Muslims, not poverty of uneducated Muslims, creates terrorists:

The known backgrounds of the September 11 terrorists suggest the same: leaders and recruits to the most fanatical terrorist groups are *not* the poor, unfairly treated, and marginalized masses of the Islamic world, but rather—just as in Latin America, Sri Lanka, and the Philippines—young and radicalized university graduates who have lost their traditional employment in government-paid universities and other public sector positions and find their career aspirations blocked. The same syndrome applies to unassimilated and unassimilable young, well-educated, usually second-generation Muslim immigrants in the West.[44]

Radu argues from this that:

Nothing in the background of the Western-born or -based Muslim terrorists supports the widespread fantasy that Islamic terrorism can somehow be explained by injustice, poverty, or discrimination. On the contrary, terrorism on the scale of the September 11 attacks *requires* elaborate coordination by multilingual, adaptable, and highly educated people. No impoverished, ignorant victims of Western imperialism need apply. At bottom, therefore, international fundamentalist Islamic terrorism is not a social or economic, but rather a cultural, phenomenon.[45]

But this is a *non sequitur*. Far from showing that "nothing" about economic justice contributes to the motivation of terrorists, Radu himself has cited the economic joblessness of educated Muslims. Surely their widespread setbacks, and not just the plight of the destitute, are symptoms of economic injustice. Seeing the oppression of their poor and uneducated compatriots only heightens their anger. As just peacemaking theory points out, it is those who have developed some expectations but then see their own or their fellows' conditions dropping well below those expectations who tend to turn to violence.[46]

This is not to contest altogether the cultural sources of terrorism. But "cultural sources" include the culture of authoritarianism. That is why just peacemaking practices focus *both* on human rights and democracy, *and* on sustainable economic development.

Zachary Abuza has written an impressive study of terrorist networks in Southeast Asia. He combines relative economic deprivation with authoritarian religion as causes of terrorist recruitment. In Southeast Asia, "radical Islam is growing for a variety of reasons. These include economic dispossession, the lack of political freedom, the spread of Wahabbism and Salafi Islam, the failure of secular education, and an increased number of religious students studying in Middle Eastern and south Asian *madrasses* (Islamic schools)."[47] This suggests to Abuza that:

The growth of Islamic extremism around the world, since the Iranian revolution in 1979, has less to do with theology and more to do with the failure of the domestic political economies of respective Muslim countries. Increasing gaps between the rich and poor, inequitable distribution of wealth, poverty, a lack of economic diversity, unemployment, corruption, and the lack of a viable political alternative, have all given rise to Islamic extremism. People literally have become so desperate that they have nowhere to turn to except extremist religious politics.[48]

Yet Abuza's main theme is the intricate international interconnections of the international terrorists. It is an astounding web of financing, money-raising, recruiting, teaching, organizing, encouraging, inspiring, that connects the terrorists across the many countries in which they live.

The conclusion seems clear that combating terrorism cannot be the work of one powerful country with a large military force. It requires work with the international forces of justice and peace, and a cooperative foreign policy. By contrast, a unilateral policy alienates other nations with what they perceive, in Fareed Zakaria's words, as "the arrogant empire."[49]

The Limits of Unilateral Power and
the Need for a Cooperative Foreign Policy

There is a limit to how much the United States can do or will do, and there is a limit to how much military power can do. Many of us recall Reinhold Niebuhr's realistic essay, "The Limits of Military Power," when the Eisenhower administration was deciding whether to replace the French in the Vietnam War.[50] That administration must have read Niebuhr's essay; it wisely decided not to enter the Vietnam War at that time.

Many of us also recall the debate between George W. Bush and Al Gore, when Bush said, "It is time for the Europeans to do their share in Kosovo." Apparently he did not know that eighty-five percent of the troops doing the peacekeeping in Kosovo then were European and fifteen percent were American—but Gore did not challenge his facts either. In any case, even in ignorance, Bush was right that the United States should not be expected to do it all alone; the U.S. needs the Europeans, Asians, Africans, Middle Easterners, and all the world to do their share. Then-candidate Bush also said that the United States needs "a more humble foreign policy." He was right. But his statement is ironic now. The world's

"sole remaining superpower" needs a new foreign policy of cooperation, in which it cooperates with other nations so that they cooperate in
bringing their skills and capabilities to these complex problems.

The world is in flux, and the U.S. relationship with the Muslim world
is too complex for "going it alone." The United States was already involved in rebuilding Kosovo, Bosnia, and Serbia, pre-9/11. It is now
involved in rebuilding Afghanistan. The rise of the Taliban and al Qaeda
had much to do with the lack of U.S. support in rebuilding Afghanistan
after the Soviet Union was driven out. The negative example of no nation-building in Afghanistan after the expulsion of the Soviets shows that
failing to invest in sustainable economic development and human rights
can create the conditions for military war-fighting later. The Muslim
world is watching to see if the United States only wants to make war on
Muslim nations or will be committed to building justice and peace and
a semblance of government, education, and economic opportunity in
Afghanistan. Thus far it is under-investing and underproducing.

And now the United States must help rebuild Iraq. A State Department
committee had developed lessons from past nation-building efforts and
had a plan to guide the rebuilding in Iraq. They included the need for
international cooperation. Instead, the Bush administration disbanded
the State Department committee and instead put the Pentagon in charge
of the effort. Almost all can see that was a disastrous mistake. The military under orders from Bush was not prepared for the task; it positively
neglected international cooperation both in making the war and in letting
contracts for reconstruction. A little less trust in militaristic solutions and
a little more respect for civilian involvement and international cooperation can prevent much war later on.

By disengaging from work for justice for Palestinians, by engaging in
war in Muslim Afghanistan without adequate follow-up to help build
democracy, and by initiating war in Muslim Iraq and dominating Iraq
after the war without U.N. leadership, the U.S. government is effectively
persuading many Muslims and Arabs that bin Laden is right: the United
States is making war against Muslims wherever it can and seeking to
dominate them. The resulting anger and resentment make terrorist recruitment significantly more successful.

Forces of flux also create significant opportunity for change toward
peace, however. The Greater Middle East, reaching all the way to Pakistan, needs more responsive governance, more effective economics, and
a strengthening of the peaceful side of Islam rather than the authoritarian and radical side. Things could move in this direction, if they receive

wise and consistent help. But that is more than the United States can do alone, and more than military power can achieve. The United States needs to work consistently with the United Nations, and the international forces for human rights and cooperation—two key practices of just peacemaking—so that those forces help nudge the world in the direction of peace.

Change is in the air. There is great danger, and great opportunity. Imagine a United States aligning its power with the cooperative forces in the international system, and with the United Nations. Imagine the United Nations leading the actions in Iraq, with much-needed U.S. support, so that Muslims and Arabs do not see the action as U.S. colonialism but as U.N. liberation from colonialism and dictatorship. The United Nations has zero reputation for colonialism and much reputation for helping nations achieve self-determination: the U.N. Trusteeship Council oversaw the achievement of self-determination for many nations. As in Kosovo and Bosnia, U.N. leadership in Iraq, with U.S. support and the support of many nations, would be much less resented and much more hopefully received. Imagine much-decreased Arab and Muslim resentment and anger. Imagine the motivation for terrorism dramatically decreasing. Imagine strengthened international cooperation opening up realistic alternatives to bitterness and war.

Notes

1. *Time*, March 3, 2003, 44–45.
2. John E. Mueller, *War, Presidents, and Public Opinion* (New York: Wiley, 1973).
3. According to Mueller, what did have influence was the number of body bags coming home. In spite of increasing demonstrations against the war by both pacifists and persons convinced the war was unjust, and despite intellectuals' arguments that the war was unjust, these did not seem to affect the polls about the war. His "body-bag hypothesis" has had much influence both in government policy and in the public mind. (Hence the Bush administration does not allow photographs of body bags coming home from the Iraqi War or from the guerrilla war continuing after the mission was allegedly accomplished.) But in order to make his argument fit data, Mueller must hypothesize that the support declined with a logarithm of the total number of casualties. "A rise from 100 to 1000 is taken as the same as one from 10,000 to 100,000" (60). But both in the Korean War and World War II, the body-bag hypothesis fails. During the long-lasting and very costly World War II, far more body bags came home. But it was widely judged to be a just war (in spite of the obliteration bombing). Did the support decline with the body bags, or did it stay high with the perceived justice of the war? It stayed high through the end of the war. Support did not decrease (as it did not decrease for the Korean War after a temporary drop when China entered the war in 1950). The threat-from-the-enemy factor was higher for WWII, support

for FDR was higher, nationalism was higher with total mobilization, and the justice of the war was higher, because Hitler was so thoroughly evil.

4. 59% to 37% in the February 10 poll; 62% to 36% on February 24; and 60% to 35% on March 4.

5. Similarly, Americans thought—by about a two-to-one majority—that the United States should wait for approval from the United Nations before waging war. Hence President Bush shifted from originally contending that he did not need a U.N. vote to going to the U.N. and promising he would ask for U.N. approval before waging the war.

6. Norman K. Gottwald, *All the Kingdoms of the Earth: Israelite Prophecy and International Relations in the Ancient Near East* (New York: Harper & Row, 1964) is highly insightful and realistic, and forty years later, still is must reading for ethicists.

7. Glen H. Stassen, *Just Peacemaking: Transforming Initiatives for Justice and Peace* (Louisville, KY: Westminster/John Knox Press, 1992), chapters 2 and 3.

8. For a full introduction to these practices, see Glen Stassen, *Just Peacemaking: Ten Practices for Abolishing War* (Cleveland: Pilgrim Press, 1998 and 2004).

9. I have written a somewhat systematic overview in Glen H. Stassen, "Turning Attention to Just Peacemaking Initiatives That Prevent Terrorism," *The Council of Societies for the Study of Religion Bulletin* 31, no. 3 (September 2002): 59–65. Susan Brooks Thistlethwaite has written an incisive essay on just peacemaking practices that combat terrorism, "New Wars, Old Wineskins," in *Strike Terror No More: Theology, Ethics, and the New War*, ed. Jon L. Berquist (St. Louis, MO: Chalice Press, 2002).

10. Fareed Zakaria, "Suicide Bombers Can be Stopped," *Newsweek*, August 25, 2003, 57.

11. Svante E. Cornell, "The Kurdish Question in Turkish Politics," *Orbis* 45, no. 1 (Winter 2001): 42.

12. See Glen Stassen, *Just Peacemaking: Ten Practices for Abolishing War*, chapter 6.

13. Michael Radu, "The Rise and Fall of the PKK," *Orbis* 45, no. 1 (Winter 2001): 58.

14. Cornell, "The Kurdish Question in Turkish Politics," 37.

15. See Glen Stassen, *Just Peacemaking: Ten Practices for Abolishing War*, chapter 5.

16. Cornell, "The Kurdish Question in Turkish Politics," 40.

17. Ibid., 45.

18. See Glen Stassen, *Just Peacemaking: Ten Practices for Abolishing War*, chapter 7.

19. See Glen Stassen, *Just Peacemaking: Ten Practices for Abolishing War*, chapter 3.

20. Radu, "The Rise and Fall of the PKK," 47.

21. Peter Woodman, "Stay Away from Istanbul, Britons Told," *The Press Association Limited*, 20 November 2003. There had also been several small attacks on UK and US diplomatic premises April 3, April 8, May 31, and June 11.

22. Modern marketing techniques, and the consumeristic ideology they support, are a version of this view of human nature. Authoritarian political philosophy, with its punitive and retributive understanding of justice, is an older version of this view.

23. Rob de Wijk, "The Limits of Military Power," in *The Battle for Hearts and Minds: Using Soft Power to Undermine Terrorist Networks*, ed. Alexander T. Lennon, A Washington Quarterly Reader (Cambridge, MA: MIT Press, 2003), 16. Though, as Susan Thistlethwaite points out, "the airdrops are not coming anywhere close to meeting the need for food," and picking them up in that heavily mined country involves much danger.

24. Thistlethwaite, "New Wars, Old Wineskins," 264.

25. As attested to in Alexander T. Lennon, ed., *The Battle for Hearts and Minds: Using Soft Power to Undermine Terrorist Networks*, A Washington Quarterly Reader (Cambridge, MA: MIT Press, 2003), 69, 286, et passim; and Arnold M. Howitt and Robyn L. Pangi, eds.,

Countering Terrorism: Dimensions of Preparedness, BCSIA Studies in International Security (Cambridge, MA: MIT Press, 2003), chapter 5 et passim.

26. Anthony J. Blinken, "Winning the War of Ideas," in *The Battle for Hearts and Minds*, 285.

27. Mark Wheelis, Malcolm Dando, and Catherine Auer, "Back to Bioweapons?" *Bulletin of the Atomic Scientists* 59, no. 1 (January–February 2003): 40–47. The following information and quotes come from this well-informed essay. It assesses motivations for U.S. rejection of enforcement, and concludes the United States should re-enter the treaty.

28. See Glen Stassen, *Just Peacemaking: Ten Practices for Abolishing War*, chapter 9.

29. Robert Pape, "The Strategic Logic of Suicide Terrorism," *American Political Science Review* 97, no. 3 (August 2003).

30. Ibid., 351–52.

31. Bruce Hoffman, "The Logic of Suicide Terrorism," *Atlantic Monthly* 291, no. 5 (June 2003): 44.

32. See Glen Stassen, *Just Peacemaking: Ten Practices for Abolishing War*, chapter 2.

33. Lennon, *The Battle for Hearts and Minds*, 73, 79, 91, 153, et passim.

34. Ibid., 235.

35. Quoted in ibid, 175.

36. Ibid., 175–6.

37. Ibid., 242; 201 et passim.

38. Ibid., 108ff.

39. Ibid., 362ff.

40. Ibid., 103–4 et passim.

41. Ibid., 362–6.

42. Ibid., 364–5.

43. Ibid., 150ff. 162–3, 166.

44. Michael Radu, "Terrorism After the Cold War: Trends and Challenges," *Orbis* 46, no. 2 (Spring 2002): 286.

45. Ibid.

46. Glen Stassen, *Just Peacemaking: Ten Practices for Abolishing War*, 112.

47. Zachary Abuza, "Al Qaeda's Southeast Asian Network," *Contemporary Southeast Asia* 24, no. 3 (December 2002): 428.

48. Abuza, "Al Qaeda's Southeast Asian Network," 433. For a wider-ranging historical study of terrorism in a readable format, see Walter Laqueur, *The New Terrorism: Fanaticism and the Arms of Mass Destruction* (New York: Oxford University Press, 1999), 79–156; and Paul Gilbert, *New Terror, New Wars* (Washington, DC: Georgetown University Press, 2003). More comprehensive and systematic, and I think best informed is Audrey Kurth Cronin and James M. Ludes, *Attacking Terrorism: Elements of a Grand Strategy* (Washington, DC: Georgetown University Press, 2004).

49. Fareed Zakaria, "The Arrogant Empire," *Newsweek*, March 24, 2003, 19–33.

50. Reinhold Niebuhr, "The Limits of Military Power," *New Leader*, May 30, 1955, 16ff.

PART II

Just Policing: The Proposal

Chapter 4

Warfare vs. Policing:
In Search of Moral Clarity

Gerald W. Schlabach

The differences between war and policing make a difference. So I will argue. But this is not to deny all similarities.

To distinguish sharply between the two phenomena is to employ what sociologists and ethicists call "ideal types." Any "typology" is valuable precisely because it helps us to simplify, describe, and evaluate realities that are more complex than the types themselves. War and policing have often merged in reality, of course, as communities and nations have attempted to use warfare as a tool for policing. But just because such a merger has been common historically and down to our day does not make it ethical. And in any case, simply to study carefully the ways that war and policing may merge will require us to distinguish between their two dynamics more carefully than we have done. In broad strokes, then, we can begin to chart the difference between war and policing in the following way:

Policing seeks to secure the common good of the very society within which it operates; because it is embedded, indebted, and accountable within that community, according to the rule of law, it has an inherent tendency to minimize recourse to violence.

Warfare may also seek to secure the common good of a society, of course. But because it extends beyond that society through threats to other communities, it has an inherent tendency to break out of the rule of law. It thus cuts whatever slender bonds of accountability that would truly limit its use to "last resort." And this difference is only the beginning. For having cut loose, war usually jeopardizes not only the common good of international community, but even that of the society in whose name it is being waged.

Neither pacifists nor just warriors have explored this difference adequately.[1] Pacifists and just warriors have rarely even argued over the similarities between war and policing with enough rigor to expose the limits of those similarities and thus reveal crucial differences.[2] If they would do so together and thus all-the-more accountably, however, war might in fact cease to be a church-dividing issue. How so?

If both pacifist and just-war-affirming churches attended more fully to the differences between war and policing, then (1) what once was claimed to be "just war" would finally be just because it would just be policing not war; (2) pacifists could fulfill, not betray, their vocation to call all Christians to the nonviolent way of Jesus Christ by helping societies respond more effectively to the challenges that have historically led to war; and (3) in the process both would have practically yet decisively rejected war. To begin moving in this direction, however, both traditions of moral reflection need to recognize their respective failures to think in clear and forthcoming ways about policing.

Policing and the Just War Tradition

The just war tradition of moral deliberation suffers from a kind of slipperiness.[3] It claims that war can sometimes be morally justifiable, and attempts to use reason to limit war to cases that are exceptional and morally justifiable. But as it does so, it gets much of its credibility by imagining war to be like police action. It thus seems mere "common sense" that war may sometimes be necessary to protect innocent third parties and maintain order between nations, just as police force does within a given community. Once wars have been justified in this way, however, very different psycho-social dynamics take over, which move it farther and farther away from policing.

The intention of the just war theory's more conscientious proponents has been to keep violence at the bare minimum that human societies apparently need if they are to maintain order in a sinful world. Beginning with a strong presumption against violence,[4] which the tradition shares with pacifism, just war thinkers would allow recourse to lethal violence only as an exception and only as a concession to the realities of our world.

Ours is a world, after all, that does not yet enjoy the fullness of God's Reign. Instead it suffers from crime, unjust aggression, exploitation, abuse of human rights, and thus from a general lack of mutual trust. In such a world, love of neighbor and protection of the innocent seem at times to require the judicious use of violent force. To be moral and judicious in fact, any recourse to violent force must come only in the wake of sincere attempts to resolve conflicts and to sanction the recalcitrant by first using other kinds of force. Only when the criterion of last resort and other criteria are met may war be justifiable.[5]

Yet skeptics have reason to wonder whether just war reasoning consistently delivers upon its promise to limit the violence of war. Before John Howard Yoder became both a leading advocate of Christian pacifism *and* a major scholar of just war thinking, he was a student of the renowned Protestant theologian Karl Barth. Yoder has recounted an incident that represents all too well the way in which just war reasoning loses whatever grip it had on Christian conscience and devolves into something else. Yoder was in the lecture hall at the University of Basel around 1951 when Barth delivered lectures on war that would later go into volume III/4 of his *Church Dogmatics*. As Barth condemned virtually every rationale for war and declared that pacifism is "almost infinitely right," his students squirmed—until, at the last moment, Barth allowed an exception: A Christian republic like his own Switzerland might fight a strictly self-defensive war.

First came a palpable release of tension, then applause. "What is significant here," noted Yoder, "is the difference between what Barth said and what the students understood." Barth had condemned all but the rarest war. He later came to oppose nuclear weapons categorically and he even called himself "practically pacifist." Yet "every half-informed Christian thinks Karl Barth is not opposed to war." If theologians are going to claim their positions are realistic, concluded Yoder, they must acknowledge that this "tendency of theologians' statements to be misinterpreted is also part of "political reality."[6]

Just so, just war reasoning all too often devolves functionally into propaganda. It becomes permissive rather than stringent. It sometimes becomes permissive precisely through the reassuring guise of having been stringent. It serves to condone wars by establishing the general principle that wars *can* be just. Its best-intended practitioners may wish to curtail wars through rigorous moral deliberation over particular wars. But that is not the message that reaches the pews.

Just war deliberation *should* require disciplined (even heroic) political action when particular wars fail to meet just war criteria. If that is not happening, what we have here is a just war rhetoric or theory, at best. What we do *not* really have is a just war *tradition* in the full communal sense of which Aristotelians such as philosopher Alasdair MacIntyre speak, a living tradition with operative practices shaping a community through time.[7] In their 1993 statement, *The Harvest of Justice is Sown in Peace*, U.S. bishops recognized the need for such an operative, living, tradition when they followed up their rehearsal of the just war criteria by noting: "In the absence of a commitment of respect for life and a culture of restraint, it will not be easy to apply the just-war tradition, not just as a set of ideas, but as a system of effective social constraints on the use of force."[8]

Yet despite these failures just war thinking continues its hold on moral discourse because it seems to make simple "common sense" and appears "realistic," while pacifism apparently does not. We need not rehearse the principles and precepts of the natural law (in accord with Catholic just war thinking) in order to notice why.[9] All we must do is notice a telling phenomenon: Non-pacifist Christian theologians and ethicists may treat the need for the police function as self-evident and needing no argument,[10] or they may sometimes argue at length for the legitimacy of the police function based in biblical texts such as Romans 13 and 1 Peter 2.[11] In either case they may then go on to argue analogically for the legitimacy of Christian participation in warfare using the police function as a metaphor. But rarely if ever do they do the reverse and use war as a metaphor for policing.[12]

The point here is not that there is *complete* discontinuity between the role that civic authorities take in ordering the life of communities through the police function and the role that they play in protecting those communities through the military function.[13] If the core arguments of the present project prove convincing and fruitful, Christians will need to discriminate carefully among the continuities and the discontinuities in war and policing on their way toward eliminating war as a church-dividing issue. The point for now is simply that the easy assumption of continuity, based on using policing as a metaphor to explain the work-ings of war, obscures some very serious differences between policing and war. That obscurity in turn keeps the just war tradition from con-sistently working, even on its own terms, to limit rather than provide a blank check to wars.

For once war is justified as an extension of the self-evident need for policing, war consistently becomes something other than policing, and the just war tradition tends to devolve into either "war realism" or crusading. War realism (alternately, "warism"[14]) is the very position that the just war theory has tried to disprove, namely, that war has a life and logic all its own, impervious to any moral considerations beyond self-interest. Crusading is the real dynamic that drives allegedly just wars whenever their defenders cite just cause to the exclusion of all other criteria for a just war, or whenever unconditional surrender is demanded, or whenever the preservation of personal or national honor keeps people fighting long after they have reasonable grounds to expect "probable success," or whenever claims to righteous causes or sacred duties trump in any other way the demands that just war criteria would impose.[15]

In all of the following ways war takes on a significantly different psycho-social dynamic from policing, so that even in those cases where the two merge, amid the complexity of real life, we can distinguish two "types" of phenomena at work, and make ethical or policy evaluations accordingly.

1. *Untethering from the common good.* Military weapons and organizations are designed to be expeditionary. In other words, they take the capacity to kill and destroy (or to *threaten* to kill and destroy) into someone else's territory. They then use that capacity to hold the territory without depending any more than necessary on ties to the local society.[16] By contrast, those who do police work are seeking to preserve the public safety of their own locales. If they are not to act as vigilantes they must be accountable to their neighbors through the rule of law. Police cannot operate in another jurisdiction without permission except in cases of "hot pursuit," and even then they must cooperate with that jurisdiction to extradite any suspect they apprehend. U.S. efforts to "root out" terrorists in the Middle East and South Asia following the attacks of September 11, 2001 only began to be analogous to policing insofar as they relied on international law and U.N. approval.[17] Following "successful" military invasions of Afghanistan and Iraq, however, the U.S. military has been the first to admit that it is ill-prepared to do police work in those nations. If the purported goal of military operations has been to establish democratic civil society through "nation-building," then in post-war Afghanistan and Iraq their improvisational nature at best, or their ineptness at worst, has only confirmed how disconnected war can be from policing and the common good, even when on purely military terms it succeeds.[18]

2. *The rally-'round-the flag phenomenon.* It was not simply a slip-up when President George W. Bush initially spoke of responding to the

September 11 attacks with a "crusade" and the U.S. military initially named its war in Afghanistan "Operation Infinite Justice." Political leaders usually draw on the rhetoric of national pride, honor, *and thus* crusading in order to marshal the political will and sustain the sacrifices necessary to fight wars, even if their deliberations initially ran the war through the grid of just war criteria. This is the phenomenon we associate with phrases such as "rally around the flag" and "war fever." While the rituals surrounding police work include flags, oaths, and appeals to honor, they proceed in far less feverish ways.

3. *The blunt instrument problem.* Even circumscribed warfare, aiming to meet the criterion of noncombatant immunity,[19] is too blunt of a tool to serve the police officer's basic task of identifying and apprehending criminals. As Stanley Hauerwas once put it, "B-52s turn out to be very crude police officers."[20] His remark received tragic confirmation a few months later when on June 30, 2002, B-52s bombed a wedding in the village of Kakarak, apparently after mistaking traditional fireworks for anti-aircraft fire. In another incident on July 22, 2002, the Israeli government dropped a one-ton bomb on a house in a Gaza City neighborhood in order to assassinate Salah Shehada, who was on Israel's "most wanted" lists of Palestinian terrorists. However legitimate a target he might have been for a police action to apprehend him, the bombing not only killed him and his family but at least ten more noncombatants, while wounding at least a hundred others. The very need to appeal to the principle of double effect in order to explain why a nation and its soldiers are not blameworthy when their targeting results in "collateral damage" amounts to a tacit recognition of the blunt instrument problem.

4. *Failure to meet minimal requirements for the rule of law.* Warfare can never be subject to the rule of law in the way that policing can be. If the development of democratic processes since ancient Greece teaches us anything it is that no rule of law is possible without separating the roles of "judge and executioner." Hauerwas probably overstated his case when went on to say that in good policing the "arresting agent is not the same as the judging agent," while in war "those two are the same."[21] With civilian-controlled militaries, at least, soldiers are not to go into action until someone else in the chain of command has given the order. Yet in a way the deserts of Iraq have confirmed Hauerwas's point nonetheless. Anti-personnel munitions have chewed up thousands upon thousands of Iraqi conscripts, judging and executing them for supporting Saddam Hussein without any mechanism to determine

whether the regime was keeping them in uniform against their will. Since they were combatants, technically this was not a violation of the just war theory's condemnation of indiscriminate targeting. Yet the more certain it is that the regime was tyrannizing its people, the less certain it is the death of any given conscript was fair. Thanks to the "blunt instrument phenomenon" they were being judged and executed indiscriminately, without benefit of any judicial process to sort the guilty willing from the innocent unwilling. Should a militarist shrug in reply, saying, "That's war; what else can you expect?" there is no need to refute him. The dynamics of war *may* in fact offer no other choice but to shoot now and ask questions later. But that's the point: war is not policing.

5. *The football phenomenon.* Coaches and generals both have reasons to insist that the "best defense is a good offense." But those then become reasons why "good" military strategy intrinsically tends toward greater and greater firepower while "good policing" inherently narrows the use of violence to last resort. Since the first Gulf War, some military strategists have referred to the overwhelming, decisive use of firepower as "hyperwar." If the best defense is a strong offense, then striking hard and striking first make sense. Very quickly, however, key just war criteria such as last resort, proportionality, and noncombatant immunity lose out.

6. *Adrenaline rush.* We have words like "frenzy," and "berserk" in the English language precisely because our linguistic ancestors noticed what the heat of battle can do to the psyche of warriors.[22] Irrationality sets in. Warriors simultaneously experience deep fatigue and intense focus, power and vulnerability, love of comrade and hatred of foe. Amid this volatile psychological mix they may strike indiscriminately, continue against impossible odds (i.e. *im*probable success), and survive by drawing on every emotion that Augustine's theory of "right intention" amid war would rule out. Those who do not "go berserk" need the rush of adrenaline to survive; those who guide their battles from capital cities far from the front lines vicariously feel that rush. Though adrenaline surely courses through the veins of police SWAT teams too, and constant exposure to danger and frustration can lead to police brutality even without factors like racism, war changes the chemistry in significant ways. The setting is more likely to be outside of the soldier's own community, so that neither bonds of identification nor the rule of law constrain the psychology of frenzy.[23] Further, the military campaigns that create the conditions for frenzy are prolonged

so that those conditions become endemic, whereas the high-intensity occasions for SWAT team police actions are just that, occasional.

7. *The let-them-not-have-died-in-vain phenomenon.* Even if one no longer has good reasons to be at war, and even if that war never passed the muster of just war criteria, the death of one's forebears or comrades in an otherwise untenable war gives "reasons" to fight on. For although the defense of honor is *not* a just cause in the modern canon of just war criteria, it is probably the most forceful reason to fight in the collective mind of any general populace (cf. no. 2 above.) That late-twentieth-century Serbian nationalists cited a thirteenth-century defeat in order to stoke their sense of heroism suggests how powerful this phenomenon can be. But this is only an extreme case of how far the psycho-social dynamics of real wars can take us from the dispassionate rationality of just war theory and the practical precision of good policing. This and the adrenaline phenomenon consistently make it unimaginable for a nation to sue for peace, even though surrender *should* be a moral obligation whenever one's own war effort fails to meet the criteria for a just war.[24]

8. *Militarization.* The more that a civilian population and a military force engage with one another, the more violent and indiscriminate warfare becomes.[25] Militarizing civilian populations makes them more vulnerable to attack, makes it harder for the *other* side to fulfill the criterion of noncombatant immunity, and tends to weaken the social fabric by obscuring the deeper causes of conflict and injustice while offering military solutions to social problems. On the other hand, the more that a community and its police are engaged with one another, the less violent policing can become. "Community policing" is a new name for a return to an old strategy that gets police out of their patrol cars, onto the street, into town meetings, and integrated into the neighborhoods they seek to protect.[26] Police cannot do it well without attending to the deeper causes of crime and thus strengthening the social fabric of a community.

This list is probably not unassailable and surely not exhaustive.[27] Critics might note counter-evidence pointing out psycho-social continuities between policing and war. Sympathizers may extend the list and corroborate it with further research.[28]

Still, the list should be sufficient to demonstrate that, contrary to long usage, policing cannot serve in any kind of facile or automatic way as a metaphor to justify warfare. For the just war theory to stand any chance of fulfilling its advocates' best intentions, it must retrace its steps and attend far more closely to the ways in which war is *not* like policing. Meanwhile, policing itself must be called back from the brink of militarization. "Just war" is probably a misnomer for what can just be just policing if it is to establish a real tradition of actually reducing violence to the minimum possible for a fallen world.

Policing and the Pacifist Tradition

What pacifists think about policing is no more clear, however. The Society of Friends, or Quakers, has within its tradition the historical experience of generally unarmed policing in colonial Pennsylvania. Some twentieth-century Quakers have been open to Christian participation in policing, including international police forces.[29] Mennonite positions against any use of violent force have been more resolute and one might expect this to make them an example of strict pacifist clarity about policing. But if anything, Mennonites only show more clearly the need for pacifist deliberation on the ethics of policing.

Mennonites are not likely to find their early Anabaptist forebears making clear distinctions to guide them here, because sixteenth-century magistrates combined the roles of police and warrior.[30] With less of a tradition of civic involvement than Quakers, Mennonites have been less inclined to participate in local policing and have not seen international policing as different enough from the military for them to alter their official position of nonparticipation.[31] That much is clear. But twentieth-century Mennonites have directed most of their attention against military conscription, militarism, and warfare.

Influential Mennonite answers as to why members of their churches should not be police officers, therefore, have sometimes simply been that Christians have more important things to do. This carries an intriguing implication. It suggests that while their pacifism vis-à-vis military action was principled, their pacifism vis-à-vis police action was vocational. And vocational discernment will turn out to be crucial for an adequately Christian ethic of policing, whether approached from the pacifist or the just war side.

First, though, let us notice how September 11, 2001 exposed the need for pacifists to think through an ethic of policing more clearly. The al Qaeda terrorist attack that day upon New York's World Trade Center and the U.S. Pentagon certainly did *not* "change everything" for Christian believers who know that Calvary is the day that changed everything.[32]

And yet 9/11 certainly *did* dislodge neglected issues of all sorts and force even people of firm faith to examine their assumptions anew. For Christians committed to the thoroughgoing practice of nonviolence, the place of policing has been one of those issues.

Strikingly, after all, the best immediate alternative to vengeful retaliation that many pacifist voices could advocate was that nations treat the 9/11 attacks as a crime against humanity and try terrorists in courts of international law. On September 22, the Mennonite Central Committee's Executive Committee issued a statement that focused on upholding "the call of Jesus to love enemies and live as peacemakers" while praying for and reaching out to people affected on all sides of the conflict. Following the exhortation of Jeremiah 29:7 that Israelites exiled in Babylon should "seek the welfare of the city," the statement reiterated that the primary citizenship of Jesus' followers requires them to live "as citizens of a new Kingdom," yet also means being "advocates and builders of peaceful systems and institutions" wherever they live. What then to advocate? While praying for national leaders, people of faith should "call on governments to exercise restraint and respect for the process of international law and diplomacy."[33]

Pacifist theologians, ethicists, and international specialists made similar moves. Mennonite ethicist Duane K. Friesen of Bethel College (KS), author of *Christian Peacemaking & International Conflict: A Realist Pacifist Perspective,*[34] urged students and colleagues to view 9/11 within a crime framework, not a war framework.[35] Veteran Mennonite peacemaker John Paul Lederach, Professor of International Peacebuilding at Notre Dame's Kroc Institute for International Peace Studies, called for a multifaceted response that would address root causes and strengthen the international system; still, his proposals also included recourse to the United Nations or Islamic courts of law, and explicitly, "domestic and international policing."[36] Theologian Stanley Hauerwas, a pacifist ally of Mennonites, said he would like to start envisioning ways to take the police function into the international arena, so long as societies learn to do a better job of providing local police with the resources and social cooperation they need to make killing a truly rare event.[37]

What broad appeals to international courts of law do not always clarify, however, is who would apprehend the criminals, how they would operate, and whether the political bodies that conduct international policing would have the support of pacifist churches.[38] Jim Wallis, editor of *Sojourners* magazine, stated the problem clearly. He had advocated "the most extensive international and diplomatic pressure the world has ever seen against bin Laden and his networks of terror—focusing the world's political will, intelligence, security, legal action, and police enforcement against terrorism." Such mobilization would dry up the terrorists financially and politically, and expose their "ugly brutality" before an international tribunal. "But when the international community has spoken, tried, and found them guilty, and authorized their apprehension and incarceration, we will still have to confront the ethical dilemmas involved in enforcing those measures. The terrorists must be found, captured, and stopped. This involves using some kind of force."[39]

Wallis was not simply ceding to the claims of that amoral school of international relationships known as *Realpolitik*, nor to Christian Realism so-called. The editorial stance of his magazine and his article as a whole make clear that his first priorities remained policies to focus on the conditions of global inequity and superpower hubris that breeds resentment and terrorism, initiatives that utilize culturally-sensitive conflict resolution of the sort Lederach practices, and strategies that develop forms of force which remain compatible with nonviolence. True "realism" would recognize that these may be the *only* ways to combat rather than breed terrorism, after all. Nonetheless, Wallis was squarely facing the fact that even a society that did everything he as a longtime peace activist was calling for would still require the police function.

To see his point, consider the following scenario: Let us wildly assume that the United States of America that was struck on September 11 had political leaders who had somehow been impressed by the nonviolent victories against tyrants in the twentieth century,[40] had become convinced by arguments in favor of civilian-based defense put forth by political scientists such as Harvard's Gene Sharp,[41] and had begun a process of "transarmament" toward increasing reliance on such strategies.[42] Such a United States would embark on a sturdier and more authentic course of coalition-building, taking European and Arab League concerns far more seriously. It would thus recognize the 9/11 strikes as a tragically late wake-up call reminding Americans that in a globalized world, true security can only come by building upon interdependence not spurning it,[43] and by addressing global inequities rather than flaunting them.[44] This imagined U.S. would already have welcomed and strengthened the institutionalization of international tribunals for cases of genocide and war crimes, rather than bowing out of relevant treaties. And while we are at it, let us imagine that Christians in the West had paid far greater attention to Pope John Paul's Jubilee Year calls for repentance from historic sins such as the Crusades, and were communicating far more broadly their remorse and desire for qualitatively new relationships with the Muslim world.

No doubt all of this would already have gone far toward removing the causes of terrorism. But proponents of *Realpolitik* have a point when they argue that socioeconomic change can never come fast enough to eliminate *all* resentment and threats. So let us concede that the 9/11 strikes *could* still have happened. Fortunately, all of this would also have cleared the way for waging a nonviolent campaign on various fronts. While diplomats appealed to Afghani tribal elders to turn over al Qaeda leaders to an international tribunal, culturally sensitive nonviolent practitioners and mediators would disperse throughout Afghanistan and the Muslim world to communicate Western and Christian willingness to learn and correct the reasons "why they hate us." Combined, these efforts would do enough to begin drying out the social network of support for al Qaeda that Afghani leaders would then have the political cover they needed to remove their support for al Qaeda. Still, since the premise of all these alternative policies is that terrorist crimes against humanity should be treated within the rubric of prosecuting criminals not waging war, we must assume that *as* criminals, the perpetrators would probably refuse to turn themselves in.[45]

So what now? It actually turns out to be far easier to imagine the conditions in which societies could dispense with war than it is to imagine dispensing with the police function. It is in fact *realistic* to imagine dispensing with war because all of the strategies to which I have alluded are in development by theorists and practitioners employing pilot projects.[46] Further, global interdependence makes successful military strategies increasingly unimaginable (if success means proportionately less violence, not simply winning wars).[47] Yet to complete the final phase of the scenario I have imagined, some kind of SWAT team with recourse to lethal violence still seems necessary. So too for the prison guards to hold the criminal terrorists they apprehend. Thus we must press the question of whether post-9/11 calls for turning to international legal procedures do not imply positive support for police action.[48]

Though Mennonites have not been much more forthright about policing than just war thinkers, there are precedents both in Mennonite practice and among leading Mennonite thinkers for seeing policing as a different question than war and soldiery, leading to different possible answers. Within and among the historic peace churches that have opposed Christian participation in warfare and militaries, the same level of consensus does not exist concerning Christian participation in policing.[49] Mennonite institutions such as colleges, with responsibility for the security of hundreds of residents, have quietly cooperated with local police—and even the strongest advocates of nonviolence on their faculties have rarely objected.

In fact, some Mennonites have been working very deliberately with criminal justice systems. Along with a general trend among Mennonites to label themselves as "nonviolent" or "pacifist" rather than "nonresistant," and in turn to accept nonviolent direct action as compatible with Jesus' teachings, Mennonites have been leaders in developing nonviolent alternatives that humanize the criminal justice system. Parallel to the work of John Paul Lederach in international conflict transformation, Mennonites such as Howard Zehr have launched programs for victim-offender reconciliation—with restitution rather than retributive punishment as the judicially-recognized consequence of crime wherever possible. Along the way they have helped launch and provide a conceptual basis for a much larger movement advocating what many now know as "restorative justice."[50]

Such efforts have gone forward in the same spirit as efforts to conceptualize and then launch pilot projects in unarmed civilian-based defense, which would allow nations to imagine and then begin the process of transarmament away from the violent weaponry upon which their militaries depend today. But there is one subtle difference. That difference might allow Mennonites and other pacifists to participate in policing institutions in a way that they cannot conscientiously do within military institutions. The difference it is this:

On one hand, military transarmament would require military institutions to become something qualitatively other, organizers and mobilizers of the broad civic participation needed to make societies unconquerable, with last resort recourse only to the potentially lethal force of true policing on the international level. On the other hand, transarmament for the criminal justice system requires police institutions to do a better job of what their mandate is already to do—preserve community order and secure the safety of all citizens with only rare, minimal, and judicious use of violence. In short, nonviolent strategies for responding to international conflict constitute alternatives to war that would displace the military as we know it,[51] while nonviolent strategies for reforming the criminal justice system simply make the police into better and better police. Thus, cooperation with—and eventually within—the policing system can be imaginable for Christian pacifists in a way that working within the military system is not.

Even when leading Mennonite thinkers have explained why they believed faithful Christians could not serve as police, they have offered precedents for thinking the question of policing through to a different answer. At mid-twentieth century, Guy F. Hershberger was the leading spokesperson for Mennonite "nonresistance" and conscientious objection to military service. The *no* he gave to policing was clear. The state and its "sword" are ordained by God according to Romans 13, but as a "sub-Christian" measure that God provides for a sinful world.[52] Policing was incompatible with Christian discipleship, therefore. When pressed that police operations "may be necessary for the successful operation of a state in a sinful society," Hershberger's simplest and most elegant answer was that "the Christian is called to live a life on a higher level than this" and thus has better things to do by witnessing to Christ in word, deed, and ministries of reconciliation.[53]

Within a few years John Howard Yoder would identify the question of calling as potentially decisive, but would on principle refuse to decide. Deciding, after all, must be the case-by-case task of discerning communities who hold their members accountable, offer them binding pastoral guidance in particular historical circumstances, and make those judgments by the Christian community's own standards of gospel proclamation.[54] The standard must not be a reading of the "natural" order that is so easily confused with the limited standards of a fallen world.[55] Like Hershberger, Yoder was prepared to affirm the legitimacy of the state, with its police function, as God's provision to limit evil in a world estranged from God.[56] And though far readier to approve of Christian political advocacy and to consider participation in some governmental functions,[57] Yoder certainly agreed with Hershberger (and early Anabaptists) that God's ordering *of* the state did not automatically warrant Christian participation *in* the state.

Yoder, however, used this basic Anabaptist-Mennonite framework to make somewhat different points. Affirming the legitimacy of the police function provided a wedge for more pointed critiques of war and militarism. Since the biblical standard for judging a magistrate's legitimacy was protection of the innocent and punishment of the guilty, "the state never has a blanket authorization to use violence."[58] Indiscriminate warfare and the use of war for any purpose beyond "the localized readjustment of a tension" are therefore "wrong for the state, not only for a Christian." Though limited police action within society or by the United Nations could not be condemned in principle, "all modern war" stood condemned "on the realistic basis of what the state is for."[59] While keeping Christian social ethics focused primarily on witness to Christ's reconciling lordship according to the standards of Jesus' gospel proclamation of God's Reign, Yoder was widening that focus enough that Mennonites could recognize social and political engagement to promote social justice and limit violence as *part* of this very witness.

Having suggested that limited police actions—domestic or international—might not be condemned in principle, however, Yoder then needed to revisit the question of whether a Christian could be a police officer. Characteristically, his answer reframed the question:

> The question, May a Christian be a policeman? is posed in legalistic terms. The answer is to pose the question on the Christian level: Is the Christian *called* to be a policeman? We know he is called to be an agent of reconciliation. Does that general call, valid for every Christian, take for certain individuals a form of a specific call to be also an agent of the wrath of God?[60]

If Yoder was moving the discussion of policing from the domain of principle to the domain of vocational discernment, the immediate result was not to make it any more likely that Christian pacifists would apply to become police officers.[61] Rather, Yoder drove home the point that the conditions do not now exist to make this morally possible:

> Stating the question in this form makes it clear that if the Christian can by any stretch of the imagination find his calling in the exercise of state-commanded violence, he must bring us (i.e., lay before the brotherhood) the evidence that he has such a special calling. Long enough we have been told that the position of the conscientious objector is a prophetic one, legitimate but only for the specially called few; in truth we must hold that the nonresistant position is the normal and normative position for every Christian, and it is the use of violence, even at that point where the state may with some legitimacy be violent, that requires an exceptional justification.[62]

Yoder reported never having met anyone "testifying to such an exceptional call."

But could he—ever? Yoder was writing primarily for his own Mennonite Church at the time, and secondarily for other historic peace churches. Testimonies to a sense of vocation for policing, whether domestic or international, were unlikely in that context.

Still, Yoder was already involved in wide-ranging ecumenical conversations that would continue throughout his career. Engagement with just war thinkers was one such conversation. As we continue that conversation by pursuing the notion of just policing, the question of vocation that Yoder once posed turns out to remain crucial. Some members of just-war-affirming churches would in fact claim that policing and military service is a calling—a "higher calling," even—to which they have responded. With Yoder we must then inquire into the discernment practices by which their churches have tested such vocational claims. To this, and to other practices necessary for Christians of various traditions to continue converging around the just policing agenda, we thus turn in the next chapter.

List of Just War Criteria
from USCCB Statement, 1993

THE HARVEST OF JUSTICE IS SOWN IN PEACE I.B.2

First, whether lethal force may be used is governed by the following criteria:

- *Just Cause:* force may be used only to correct a grave, public evil, i.e., aggression or massive violation of the basic rights of whole populations;
- *Comparative Justice:* while there may be rights and wrongs on all sides of a conflict, to override the presumption against the use of force the injustice suffered by one party must significantly outweigh that suffered by the other;
- *Legitimate Authority:* only duly constituted public authorities may use deadly force or wage war;
- *Right Intention:* force may be used only in a truly just cause and solely for that purpose;
- *Probability of Success:* arms may not be used in a futile cause or in a case where disproportionate measures are required to achieve success;
- *Proportionality:* the overall destruction expected from the use of force must be outweighed by the good to be achieved;
- *Last Resort:* force may be used only after all peaceful alternatives have been seriously tried and exhausted.

These criteria (*jus ad bellum*), taken as a whole, must be satisfied in order to override the strong presumption against the use of force.

Second, the just-war tradition seeks also to curb the violence of war through restraint on armed combat between the contending parties by imposing the following moral standards (*jus in bello*) for the conduct of armed conflict:

- *Noncombatant Immunity:* civilians may not be the object of direct attack, and military personnel must take due care to avoid and minimize indirect harm to civilians;
- *Proportionality:* in the conduct of hostilities, efforts must be made to attain military objectives with no more force than is militarily necessary and to avoid disproportionate collateral damage to civilian life and property;
- *Right Intention:* even in the midst of conflict, the aim of political and military leaders must be peace with justice, so that acts of vengeance and indiscriminate violence, whether by individuals, military units or governments, are forbidden.

Notes

1. Corroborating this claim on the basis of a much wider literature review is Tobias Winright, "From Police Officers to Peace Officers," in *The Wisdom of the Cross: Essays in Honor of John Howard Yoder*, eds. Stanley Hauerwas, et al. (Grand Rapids, MI: Wm. B. Eerdmans Publishing Co., 1999), 86, 91–92. A partial exception was John H. Yoder, who was noting the difference more and more regularly in the latter years of his career (see for example the emendation to the revised edition of *The Politics of Jesus*, 2nd ed., reprint, 1972 [Grand Rapids, MI: Wm. B. Eerdmans, 1994], 205), and encouraging students such as Winright to pursue its implications at the time of his death.

2. Tobias Winright is becoming a leading exception. See: "The Perpetrator as Person: Theological Reflections on the Just War Tradition and the Use of Force by Police," *Criminal Justice Ethics* 14, no. 2 (Summer/Fall 1995): 37–56; "Two Rival Versions of Just War Theory and the Presumption Against Harm in Policing," *Annual of the Society of Christian Ethics* 18 (1998): 221–39; "From Police Officers to Peace Officers"; "The Challenge of Policing: An Analysis in Christian Social Ethics," Ph.D. dissertation (University of Notre Dame, 2002).

3. Cf. John Howard Yoder, *When War is Unjust: Being Honest in Just-War Thinking*, rev. ed., foreword by Charles P. Lutz, afterword by Drew Christiansen (Maryknoll, NY: Orbis Books, 1996), 50–70.

4. See James F. Childress, "Just-War Criteria," in *Moral Responsibility in Conflicts: Essays on Nonviolence, War, and Conscience* (Baton Rouge: Louisiana State University Press, 1982), 63–94; United States Conference of Catholic Bishops (USCCB), *The Challenge of Peace*, §§70, 80; Richard B. Miller, "Aquinas and the Presumption Against Killing and War," *Journal of Religion* (April 2002): 3–35.

5. For classic catalogs of the criteria for a just war, see: Augustine, *Contra Faustum Manichaeum* [Reply to Faustus the Manichaean] 1.22.74-76; Aquinas, *Summa Theologica* II-II 40.1; Francisco de Vitoria *De iuri belli* [On the law of war]. John Yoder provided a quite detailed catalog in appendix 5 of the revised edition of *When War is Unjust*, 147–61 (note that this is *not* available in the first edition, Augsburg Publishing House, 1984). Also see the 1992 *Catechism of the Catholic Church*, §§2307–2317, and the U.S. Conference of Catholic Bishops, *The Harvest of Justice is Sown in Peace*, statement (Washington DC: United States Catholic Conference, 1993), section I.B.2. *The Harvest of Justice* offers a list that is commendable for thoroughness yet brevity. See Appendix A on p. 85.

6. John Howard Yoder, "Peace Without Eschatology?" in *The Royal Priesthood: Essays Ecclesiological and Ecumenical*, ed. Michael G. Cartwright (Grand Rapids, MI.: Wm. B. Eerdmans, 1994), 166–67.

7. Cf. note 9 on p. 107.

8. U.S. Conference of Catholic Bishops, *The Harvest of Justice*, section I.B.2. Drew Christiansen calls attention to this paragraph and confirms its importance in his afterword to John Howard Yoder, *When War is Unjust*, 108. Ronald G. Musto has likewise commented: "Stalin might well have scoffed at the 'leverage' of the Vatican [as a peacemaker through international diplomacy], for without the pope's 'divisions,' that is a Catholic laity educated for and committed to active peacemaking, all the pope's words of influence and exhortations to peace were doomed to impotence." Musto, *The Catholic Peace Tradition* (Maryknoll, NY: Orbis Books, 1986), 168.

9. Nor need we belabor the objections that arise (in accord with Mennonite pacifist doubts about the reliability of common sense) as to whether the natural law is universal or accessible enough to guide us. For a standard version of those objections, however, see John Howard Yoder, *Christian Witness to the State*, 33–34.

10. Augustine, in *Ep.* 47.5 to Publicola, provided an argument that a public functionary was no more guilty of homicide when acting to defend his city against villains who would threaten public order than the builder of a wall would be if it fell upon someone trying to tear it down—but he first took it as axiomatic that a Christian who was not to defend his own life might "happen to be a soldier or public functionary acting, not for himself, but in defence of others or of the city in which he resides." In *City of God* 19.6 Augustine began the chapter with a rhetorical question that took civil judgment and thus policing to be a self-evident need: "What of those judgements passed by men on their fellow men, which cannot be dispensed with in cities, however much peace they enjoy?" Once he had established that a just man would reluctantly sit as civil judge (thus participating in the police function), Augustine argued that this same man would participate in just wars.

Martin Luther, in arguing that soldiers could be Christians, exclaimed that if he gave in on this point he would have to conclude that policing was wrong too (Martin Luther, "Whether Soldiers, Too, Can be Saved," 1526, trans. Charles M. Jacobs and Robert C. Schultz in *The Christian in Society III*, vol. 46 of *Luther's Works*, ed. Robert C. Schultz, gen. ed. Helmut T. Lehmann [Philadelphia: Fortress Press, 1967], 98–99). Though Luther did go on to refer his readers to another treatise on *Temporal Authority* for a fuller explanation, his exclamation suggested a working assumption that the legitimacy of policing was basically self-evident.

For other standard examples of arguments that have used policing to justify warfare see James Martineau, "The 'Police Analogy,'" exerpt from *National Duties and Other Sermons and Addresses*, 1903 in *War and the Christian Conscience: From Augustine to Martin Luther King, Jr.*, comp. Albert Marrin (Chicago: Henry Regnery Company, 1971), 119–24 and, in a less straightforward way, Reinhold Niebuhr, *Moral Man and Immoral Society*, reprint ed., The Scribner Lyceum Editions Library (New York: Scribner's, 1960), 238–40. For a recent turn to the apparently self-evident "analogy" of the police function in order to explain the need for just war criteria to restrain the ferocity of war, see Charles P. Lutz's forward to John Howard Yoder, *When War is Unjust*, xiii.

Also see footnote 13 on John Calvin.

11. John Calvin, *The Institutes of the Christian Religion*, vol. 2, ed. John T. McNeill, trans. Ford Lewis Battles, The Library of Christian Classics, vol. 21 (Philadelphia: Westminster Press, 1960), IV.20.

12. Certainly within the ranks and the culture of police forces, as well as in popular culture, war does sometimes serve as a metaphor for policing, as reflected in the language of "crimefighting," "the war on crime," and so on. It is precisely the danger of militarizing police work that has led Tobias Winright (see note 2) to bring the logic of the just war theory to bear on the ethics of policing, as he noted in "The Perpetrator as Person," 37–39. But if, as I am arguing, the just war tradition at its best should just have been about just policing all along, the militarization of policing merely demonstrates the urgency of our task. In any case, in the present paragraph I am referring here to Christian theologians and ethicists, not popular culture.

13. John Calvin articulated the continuity that many people take to settle the matter when, after many pages defending the legitimacy of civic authority, he summarily justified warfare in a few sentences. See Calvin, *Institutes*, 4.20.11.

14. Duane L. Cady, *From Warism to Pacifism: A Moral Continuum* (Philadelphia: Temple University Press, 1989).

15. See John Howard Yoder, *When War is Unjust*, 12–14, 130–35.

16. Civil wars are of course an apparent exception, but in their own way they demonstrate the tendency of war to become untethered from the common good. Civil wars both result from and cause further deterioration of civil society. Parties to a civil war

must usually treat the territory and population of their own nation as if it were foreign. So-called national security states increasingly treat all but their ruling class as a captive population in an occupied territory whose undercurrent of resentment may at any time seethe into open insurgency.

17. Increased airport security, detaining suspected terrorists inside the United States, and cooperating with other nations in order to restrict the movement of potential terrorists would all have qualified as standard police work and would not have required expeditionary forces.

18. I am grateful to J. Denny Weaver of Bluffton University for pointing out (in personal correspondence of February 4, 2002) how the expeditionary character of war differs from the jurisdictionally limited character of policing, and for some of the illustrations of that difference in this paragraph.

19. For an especially influential and ground-breaking article insisting that the principle of noncombatant immunity be upheld as a moral absolute, see Ford, "The Morality of Obliteration Bombing." Also see Paul Ramsey, *War and the Christian Conscience: How Shall Modern War be Conducted Justly?* Published for the Lilly Endowment Research Program in Christianity and Politics (Durham, NC: Duke University Press, 1961).

20. Jim Wallis, "Interview with Stanley Hauerwas," *Sojo.Net: The Online Voice of Sojourners Magazine*, January–February 2002, Http://sojo.net/index.cfm?action=news. display_archives&mode=current_opinion&article=CO_010702h.

John Yoder made this same point at greater length in *Christian Witness to the State*, 46–47.

21. Wallis, "Interview with Stanley Hauerwas." The larger context of this quote relates directly to the larger context of this paper, as it expresses his sympathy for domestic police, calls upon society to provide them with the resources they need to avoid killing, and envisions extending that sort of policing into the international sphere.

22. For an elegant and historically literate essay on some of these dynamics, see Lee Sandlin, "Are we Finally Losing the War? / Losing the War," two-part series, *Chicago Reader*, March 1997.

23. Racism and racial disparity increase the prospect of police brutality precisely because they give police the sense of being at war with the neighborhoods they are sworn to keep safe.

24. John H[oward] Yoder, "Surrender: A Moral Imperative," *The Review of Politics* 48 (Fall 1986): 576–95.

25. Along with the development of increasingly lethal technologies of war, this has been the story of modern warfare, whether we are talking about the creation of mass armies since the French Revolution, the interpenetration of guerrilla movements with their civilian bases, or expansion of "military-industrial complexes."

26. Although the various tactics of low-intensity warfare (creating lightly-armed civilian patrols, engaging in nonmilitary projects to win over the loyalty of a suspicious populace, etc.) may seem analogous to community policing, low-intensity warfare weakens the social fabric of communities by inviting neighbors to inform on one another, or use martial procedures to settle old grudges.

27. For a similar list, overlapping in part with my own, see Tobias Winright, "From Police Officers to Peace Officers," 102. The two lists are complementary not competitive because Winright's focuses on differences in legal status, while mine focuses on what I am calling psycho-social dynamics. Also note John Howard Yoder, *The Politics of Jesus*, 205.

28. Note for example the passing statement by Drew Christiansen S.J. in a 1999 article in the context of Kosovo bombing: "Clarity and certainty are far less easy to attain today

on the ethics of using force than at times when the international system was more stable." Might this point to yet another psycho-social dymanic, by which the more policy-makers need the just war tradition, the less likely it is to provide them with clear guidance? See Drew Christiansen, S.J., "Peacemaking and the Use of Force: Behind the Pope's Stringent Just-War Teaching," *America* 180, no. 17 (15 May 1999): 13–18.

29. See Guy Franklin Hershberger, *The Way of the Cross in Human Relations* (Scottdale, PA: Herald Press, 1958), 178–79; Tobias Winright, "From Police Officers to Peace Officers," 105. Winright also notes Quaker openness to international policing and cites James F. Childress, "Answering That of God in Every Man," *Quaker Religious Thought* 15 (1974): 25.

30. On the origins of modern, separate, police forces in the nineteenth century, see Tobias Winright, "From Police Officers to Peace Officers," 87–89.

31. Where Mennonites have lived in near total isolation, and thus had to govern themselves in civil as well as religious matters, some intriguing models of nonviolent policing have emerged, but these need further historical research. Examples are the German Mennonite colonies in pre-Soviet Russia, partially translated into the Paraguayan Chaco in the twentieth century.

32. During the months following September 11, 2001, Stanley Hauerwas sought repeatedly to remind U.S. Christians of that (see quotation, e.g. in Jim Wallis, "Hard Questions for Peacemakers," *Sojourners*, [January–February 2002]: 32).

33. On October 15, the Mennonite Church USA Peace and Justice Committee also issued a "Statement to Mennonite Congregations" along similar lines. Appropriate to the focus that Mennonite social ethics has on the distinctive witness of the Christian community itself, the statement expanded most upon personal and congregational ways of praying and working for peace. Those not only included calling "on our government to address the root causes of the problem," however, but also encouraging "the governments of the world to use the existing mechanisms of the United Nations Security Council and world court system to deal with the present crisis."

34. Duane K. Friesen, *Christian Peacemaking & International Conflict: A Realist Pacifist Perspective*, foreword by Stanley Hauerwas, Christian Peace Shelf Selection (Scottdale, PA: Herald Press, 1986).

35. This was at a campus forum already on the afternoon of September 11. This handout was later published as a sidebar in an MCC publication. See Duane K. Friesen, "Naming What Happened and How We Respond," *Peace Office Newsletter* 32, no. 1 (April–June 2002): 7.

36. John Paul Lederach, "Quo Vadis? Reframing Terror from the Perspective of Conflict Resolution," Town Hall Meeting, October 24, 2001 (University of California, Irvine, 2001), Http://www.nd.edu/%7Ekrocinst/sept11/ledquo.html. Also see John Paul Lederach, "The Challenge of Terrorism: A Traveling Essay" (2001), Http://www.mediate.com/articles/terror911.cfm, and Jim Wallis, "An Interview with John Paul Lederach," *Sojo.Net: The Online Voice of Sojourners Magazine*, January–February 2002, Http://www.sojo.net/index.cfm?action=news.display_archives&mode=current_opinion&article=CO_010702l.

37. Wallis, "Interview with Stanley Hauerwas."

38. The American Friends Service Committee did release a paper detailing legal remedies available to the United States through international courts and tribunals. See AFSC, "International Legal Remedies in Response to the Attacks of September 11th, 2001" (2001), Http://www.wcc-coe.org/wcc/behindthenews/analysis20.html.

39. Wallis, "Hard Questions for Peacemakers," 31.

40. India, KKK terrorists in the U.S., Philippines, Poland, Czechoslovakia, the Soviet Union, South Africa, etc.

41. Gene Sharp, *Making Europe Unconquerable: The Potential of Civilian-Based Deterrence and Defence* (Cambridge, MA: Ballinger Pub. Co., 1985); Gene Sharp and Bruce Jenkins, *Civilian-Based Defense: A Post-Military Weapons System* (Princeton, NJ: Princeton University Press, 1990).

42. In this context, everything that the actual Washington leadership has said about terrorism constituting a new kind of threat and requiring a new kind of war would mean something very different but be more not less appropriate!

43. Cf. Michael Joseph Smith, "Strengthen the United Nations and International Efforts for Cooperation and Human Rights," 146–51.

44. In speaking here of global inequities, I am not referring only to economic disparities but to forms of political and cultural power that are threatening to homogenize cultures around the globe. I am in agreement with those who argue that it is far too simplistic to say that poverty is the cause of terrorism. Influenced by Benjamin R. Barber, *Jihad Vs. Mcworld* (New York: Random House, 1995), my own view is that while economic factors are certainly in play, the driving influence behind terrorism is the sense within many traditional societies around the world that the acids of global homogenization are corroding the integrity of local cultures at a pace that does not allow them to adjust and evolve at their own pace. Analyses associated with both the left (seeking to alleviate poverty by righting global economic injustice) and the right (seeking to alleviate poverty by promoting global free trade) are often blind to these cultural dynamics and to the ways that their proposals may actually exacerbate resentment within traditional cultures.

45. Theorists of nonviolence themselves have stressed that their strategies do not require the conversion of adversaries—though they do leave open that possibility in a way that violent action does not—but rather aim at altering the system of social supports that allows adversaries the power to continue committing their injustices.

46. See especially the work of Gene Sharp: *The Politics of Nonviolent Action*, 3 vols., ed. Marina Finkelstein (Boston: Extending Horizons, 1973); *Social Power and Political Freedom*, Extending Horizons Books (Boston: P. Sargent Publishers, 1980); Sharp, *Making Europe Unconquerable*.

47. See Friesen, *Christian Peacemaking & International Conflict*, Paul W. Schroeder, "Work with Emerging Cooperative Forces Within the International System," in *Just Peacemaking: Ten Practices for Abolishing War*, ed. Glen Stassen (Cleveland: Pilgrim Press, 1998), 133–46, and more recently, Schell, "No More Unto the Breach."

48. "Positive" here would contrast with the "double negative" logic by which pacifists have sometimes taken a stance that does *not oppose* police actions (or military operations more closely approximating police action) when they fall within the legitimate functions of the state according to Romans 13.

49. For a succinct survey of representative positions, see Tobias Winright, "From Police Officers to Peace Officers," 96–108.

50. Howard Zehr, *Changing Lenses: A New Focus for Crime and Justice*, Christian Peace Shelf Selection (Scottdale, PA: Herald Press, 1990).

51. There are of course instances such as Bosnia and Kosovo in which the U.S., U.N., NATO and other militaries have themselves acted more like police: rebuilding infrastructure, collecting garbage, investigating allegations of human rights abuses, mediating between mutually suspicious ethnic groups, and so on. In other words, the "military as we know it" continues to evolve within an international system in which (quite apart from the urgings of pacifists) "humanitarian intervention" for the protection of human rights is becoming increasingly important. On the other hand, the difficulty that the U.S. and coalition forces have had policing and restoring civil society in Iraq indicates the degree of

adjustment that "the military as we know it" may need to make in order to take on policing roles. Thus, ongoing debates among military strategists about whether and how the military role should change will undoubtedly continue. In any case, these internal debates are not likely to change the main point of the current paragraphs, that conscientious members of the churches in pacifist traditions can already participate in police functions in ways that they cannot be expected to participate in militaries.

52. Guy F. Hershberger, *War, Peace, and Nonresistance*, 3rd ed., Christian Peace Shelf Selection (Scottdale, PA: Herald Press, 1969), 54, 156, 311. Police operations might well be less violent than warfare (*War, Peace, and Nonresistance*, 311; *Way of the Cross*, 179), and the use of force within a system of international law and policing might be "much less objectionable than that now exercised in our world at war," (*War, Peace, and Nonresistance*, 174) but Hershberger was sure that the basic task of the police and military was fundamentally the same, to maintain order using methods of force that "do not harmonize with the New Testament way of nonresistance" (*War, Peace, and Nonresistance*, 162, 311).

53. Guy F. Hershberger, *War, Peace, and Nonresistance*, 162. This response might seem curt or aloof in some contexts, but it grew from Hershberger's vision of the Christian community richly contributing people of moral character and ministries that are always in far shorter supply than are soldiers. See pp. 252–53, toward the end of a later chapter answering charges like those of Reinhold Niebuhr that a nonresistant people is socially irresponsible or even parasitic.

54. This was characteristic of Yoder's lifelong approach (he would not have wanted to say "methodology") for theological reflection and ethical discernment. On the implications of this approach for the specific issue of policing, see Tobias Winright, "From Police Officers to Peace Officers," 108–14.

55. On this last point, see John Howard Yoder, *Christian Witness to the State*, 36.

56. John Howard Yoder, *Christian Witness to the State*, 12ff., 36; *The Politics of Jesus*, 196–98, 201–2, 203–5.

57. See John Howard Yoder, *Christian Witness to the State*, 28 (and cf. 56) for signals of Yoder's willingness to consider the latter. The book as a whole represents Yoder's argument for the former.

58. John Howard Yoder, *Christian Witness to the State*, 36. Yoder continued: "The use of force must be limited to the police function, i.e., guided by fair judicial processes, subject to recognized legislative regulation, and safeguarded in practice against its running away with the situation. Only the absolute minimum of violence is therefore in any way excusable. The state has no general authorization to use the sword independently of its commission to hold violence to a minimum." Also see pp. 5, 46-47.

59. John Howard Yoder, *The Original Revolution: Essays on Christian Pacifism*, Christian Peace Shelf (Scottdale, PA: Herald Press, 1971), 74ff., John Howard Yoder, "Peace Without Eschatology?" 159–60; self-quoted in John Howard Yoder, *Christian Witness to the State*, 5.

60. John Howard Yoder, *Christian Witness to the State*, 56–57.

61. The logic of Yoder's position is a kind of *triple* negative: Christian policing was *not unthinkable*, but he was *not* yet convinced, so three negatives calculated out to a continuing negative. And even if he were to become convinced, a double-negative could never mean unqualified affirmation.

62. John Howard Yoder, *Christian Witness to the State*, 57.

Chapter 5

Practicing for Just Policing

Gerald W. Schlabach

Let us be clear: Should the concept of "just policing" gain currency, the first task of advocates will continue to be resistance to the militarization of currently constituted police forces. None of the arguments in this book aims to affirm all that goes by the name of policing, nor to urge Mennonites, other historic peace churches, or other Christian pacifists to join their local police forces as currently constituted, nor to discourage those who hold to either the just war or the pacifist position from denouncing police brutality and human rights abuses wherever they occur.

Nor is our intention to justify any nation taking on the role of "policeman of the world," which is actually a euphemism for imperialism, not a name for international police forces accountable to the rule of international law. The militarization of police forces poses real dangers in many urban areas of the United States, for example, where racism and endemic social ills have too often conspired to place police on a war footing vis-à-vis minority populations. On one hand, all of the just war criteria for assessing whether the exercise of violent force is acceptable should continue to apply for the purpose of minimizing not rationalizing violence.[1] On the other hand, pacifist work to strategize alternatives to war and the overall criminal justice system should not neglect the need for nonlethal and nonviolent tactics to apprehend and detain criminals. Thus, both traditions have contributions to make simply in the improvement of ordinary policing.

But that is how it goes! That is how divided Christian traditions have already found themselves collaborating, each on the basis of its own moral convictions, without waiting for complete consensus on long-standing moral debates, yet finding that they have built more mutual understanding than they once expected. This is how the patterns may emerge by which war might yet cease to be a church-dividing issue.

Taking Stock of Current Practices

Looking back, two trends have already brought us to a point from which to envision a way toward further convergence. Coming from a direction that pacifists can recognize and own is the development of nonviolent action. Coming from a direction that non-pacifists can recognize and own is the development of community policing.

As Tobias Winright has pointed out, the development of efficacious nonviolent action for political ends in the twentieth century, coupled with a shift that has led many pacifists to identify their position as Gandhian *nonviolent resistance* rather than Tolstoy's *nonresistance*, has already begun to change the shape of debates about policing: "With this type of pacifism in mind, then, the efficacy of violence in policing, generally assumed by nearly everyone [until recently], is called into question. That is, when the greater efficacy of nonviolence is granted, policing itself can be envisioned in a completely different way."[2]

Converging from the other direction is the model of "community policing." By extending it into the international arena Catholics may be able to fulfill the mandate of the Second Vatican Council to "undertake a completely fresh appraisal of war,"[3] to make the enforcement of international law into "just policing," and to integrate the contributions that pacifists have already been making to international peacemaking. This in turn makes it possible to invite their further participation in "just policing" without requiring pacifists to condone warfare even in exceptional cases.

Though the concept of community policing is only a decade or two old, it has already produced a large literature, with debates over both the best ways to implement it and the worst case dangers that can come with its abuse.[4] What makes it an appropriate model to extend by analogy into the sphere of international policing is the way that it integrates (1) the very sort of work on root causes of violence and conflict that pacifists have advocated as basic for achieving real peace with justice, (2) a continued but modified role for apprehending criminals, and (3) ample room for developing less-violent and nonviolent tactics for even that apprehension. Community policing, wrote one commentator,

> refers to a shift from a military-inspired approach to fighting crime to one that relies on forming partnerships with constituents. It employs health and human service programs as well as more traditional law enforcement, with an emphasis on crime prevention. It represents a change from a reactive model of law enforcement to one dedicated to developing the moral structure of communities.[5]

"Moral structure of communities," yes, and the web of community relationships that constitutes healthy society.

But notice: This is the very way that analysts like John Paul Lederach would urge nations to respond to terrorism: holding criminals accountable to international law; strengthening the preventive system by beginning the hard work of changing "patterns of political, religious, and economic roots of social exclusion, isolationism, and oppression that contribute to the origins of terrorism;" and integrating these immediate and long-term approaches by relying upon (not resisting) the interdependence of nation with nation.[6] Terrorism is not located in any one territory, after all, Lederach has noted. Instead it uses "the power of a free and open system" for its own benefit. This makes its threat comparable to a virus, which enters into a system and uses the resources of its host against that host. "And you do not fight this kind of enemy by shooting at it. You respond by strengthening the capacity of the system to prevent the virus and strengthen its immunity."[7]

Lederach warned that to understand terrorism otherwise and to attack it with a "war on terrorism" would be like targeting mature dandelions with a golf club. Tragically, a year after the U.S. invasion of Iraq, Lederach's words were echoed in the hearing rooms of Washington and in mainstream media. *Newsweek* used the same metaphor as Lederach when it wrote: "The United States is not up against one unified enemy, in fact, but a mutating virus of anti-American hatred." Likewise, it reported, "Controversial former counterterrorism coordinator Richard Clarke likens the aftermath of the Afghan war to 'smashing a pod of seeds that spread round the world,' allowing bin Laden and his deputies 'to step back out of the picture and have the regional organizations they created take their generation-long struggle to the next level.'" Clarke has described the war in Iraq not simply as a distraction and a drain from the real struggle against terrorism. "Worse, 'we delivered to Al Qaeda the greatest recruitment propaganda imaginable,'" according to Clarke.[8]

It is the need to strengthen "the capacity of the system to prevent the virus and strengthen its immunity," as Lederach put it, that makes the extension of community policing models into international policing so urgent. Admittedly, military strategists and just war thinkers have sometimes attempted pale versions of community policing when they have turned to "low-intensity warfare" replete with public works to "win the hearts and minds" of populations who might be harboring clandestine adversaries, or when they air-dropped food aid into Afghanistan at the start of the post-9/11 invasion there. But if Lederach's recommendation is to strengthen the viral immune system of the international body politic, then public works programs coordinated with low-intensity warfare are like sending an impoverished patient home after a shortened hospital stay because she does not have health insurance. And the air-drops over Afghanistan in late 2001 were like using antibiotics to treat a viral infection, which every physician knows to be a useless misdiagnosis. Upon closer examination the *intent* of low-intensity warfare is *not* the same as policing at all. While some of its tactics may superficially seem to coincide with policing, the intent of low-intensity war is the very opposite of policing—not to reduce violence but to turn the population into a war society.

Even if the community policing model can be manipulated and abused, what distinguishes it from warfighting strategies is this: Committing greater resources will make police more attuned to community needs and make policing less violent over all, whereas committing more resources to military strategies will increase their store of destructive weaponry, tempting soldiers and civilian leaders toward short-cuts that ignore social needs. The psycho-social dynamic of policing moves those who invest in it towards less violence because community policing has always been integral to good policing, even without the name. What prevents good police from taking a war footing toward the populations they are sworn to protect is that their relationships are intra-community—not *we-versus-them* but *we-are-they*. Community policing only underscores what was already the case, that any violent consequences to "them" will be consequences for "us." This reduces the chance that violence will desensitize police officers to further violence, and increases the likelihood that any use of violence will truly be last resort.

The framework of community policing, then, is one within which members of both the just war and pacifist traditions can contribute, and can in fact "provoke one another to love and good deeds" (Heb 10:24). Any further convergence of the two, however, will require more than theory or pronouncements, more than right intentions. It will require practices, a firm pastoral commitment to engendering and forming communal practices down to the parish level.

I choose the more Catholic word "parish" here because in the formation of those practices we need in order to make war into less and less of a church-dividing issue, the Catholic Church and other representatives of the just war tradition bear a somewhat greater burden of proof. "Proof" connotes reason, and the strength of the just war tradition down through the centuries has been its claim to reason. Reason, reflecting upon common human experience, rightly ordered through the teaching authority of the church, is supposed to have been strong enough to minimize recourse to war. Yet it is not at all clear that just war thinking has established enough of a track record of doing so that it really constitutes a communal (rather than merely intellectual) tradition. In order to convince pacifists that the just war approach offers a legitimate resource for Christians, Catholics will need to embody their "proof" with practices that would transform the just war tradition back into what it has claimed to be, in effect, just policing.[9]

If the bearing of burdens here is asymmetrical, however, it is nonetheless balanced, for Mennonites and other historic peace churches in turn bear a somewhat greater burden of charity. The strength of their pacifist tradition down through the centuries has been its claim to the power of Christ-like love. It is faith in this power that leads Mennonite pacifists to hope against hope for the reconciled healing of relationships in even the most intransigent of human conflicts. Yet it is not at all clear that the descendents of persecuted Anabaptists have established an adequate track record of applying this faith and hope for the healing of Christ's divided church. In order to convince Catholics that their tradition embodies the transformative power of love rather than the schismatic hardening of resentment, they will need to interpret Catholic willingness to take on and grapple with the problems of civic governance as charitably as intellectual honesty allows—rather than marking down every instance of the Catholic exercise of civil authority as evidence of corruption, the "Fall of the Church," or a pejorative "Constantinianism."

Vocational Discernment:
The Crucial Piece, for Both Traditions

When Mennonite theologian John Howard Yoder reported never having heard of a Christian testifying to, and testing, an exceptional sense of calling to become a police officer, he was thinking of Christians in churches that see Christlike nonviolence as normative for all forms of human relationship.[10] He was not thinking of Christians in just war churches who enter into armed military or police service believing it to be a "higher calling" than civilian life. Yet his essential point may still be applied within traditions that espouse the just war theory and assume that Christian participation in policing is appropriate.

For the claim that policing can be an appropriate Christian vocation will have far greater credibility if churches have solid practices for testing vocations. And as I will later argue, neither such vocations nor such discernment will be credible unless the just war theory's "presumption against violence" has been institutionalized in ways that provide both individuals and communities with real and concrete options for serving the common good and defending the innocent nonviolently. This is what will render the "last resort" of violence a truly last alternative.

Certainly for pacifist churches then, but arguably for just war churches as well, nothing by way of discernment is possible if Christian communities lose their frame of reference: the Gospel, not the natural order except as known through the lens of Christ's revelation of its true character; ministries of reconciliation, not the functions of state except as used instrumentally to achieve limited nonviolent ends; the mission of the church, not the self-interest of nations except perhaps as defined through the preferential option for the poor and transnational solidarity. In other words, Yoder and his Mennonite predecessor Guy F. Hershberger were right to insist that as a rule Christians *do* have better things to do than policing.[11] For even if exceptions to the rule exist, they only make sense if they stand in relationship to the ultimate purpose or end of Christian witness that defines this rule.

Whatever *is* possible here will require consistent practices for testing vocation of the sort Yoder outlined before mentioning that he knew no one who had passed the test. And whatever practices of accountability are possible will require churches in which nonviolence is the norm for all their members. To envision such practices vis-à-vis policing we can extrapolate from what Yoder recommended in a later speech for *any* Christian who holds "a position of relative power in the wider society." On one hand, such persons can only be trusted in that role if they do not claim "autonomy in that station by virtue of God's having made it an authority unto itself." Instead they "will listen to the admonition of [their] sisters and brethren regarding the way [they discharge] it."[12]

On the other side of this discernment process, the peoplehood called church should understand itself to be an *ekklesia* in the original Greek sense. When the church of the Apostles adopted this word, "it meant parliament or town meeting, a gathering in which serious business can be done in the name of the kingdom." Yoder was proposing that discernment groups and accountability procedures become standard practices so that the church would not only "model" the kind of community God intends for the world, but would offer "a pastoral and prophetic resource to the person with the responsibilities of office."

> Sometimes the function of the community will be simply to encourage him to have the nerve to do what he already believes is right. At other times, other church members, thanks to their participation in other parts of society, will bring to his attention insights he would have missed; sometimes the community's proclamation of the revealed will of God may provide for him leverage to criticize the present structures.

But in no case would the public office become "autonomous as a source of moral guidance."[13]

Practicing for just policing, Mennonite

Relative to their size, Mennonites do already have a remarkable track record of sending their people to work among the poor around the world, build relationships in nations labeled "enemy," return home with lessons for addressing the root causes of injustice, work behind the scenes at international mediation, launch pilot projects for the unarmed defense of populations subject to human rights abuse, and create alternatives to criminal justice procedures to bring restorative not retributive justice. The challenge that they face is not so much to establish a track record as to articulate what they expect to do when that very "track" leads to wider institutionalization of their initiatives, in some cases by civil authority.[14] Catholics and other Christians with fewer scruples about participating in the state may legitimately ask, *So what will you do if you win? Are you willing to help implement the changes for which you have called? Why then is governance not legitimate for Christians?*

Mennonites have faced this question with varying degrees of consistency when their own ministries have positioned Mennonites to take governmental roles in health systems, welfare programs, international development agencies, and so on. Yet these state functions already assume the rule of law, made possible through policing. What if Mennonites now propose alternative forms of policing itself?

In order to work at this challenge for other functions of state, Mennonites have increasingly seen themselves in the role of Jeremiah's exiles, whom the prophet exhorted to "seek the *shalom* of the city" in which they found themselves while remembering that their primary loyalty was to God and God's covenant people. John Yoder increasingly explained his understanding of how Christians should serve the world within the rubric of this "Jeremianic" model for being a diaspora people that needs neither territory to maintain its identity nor control of state to render its service "for the nations."[15] Mennonite Central Committee executives used this image to articulate their position following the events of September 11, 2001.[16]

What Mennonites must show in practice in order to socially embody *their* arguments, is whether and how the Jeremianic model provides a convincing response to the legitimate challenge of governance. Some of Jeremiah's exiles were civil officials, after all. This should be a model for how Christian officials can critically engage the tasks of structuring and governing society without losing their ethical moorings within the master narrative of Israel, Jesus, and the church.[17] How then will Mennonites guide their members and hold them accountable? What will happen if society's need for some kind of policing meets the possibility of non- or less-violent policing, perhaps because Mennonites have advocated for just policing?

For now, Mennonites need not answer these questions by commissioning some of their members to actually become police officers. Direct responsibility for showing how Christians can "just" participate in "just policing" without once again rationalizing war falls first upon Christians who have identified with the just war tradition. What Mennonites must do (and do before their own acculturation makes the practice even more difficult) is broadly implement the kinds of accountability groups that Yoder encouraged for Christians in positions "of relative power in the wider society." That should not only mean the few Mennonites who hold administrative positions in government bureaucracies or the even fewer who hold elected office. Just as surely it should mean Mennonites in corporations, the academy, journalism, law, and other professions.

A few Mennonite individuals and congregations have taken up Yoder's suggestions in this regard, but the practice has not become widespread. It must yet become so. For without it, the Jeremianic model of exercising social responsibility will not convince other Christians that it is an adequate response to the challenge of governance. Nor will Mennonites have a basis for calling Catholics to the practices that will transform just war into just policing. Or both.

Practicing for just policing, Catholic

As we have seen, war would already be much less of a church-dividing issue if the Catholic Church's just war *theory* were in fact—in the fullest communal sense—a just war *tradition*. To qualify as a living, communal tradition it would need a far better track record of limiting military action to operations that credibly resemble police functions, reminding Catholics to resist the claims of nationalism, and training Catholics to interrogate the legitimacy of every particular war. Above all, it would need to have elicited a far broader expectation that Catholics will refuse to participate in wars that fail to meet the just war criteria.

The 1993 statement, *The Harvest of Justice is Sown in Peace*, implicitly recognized the need for much more than a rigorous and rationally binding theory when it insisted that the just war tradition must operate "not just as a set of ideas, but as a system of effective social constraints on the use of force."[18] Furthermore, the letter places its entire discussion on the ethics of peace and war within a framework that recovers the "neglected" role of spirituality in peacemaking. It then seeks to cultivate the virtues needed to practice both active nonviolence and the just war theory, and it devotes a major section to the formation of conscience. Above all, it insists that peacemaking must be intrinsic to the vocation of every Christian. As the introduction states,

> Our biblical heritage and our body of tradition make the vocation of peacemaking mandatory. Authentic prayer, worship, and sacramental life challenge us to conversion of our hearts and summon us to works of peace. These concerns are obviously not ours alone, but are the work of the entire community of faith and of all people of good will.

If the just war tradition were truly operative along these lines, and if it were accompanied by the thoroughgoing development of nonviolent practices that would truly render war a last resort,[19] Mennonites and other historic peace churches would find the tradition far less objectionable. That is why we may begin to chart the practices needed to make war no longer a church-dividing issue by exploring what the Catholic Church needs to do to implement the just war tradition, even though we hope to displace it with a tradition of just policing.[20]

The basic proposal is quite simple: The Catholic Church needs practices that are church-wide and parish-deep enough that they correspond with the magisterium's teaching that the just war tradition begins with a strong presumption against violence, allows wars only as an exception, and does so only in last resort. Here's what that would mean throughout the church:

Bishops. Whenever bishops or their local conferences consider making pronouncements concerning the justice of particular wars, it only seems fair to expect that they will oppose the war unless arguments in favor of its justice are overwhelming. This means that in "close calls" in which "reasonable people may differ" in their "prudential judgments" concerning the justice and advisability of a war, the default mode of the bishops would logically remain one of opposition.

In the months of late 1990 that led up to Gulf War against Iraq, for example, this is precisely what did *not* happen. The bishops lacked a "sufficiently clear consensus" to declare the war unjust, admitted Archbishop John Roach of Minneapolis-St. Paul, chairman of the bishops' international policy committee.[21] Though they did offer appropriate warnings that according to Catholic teaching war must always be limited, some bishops condemned the war and others called it justifiable. This, however, meant that as a body they had in effect deferred to the judgment of government policymakers.

If anything, the presumption against use of violence should have led bishops to oblige Catholic consciences to oppose the war. Thus the "presumption against violence" would coincide with the "presumption of truth" to be accorded the magisterium and would translate into communal (not just individual) selective conscientious objection.

Advisers. The presumption against violence must also outweigh the less formal and more cultural presumption that the church can only be effective at influencing policy makers if they make enough concessions to "stay in the loop." Leading Catholic theologians act not only as advisers to the bishops but as political commentators influencing public opinion. Once the U.S. administration had resolved to go to war against Iraq in 1990–91, some of these advisers who had raised serious questions about whether it was just to *go* to war began to speak as though it had been a just war all along, no doubt hoping to maintain the access they needed to urge that the war be *waged* in a just fashion.[22]

Presumably, the intentions of these Catholic advisers and commentators were good, aimed at preserving noncombatant immunity, discouraging unnecessary use of force, and so on. But for the shaping of both public discourse and Catholic conscience, such shifts undermine the very vibrancy of that presumption against violence which the church needs. Unless just war principles are seen to "have teeth," as Yoder used to say, faithful Catholics will be confused about how seriously to take them. Meanwhile, neither the bishops nor their advisers will be able to mobilize forms of Christian opposition to unjust wars that may well be more efficacious than that "loop."

Laity. Only when the default mode of Catholics is the practice of active nonviolence, rather than the uncritical acceptance of the state's summons to war, will the logic of the just war theory be fully operative. John Yoder was merely calling Catholics and others toward accountability to their own principles when he insisted that military participation should be at least as rare for Christians as conscientious objection to the military is today, and that such participation should always require exceptional justification.[23] Moral support for military service—or eventually, international policing—should only be available to those who are willing to pass through a time of vocational testing akin to both Mennonite accountability groups and Catholic novitiates.

Catholic vocational testing for potential "just policing" officers would require them to know well the criteria that are currently associated with the just war theory. It would prepare them to uphold those criteria even when that means resisting orders. And in line with Augustine's attempt to insist on right intentions of love for enemy rather than cruelty and vengeance even in times of war, candidates who show a disposition toward retaliation or demonization of enemies would be forbidden from participation in military, police, or international police forces.

At present it may be unrealistic to expect the church to withhold full communion from Catholics who enter the military without this kind of discernment, or who participate in wars of dubious justice against the counsel of the magisterium. Still, the Second Vatican Council's "universal call to holiness" at least invites consideration of that prospect. The "universal call to holiness," after all, carries with it an expectation that ordinary Christians too will grow into disciples of the Christ whose model of life has long required consecrated Christians to follow him by renouncing violence. What is certain is this: Surely the widening catechesis and accountability procedures needed to extend "the universal call to holiness" must not only teach Catholics to make a "presumption against violence," it must form them in the skills and character they need to make an active presumption in favor of nonviolent peacebuilding.

Parishes, colleges, and universities. For all this to happen, therefore, the church's institutions of formal and nonformal education must take a lead at training Catholics in the theory and practice of active nonviolence, and form them in virtues of courage, patience, and love that correspond to that practice rather than warrior virtues. And for *that* to happen, parish level resources must be available to encourage Catholic youth who are considering military service to transfer their desire for adventure, higher purpose, and service of the common good into justice advocacy, conflict resolution, and even nonviolent peaceforces.

Todd Whitmore, a moral theologian at the University of Notre Dame, suggests that the American Catholic Church should found a "Reserve Evangelical Training Corp," aiming to make two years of service as normative for young Catholics as it is for Mormon youth to dedicate two years of their life to missionary work. Meanwhile, in the short run, Catholic campuses that host programs such as the U.S.'s Reserve Officer Training Corp (R.O.T.C.) should organize their curricula to train young officers thoroughly in the just war criteria. Training should be so thorough, in fact, that resisting unjust orders and selective conscientious objection to unjust wars becomes normative.

In the long run, R.O.T.C. programs on Catholic campuses should collaborate with Justice and Peace Studies programs more closely. The goal should be to make those campuses leading think tanks for transarmament from potentially lethal and military forms of defense to nonviolent civilian-based defense. If governments object to Catholics training their soldiers-then-international-police in this way, it will only be fair to expect institutional conscientious objection.

Transnationally. Of course, for all of this to fulfill its promise in the arena of international peacemaking, Catholics will need venues for taking strategies for nonviolent action towards the next level, in the defense of the human rights of whole populations that we currently know as national defense. Until governments invest in the strategies and institutions of nonviolent civilian-based defense, and thus commit to a process of transarmament, the church should explore doing nothing less than developing a transnational, nonviolent army or peaceforce of its own.

Such an enterprise is more realistic than first blush may suggest. For in an era of globalization, political scientists recognize that nation-states are already ceding some of their prominence as international actors. Not only are multinational corporations more prominent, but so too is a vast network of nongovernmental organizations.[24] This network constitutes the best hope for the kind of global civil society that Catholic social teaching calls for in the name of human solidarity.

Actually, the church should never have forgotten to recognize itself as history's archetypical transnational society, together with Diaspora Judaism, and in keeping with the teaching of early church fathers.[25] Thankfully, the Second Vatican Council both re-affirmed the church as a transnational "Pilgrim People of God" and renounced the church's *direct* claim to political control. Together these twin moves have opened the conceptual space in which to launch a nonviolent army or peaceforce for that transnational nation which is the church.

In any case, on many smaller levels, building on parish/diocesan social justice offices, and making fuller use of its college/university Justice and Peace Studies programs, the church catholic must take a lead in forming strategic think tanks, action groups, and pilot projects for the nonviolent defense of peoples. Otherwise, Catholic soldiers and international police stand no chance of fulfilling the criterion of last resort.

Prophetically. Admittedly, these proposals assume and add up to a thorough cultural transformation within the Roman Catholic Church. To institutionalize such practices, Catholics will need to act in ways that may be uncomfortably counter-cultural for them at first. In the context of what Pope John Paul II has called the modern "culture of death," however, there may in fact be no other way to be pro-cultural in the best and most human sense. Ultimately such labels may be irrelevant at best and misleading at worst. For sometimes the church is properly counter-cultural, sometimes properly inculturated, always properly multicultural, and always a defender of vulnerable human cultures. In every last case, however, Christians can only know which is the appropriate response when cultural acceptance is the least of their concerns.

Concluding Notes on Ecclesial Vocation

Given historic power imbalances, Mennonites and other Christian pacifists certainly have some legitimate reasons to be stubborn in defense of what they believe to be the gospel truths of nonviolence. Yet their own commitment to discipleship should also lead them to embody nonviolent ways of struggling for justice that do not create new injustices or demean their opponents. These will include ways of dissenting without tearing down the very principle of ecclesial authority and ways of creatively searching for "third options." Might all this not include dreaming and working toward fresh ecclesial models for maintaining a resolute witness for nonviolence within the church Catholic?

In charting the kinds of communal practices that the Catholic Church will need to engender in order for war to cease being a church-dividing issue, we have stressed the need for much wider practices to discern, test, and maintain accountability to lay vocations, and yet the concept of vocation can be problematic for Christian pacifists at this one point.

Putting pacifism into the category of vocation is problematic if it means the wider Christian church accepts their pacifism as legitimate only *because* it is relegated to the status of vocation. Mennonites have already encountered the patronizing attitude by which the twentieth-century Protestant thinker Reinhold Niebuhr said they were not heretics, and had a place in the Christian tradition, so long as they accepted their marginal and socially irresponsible role as living reminders of the rigorous but impracticable standards of Jesus' ethic.[26] Pacifists will not be wrong to reject gentler offers of recognition for their vocation too, if that is what vocation means.

The need to embody our arguments socially through communal practices, however, suggests the sense in which it *is* proper to speak of a pacifist vocation. In a divided Christian church, we must presume that history and circumstance have made some gifts, lessons, and words from the Lord relatively inaccessible to some Christians, though intended by God for all. In this situation, the very vocation of Christian pacifist communities may well be to offer a living, socially-embodied argument that nonviolence is normative for all. To call this a vocation is not to compromise the integrity of that very argument, but to name the urgent sense of responsibility that some community must take on in order to do what will first make it intelligible, then imaginable, then credible to other Christian communities and ultimately to the whole, catholic, body.

Notes

1. See Tobias Winright, "From Police Officers to Peace Officers," 92–96, drawing on the work of Ralph B. Potter and Edward A. Malloy, as well as other writings by Winright listed in footnote 2.

2. Tobias Winright, "From Police Officers to Peace Officers," 106. This trend was one factor in the shift we have already seen as Yoder moved away from Hershberger's categorical rejection of Christian participation in both domestic and international policing. Of course, the development of politically efficacious nonviolence has also been a factor leading the Roman Catholic magisterium toward an increasingly stringent application of the just war theory, according to Drew Christiansen S.J. See Christiansen, "Peacemaking and the Use of Force: Behind the Pope's Stringent Just-War Teaching"; "What is a Peace Church?: A Roman Catholic Perspective," paper presented at the International Mennonite-Roman Catholic Dialogue (Karlsruhe, Germany, 2000).

3. *Gaudium et Spes* §80.

4. David H. Bayley, *Police for the Future*, Studies in Crime and Public Policy (New York: Oxford University Press, 1994); James Chacko and Stephen E. Nancoo, eds., *Community*

Policing in Canada, ed. James Chacko (Toronto: Canadian Scholar's Press, 1993); Robert R. Friedmann, *Community Policing: Comparative Perspectives and Prospects* (New York: St. Martin's Press, 1992); Stephen J. Gaffigan and the Community Policing Consortium, *Understanding Community Policing: A Framework for Action* (Washington, DC: Bureau of Justice Assistance, 1994); Jack R. Greene and Stephen D. Mastrofski, *Community Policing: Rhetoric or Reality,* ed. Jack R. Greene (New York: Praeger, 1988); Kenneth J. Peak and Ronald W. Glensor, *Community Policing and Problem Solving: Strategies and Practices* (Englewood Cliffs, NJ: Prentice Hall, 1996); Robert C. Trojanowicz and Bonnie Bucqueroux, *Community Policing: A Contemporary Perspective,* 3rd ed. (Cincinnati, OH: Anderson Pub. Co., 2002); Robert C. Trojanowicz and Bonnie Bucqueroux, *Community Policing: How to Get Started* (Cincinnati, OH: Anderson Pub. Co., 1994); Robert C. Wadman, *Community Wellness: A New Theory of Policing,* A PERF Discussion Paper (Washington, DC: Police Executive Research Forum, 1990).

5. Christopher Freeman Adams, "Fighting Crime by Building Moral Communities," *The Christian Century* 111, no. 27 (October 5, 1994): 894.

6. Lederach, "Quo Vadis?" Also cf. the last four Just Peacemaking practices for building international community in Glen Stassen, *Just Peacemaking: Ten Practices for Abolishing War,* 133–88: "Work with Emerging Cooperative Forces in the International System," "Strengthen the United Nations and International Efforts for Cooperation and Human Rights," "Reduce Offensive Weapons and Weapons Trade," and "Encourage Grassroots Peacemaking Groups and Voluntary Associations."

7. Lederach, "Challenge of Terrorism." Lederach continued: "It is an ironic fact that our greatest threat is not in Afghanistan, but in our own backyard. We surely are not going to bomb Travelocity, Hertz Rental Car, or an airline training school in Florida. We must change metaphors and move beyond the reaction that we can duke it out with the bad guy, or we run the very serious risk of creating the environment that sustains and reproduces the virus we wish to prevent."

8. Christopher Dickey and John Barry, "Has the War Made Us Safer?" with Gameela Ismail, *Newsweek,* April 12, 2004, 26.

9. The notion of and need for socially embodied arguments is a major theme in the work of Catholic philosopher Alasdair MacIntyre, carried through his books *After Virtue: A Study in Moral Theory,* 2d ed. (Notre Dame, IN: University of Notre Dame Press, 1984); *Whose Justice? Which Rationality?* (Notre Dame, IN: University of Notre Dame Press, 1988) and *Three Rival Versions of Moral Enquiry: Encyclopedia, Genealogy, and Tradition,* The Gifford Lectures 1988 (Notre Dame, IN: University of Notre Dame Press, 1990). One of the most succinct statements of MacIntyre's case, however, is also one of the sources of this terminology: Alasdair MacIntyre, "The Privatization of Good: An Inaugural Lecture," *The Review of Politics* 32 (1990): 344–61, especially pp. 356–61. In the context of ecumenical dialogue, proofs embodied in practices are especially necessary if Catholics hope to convince Mennonites of their claims, since Mennonites have sometimes called discipleship the "essence of Christianity." (See Harold S. Bender, "The Anabaptist Vision," *Church History* 13 [March 1944]: 3–24.)

10. See pp. 82–84 in the previous chapter.

11. Cf. John Howard Yoder, *Christian Attitudes to War, Peace, and Revolution a Companion to Bainton* (Elkhart, IN: Dist. by Co-op Bookstore, 1983), 31, 34.

12. All quotations in this paragraph are from John Howard Yoder, "The Biblical Mandate for Evangelical Social Action," in *For the Nations: Essays Public and Evangelical* (Grand Rapids, MI: Wm. B. Eerdmans, 1997), 186–87.

13. All quotations in this paragraph are from John Howard Yoder, "The Biblical Mandate," 186–87. For a far more extensive exposition of Yoder's conception of Christian congregational discernment and discipline, see John Howard Yoder, "Binding and Loosing," in *The Royal Priesthood: Essays Ecclesiological and Ecumenical*, ed. Michael G. Cartwright (Grand Rapids, MI: Wm. B. Eerdmans, 1994), 323–58.

14. For a broader theological discussion of this question, see Gerald W. Schlabach, "Deuteronomic or Constantinian: What is the Most Basic Problem for Christian Social Ethics?" in *The Wisdom of the Cross: Essays in Honor of John Howard Yoder*, eds. Stanley Hauerwas, et al. (Grand Rapids, MI: Wm. B. Eerdmans, 1999), 449–71.

15. John Howard Yoder, *For the Nations: Essays Public and Evangelical* (Grand Rapids, MI: Wm. B. Eerdmans, 1997), 1–4, 41–42, 51–78.

16. See page 78.

17. I.e., without allowing public office to become "autonomous as a source of moral guidance," as Yoder put it ("The Biblical Mandate," 186).

18. *The Harvest of Justice*, I.B.2.

19. See *The Harvest of Justice*, section I.B, which states: "Our conference's approach, as outlined in *The Challenge of Peace*, can be summarized in this way: (1) In situations of conflict, our constant commitment ought to be, as far as possible, to strive for justice through nonviolent means. (2) But, when sustained attempts at nonviolent action fail to protect the innocent against fundamental injustice, then legitimate political authorities are permitted as a last resort to employ limited force to rescue the innocent and establish justice."

20. I wish to thank Professor Todd Whitmore of the University of Notre Dame for stimulating many of the proposals that follow by sharing in personal conversation some of his own ideas for a far more thorough study of what the Roman Catholic Church must do to operationalize the just war theory. Dr. Whitmore should not be assumed to concur with all the particulars of my own proposals, of course, particularly since our conversation took place a few years ago.

21. John Dart, "U.S. Bishops Split on War's Morality," *Los Angeles Times* February 26, 1991, A-11.

22. I recall Father Bryan Hehir posing the rhetorical question about whether to make such a tactical shift in a lecture at the University of Notre Dame at the time of the Persian Gulf War. Corroborating this recollection is the article he wrote soon after the war began: "The Moral Calculus of War," *Commonweal* 118, no. 4 (February 22, 1991): 125–26. The article charts his moral deliberation step-by-step, as the public debate shifted from *why* to *when* to *how* questions.

23. John Howard Yoder, *Christian Witness to the State*, 57. See p. 83 above.

24. Cf. Duane K. Friesen, "Encourage Grassroots Peacemaking Groups and Voluntary Associations," in *Just Peacemaking: Ten Practices for Abolishing War*, ed. Glen Stassen (Cleveland: Pilgrim Press, 1998), 176–88.

25. *Epistle of Mathetes to Diognetus* 5–6; *Shepherd of Hermas* sim. 1; Clement of Alexandria, *Stromata* 6.5–6; Tertullian, *The Apology*, 38; Origen, *Against Celsus* 8.75; Pontius the Deacon, *The Life and Passion of Cyprian* 11; Gregory Nazianzen (recounting the interrogation of Basil the Great), *Oration* 43.49; Augustine, *City of God* 19.17 and 19.26.

26. Reinhold Niebuhr, "Why the Christian Church is not Pacifist," in *Christianity and Power Politics* (New York: Charles Scibner's Sons, 1940), 1–32.

PART III

And *Just* Policing: Elaborations

Chapter 6

Whose Justice? Which Relationality?

Margaret R. Pfeil

> "The effort of . . . moral reason to fit the use of military force into the objective order of justice is paradoxical enough; but the paradox is heightened when this effort takes place at the interior of the Christian religion of love."[1]

John Courtney Murray named a paradox that continues to shape the task of just war theorists as they strive to offer an account of justice and peace consonant with the "Christian religion of love." Who defines the claims of justice at stake in a conflict situation and which social agents have the power to arbitrate them? What kind of peace does the operative conception of justice reflect? Rival accounts of just war theory yield divergent responses to these questions. Still, the very fact of such interpretative debate signals the progressive development of an overarching Christian tradition of peace. The position that U.S. bishops and the Holy See are advancing ever more emphatically presses the growing edge of that tradition toward a restorative understanding of justice rooted in the *shalom* of right relationship.

A Developing Tradition and Culture of Peace

On the eve of the 2003 U.S. invasion of Iraq, the Holy See and the U.S. Conference of Catholic Bishops were vigorously urging policy-makers to pursue alternatives to war. In their November 2002 "Statement on Iraq," the U.S. bishops argued that war in this case "would not meet the strict conditions in Catholic teaching for overriding the strong presumption against the use of military force." To support their position, they invoked their 1983 pastoral letter, *The Challenge of Peace*, which states that "just war teaching has evolved . . . as an effort to prevent war. . . ."[2] In a similar vein, Archbishop Renato Martino, president of the Pontifical Council for Justice and Peace, likened the evolution of Catholic teaching on just war theory to that on capital punishment, noting that the church is moving toward a "quasi-abolitionist stance" on war.[3]

Addressing the diplomatic corps accredited to the Vatican in January 2003, John Paul II illustrated Martino's point, zealously invoking Paul VI's 1965 address to the United Nations:

> 'No to war'! War is not always inevitable. It is always a defeat for humanity. International law, honest dialogue, solidarity between States, the noble exercise of diplomacy: these are methods worthy of individuals and nations in resolving their differences. . . . War is never just another means that one can choose to employ for settling differences between nations. As the Charter of the United Nations Organization and international law itself remind us, war cannot be decided upon, even when it is a matter of ensuring the common good, except as the very last option and in accordance with very strict conditions, without ignoring the consequences for the civilian population both during and after the military operations.[4]

Acting on the pope's behalf, Cardinal Pio Laghi personally delivered a similar message to President Bush in early March, just before U.S. forces attacked Iraq. In that message John Paul II again urged the president to explore every possible alternative to war:

> Here is why, in the face of the tremendous consequences that an international military operation would have for the population of Iraq and the balance of the entire Middle East region, already sorely tried, as well as for the extremisms that could ensue, I say to all: There is still time to negotiate, there is still room for peace; it is never too late to come to an understanding and to continue discussions. . . . We must do everything possible! We know well that peace is not possible at any cost.[5]

Perhaps John Paul II's final remark had suffered in translation, or was idiosyncratic, but that makes it all the more crucial to understand. In the days leading up to the U.S. invasion of Iraq, many were using just-war rhetoric (but not the full theory) to argue that war with Saddam Hussein's government would lead to peace. The pope was applying a corrective. Not every policy leads to peace, particularly the true peace of right relationship towards which just war deliberation ought to aim. Simply to add more and more military force to counter military force would not insure peace, for it would only increase the human cost of war and thus the resentment that breeds even more conflict. To say that "peace is not possible at any cost," then, was to insist that there were limits to what military force could achieve, limits both moral and practical.

Precisely because peace is not possible at any cost, the U.S. Conference of Catholic Bishops and the Holy See attempted in these statements to turn just war theory toward the task of preventing war. In calling for greater attention to the *ad bellum* criterion of last resort and to the anticipated consequences of war for civilian life and the common good, they appealed to a "presumption against the use of force" that underlies just war thinking.

While this phrase represents a relatively recent addition to the just war lexicon, its meaning finds resonance in the broader tradition.[6] Augustine, for example, held that vindication of justice on behalf of public authority may require use of lethal force, but such killing always represents an occasion for mourning.[7] Subsequently, Thomas Aquinas approached the issue of just war by asking, "Is it always a sin to wage war?" To some, the very phrasing of this question reflects an underlying presumption against war.[8] Aquinas' query forms part of a longer treatment on charity: Love establishes the horizon for adjudicating claims of justice, and it is the only virtue whose proper act is peace, which is effected through singleminded and wholehearted love of God and love of neighbor.[9]

To others, however, the suggestion that just war theory entails a presumption against war betrays the just war tradition itself. George Weigel, for one, has accused religious leaders of "just war forgetfulness," and ventured that the just war tradition lives more vigorously in the halls of the Pentagon than in the offices of the U.S. Catholic bishops.[10] James Turner Johnson has articulated Weigel's worries more systematically. Johnson maintains that even though *The Challenge of Peace* and other Catholic social teaching texts have cited a longstanding presumption against war within the just war tradition, no such presumption or principle existed in "just war theory in its classic form." Rather, Johnson asserts:

> the concept of just war does not begin with a 'presumption against war' focused on the harm which war may do, but with a presumption against *injustice* focused on the need for responsible use of force in response to wrongdoing. Force, according to the core meaning of just war tradition, is an instrumentality that may be good or evil, depending on the use to which it is put. The whole structure of the *jus ad bellum* of just war tradition has to do with specifying the terms under which those in political power are authorized to resort to force for good—that is, to rectify specific injustices.[11]

By insisting on a presumption against injustice, Johnson hopes to salvage what he considers to be a "broken" just war tradition, thus allowing contemporary statecraft to vindicate justice but not necessarily to prevent war.[12] Like Augustine's wise judge, those exercising legitimate political authority may find it necessary to risk harming the innocent in order to stave off societal chaos.[13] Love, in service of the commonweal, sometimes entails a "sort of kindly harshness."[14]

The dissonance between the Weigel-Johnson approach to just war theory and that of the U.S. bishops and the Holy See stems, in part, from divergent interpretations of the kind of order that makes for a just peace. Peace is not possible at any cost, the pope has said, implying that just means will find their measure in the quality of peace one is seeking. By focusing on "the need for responsible use of force in response to wrongdoing," Johnson's position risks precluding full consideration of alternatives to the use of force that would satisfy the requirements of justice as determined by the kind of peace desired. Can humankind aspire to a peace that is more than the absence of war? The Holy See and the U.S. bishops' emphasis on the presumption against war yields an affirmative response.

In *The Challenge of Peace*, the bishops root their understanding of peace in Scripture (par. 27–55). The Old Testament conception of peace unfolds in the context of Israel's covenant with God, and thus assumes a radically relational quality. The people express their fidelity to God by striving toward the realization of the peace of *shalom* within the community.[15]

The Hebrew word *shalom*, deriving from the Sumerian root *silim* and the Akkadian *šalâmu*, "to be whole, uninjured,"[16] connotes threefold right relationship. It refers, first, to adequate satisfaction of one's material and physical needs, and secondly to the embodiment of just personal and social relationships. As a prerequisite for entering into rightly ordered relationships, *shalom* also involves personal integrity.[17] Ultimately, *shalom* is God's gift to a people steadfast in righteousness (*sedeq[ah]*) before God and before other humans—particularly the poor, the oppressed, and the outcasts.[18]

Covenantal justice, as Christopher Marshall makes plain, finds fulfillment in the restoration of *shalom*, not in the pain of punishment.[19] This understanding of the relationship between justice and peace informs New Testament accounts of Jesus' life, death, and resurrection. The kind of peace that Jesus gives to his disciples flows from God's love and merciful forgiveness. By his own actions, Jesus calls his followers to go and do likewise, rectifying wrongs and healing brokenness in faithful witness to the truth of God's Reign.

Weigel also appeals to peace understood in the biblical sense of *shalom*, finding there the measure of *tranquillitatis ordinis* within the political community. But, he holds, since the fullness of peace represents an eschatological reality unattainable within human history, *shalom* does not bear practical political significance, though it may have hortatory value as an ethical ideal.[20] His argument rests on his separation of the peace of *shalom* from that of "spiritual interiority." Interior conversion to right relationship with God "by definition has nothing to do with politics."[21]

The very tradition that Weigel seeks to safeguard from betrayal, however, testifies to the essential interrelationship of personal and communal peace. Augustine's understanding of right intention in a just war, for example, hinged on the loving interior disposition of the soldier being asked to kill on behalf of the public authority.[22] Aquinas followed Augustine in noting that inadmissible intentions in waging war include revenge and the lust to dominate.[23] These architects of Christian just war thinking expected that public action, including war, undertaken on behalf of the commonweal, would spring from an interior disposition toward rightly ordered relationships consonant with the objective intention (*finis operis*) of any just war, the restoration of peace.

The integrity of this correspondence between interior disposition and outward action reveals the nature of peace as God's gracious gift. Days before the 2003 Gulf War began, John Paul II affirmed this truth: "[W]e Christians are convinced that real and lasting peace is not only the fruit, though necessary, of political agreements and understanding between individuals and peoples, but a gift of God to all those who submit themselves to him and accept with humility and gratitude the light of his love."[24] Those who humbly surrender to God's gift of peace give way to an interior wholeness that gracefully issues in work for justice directed toward the fullness of *shalom*.

Ultimately, the work of peace springs from human hearts freed by the Holy Spirit to love God and others. Guided by this holistic understanding of peace, John Paul II himself probed the meaning of "the peace of order" in his 2003 World Day of Peace message. The fortieth anniversary year of *Pacem in terris* had dawned on a world shattered by the multivalent violence of war and poverty. This prompted the pope to ask, "What kind of order can replace this disorder, so that men and women can live in freedom, justice, and security?"[25] In responding to his own question, he emphasized the relational quality of *tranquillitatis ordinis*. "Gestures of peace are possible when people appreciate fully the community dimension of their lives, so that they grasp the meaning and consequences of events in their own communities and in the world. Gestures of peace create a tradition and a culture of peace."[26]

The pope's hopes for a cohesive tradition and culture of peace on the international level may seem utopian in light of the fact that Christian just war thinkers cannot seem to find common ground on a faithful interpretation of just war theory that meets contemporary needs. Might an overarching tradition of peace exist nonetheless, integrating disparate strands of just war thinking?

Stepping back a moment to consider the meaning of "tradition," Alasdair MacIntyre's account proves salient. A tradition, he holds,

> is an argument extended through time in which certain fundamental agreements are defined and redefined in terms of two kinds of conflict: those with critics and enemies external to the tradition who reject all or at least part of those fundamental agreements, and those internal, interpretative debates through which the meaning and rationale of the fundamental agreements come to be expressed and by whose progress a tradition is constituted.[27]

Understood in this light, recent exchanges among just war theorists regarding the presumption against war, and the nature and means of attaining peaceful social order, seem to be internal to the tradition. In fact they indicate a shift in Catholic teaching on peace, or what John Thiel has called an incipient development of doctrine. Any gradual growth in doctrinal understanding begins among a minority within the church, according to Thiel. It usually starts in a particular place, and it functions prophetically. A small number of voices—in this case those emanating from the Holy See and the U.S. Conference of Catholic Bishops—invite the rest of the church to consider the need to adapt traditional teaching to respond to signs of the times out of fidelity to the tradition itself.[28] As it gathers momentum, a groundswell movement in just war thinking is pressing the tradition toward the prevention of war. It presages the emergence of a broader tradition of peace, one sufficiently capacious and supple to permit internal debate among various just war interlocutors as well as between pacifists and just war theorists.[29]

The fact of such debate implies that even if Weigel and Johnson were correct in asserting that classic just war theory entails a presumption for justice rather than against war, their conception of justice would not be self-evident. As the U.S. bishops recognized when they introduced the notion of "comparative justice" in *The Challenge of Peace*, opposing sides in a particular conflict may credibly assert claims of justice; therefore, the application of just war criteria requires great humility.[30] Openness to the possibility that different conceptions of justice may underlie a conflict situation becomes part of the work of peacemaking, particularly in a fragile international system marked by failing states and signs of sovereignty's increasing fluidity.

So who defines the claims of justice at stake in a conflict situation and which social agents and international actors have the power to arbitrate them? What conception of peace does the operative interpretation of justice reflect? Unless these issues are addressed explicitly, those who enjoy sociopolitical dominance at the national or international level will likely determine the practical meaning of justice and peace without giving due consideration to the perspectives of other stakeholders.

In the cultivation of a tradition and culture of peace, attention to the relational aspects of justice functions epistemologically. The relational aspects of justice, in other words, are key to unlocking other aspects. One's standpoint determines what one is able to see and the sort of data that will thus inform one's conception of justice. Individuals and nations located at the center of social, economic, political, and cultural power structures will find it difficult to perceive and interpret the lived reality of those on the margins. They suffer from an epistemological disadvantage that undercuts their efforts to discern the sorts of just actions required by the peace of *shalom*.[31]

Weigel's account of *tranquillitatis ordinis* labors under this kind of epistemological handicap. Taking as his departure point the center of U.S. hegemony in a unipolar international system, he understands this term to coincide neatly with defense of what he perceives as U.S. national interests.[32] In his eponymous 1987 volume, for example, Weigel argued that U.S. Catholics should have regarded U.S. intervention in Central America during the Cold War as "a geopolitical given and, even more importantly, a moral and strategic responsibility."[33]

The history of U.S.-backed repression throughout that region belies Weigel's sanguine account of *tranquillitatis ordinis*, however. In its 1993 report, *From Madness to Hope*, the U.N.-sponsored truth commission in El Salvador attributed ninety-five percent of the atrocities committed during the twelve-year civil war to state-sponsored forces. The U.S. provided $4.5 billion in military and other forms of aid to the Salvadoran government in a war that claimed the lives of more than seventy thousand people.[34] The U.S. Army's School of the Americas located in Fort Benning, Georgia—ostensibly founded to foster stable democracies throughout Latin America—provided tactical training to the Salvadoran soldiers responsible for the murder of Archbishop Oscar Romero, along with the deaths of numerous other martyrs serving the Christian churches in El Salvador. The very fact that an outside commission was asked to unearth the truth of atrocities committed during the Salvadoran civil war indicates that the protection of putative U.S. national interests did not create the conditions of a just peace in El Salvador.

"Peace is not possible at any cost." Within the developing Christian tradition and culture of peace, those who embrace this truth commit themselves to explore conceptions of justice consonant with the peace of *shalom*. Hundreds of volunteers from around the world joined Witness for Peace during the Salvadoran civil war to offer their lives in nonviolent solidarity with persecuted civilians. Christian Peacemaking Teams, begun in 1984, currently work on the U.S.-Mexico border as well as in Canada, Colombia, Hebron, and Iraq to find "faith-based nonviolent alternatives in situations where lethal conflict is an immediate reality or is supported by public policy."[35] These efforts embody a restorative understanding of justice, one that seeks to rectify the wrong done in a conflict situation by cultivating right relationship. The peace of *shalom* unfolds in the very process of re-knitting the interpersonal and communal ties that acts of injustice have sundered, and of creating new relational bonds marked by justice.

Peacemaking Circles:
A Sample Practice of Restorative Justice

To demonstrate that Weigel's and Johnson's conception of justice is not self-evident, we need only sample the indigenous peacemaking practices of another, non-European culture. A ready example comes from the literature of the restorative justice movement, which first incorporated models from First Nation (aboriginal) peoples into the Canadian criminal justice system. Now a prominent practice of restorative justice programs south of the U.S.-Canadian border as well, the "peacemaking circle" demonstrates some of their central features. Though a skeptic might think them applicable only to interpersonal ethics in local face-to-face communities, this is hardly the case. If anything, the principles and practices of restorative justice prove far more compatible with the practices of international peacemaking and the conditions for global justice as Catholic social teaching envisions them than is the case with state-centered retributive justice.

The first peacemaking circles were developed in the Yukon in the early 1980s. Designed to address the personal and communal wounds caused by crime, peacemaking circles have since been adopted as a common method in other regions of Canada as well as in eight Minnesota communities.[36] In Canada, circles have been used in both juvenile and adult cases involving offenses that range from minor crimes to sexual assault and manslaughter.

While the application of the circle method to restorative tasks of healing the effects of crime is relatively recent, the process itself has long roots in Canadian aboriginal traditions. Symbolically, the circle receives and holds the Creator's gift of vision to First Nation peoples, a manner of seeing that perceives the radical interdependence of created reality. All aspects of creation stand in relation to one another, the well-being of each one bound up with that of the rest.[37] This view of creation puts into motion a "hermeneutic of peace," in other words, an interpretive standpoint that disposes one to seek courses of action conducive to the integrity of peace. One who adopts this manner of seeing reality will let the horizon of peace guide moral discernment about particular ways of being in the world. The wholeness of peace draws the person to become one with it.

The aboriginal hermeneutic of peace is integrally relational. It thus guides the application of the circle method to the practical work of peacemaking in the wake of criminal offenses. Procedurally, a community justice committee or circle support group accepts a case on the basis of several considerations. The offender must acknowledge responsibility, demonstrate concrete efforts toward rehabilitation, and find support within the community.[38] Initially, a talking circle meets to determine whether the circle method is appropriate in a particular case and represents the victim's wishes. Later, private healing circles attend separately to both the victim and the offender. Facilitators or "keepers" who are experienced in peacemaking guide these smaller circles.

Eventually, a full circle, open to all who wish to participate, convenes to bring together the concerns and needs that have emerged within the healing circles. When deemed necessary, this process may lead to a sentencing decision. A judge may refer a case to a circle process and then accept its outcome as a recommendation, or along with the prosecutor and defense attorney, the judge may participate directly in the circle and recognize the group's consensus decision as the final sentence.[39] Subsequently, review circles convene periodically to verify that all parties are fulfilling their commitments.[40]

The integrity of the peacemaking circle depends upon the direct and voluntary participation of all stakeholders in a particular case.[41] To ensure this end, a symbol bearing meaning for the community—known as a talking piece—passes clockwise around the circle from person to person. This allows each one to exercise his or her right and responsibility to participate in the deliberations without interruption and regardless of any power differentials that may exist among them.[42]

In the Ojibway community of Hollow Water, Manitoba, the circle process has proven fruitful. In this Canadian village of six hundred people, residents gathered in 1984 to address the high rate of substance abuse, vandalism, and violent behavior among their youth. Their efforts uncovered a multivalent pattern of alcoholism and sexual abuse among the families of youth offenders. An estimated eighty percent of the residents had suffered sexual abuse and about fifty percent, both male and female, had inflicted it upon others.[43]

Through the Community Holistic Circle Healing Program, Hollow Water began to address the needs of victims and offenders by establishing an elaborate system of peacemaking circles. By 1995, the process included 48 offenders, 62 victims, and 236 relatives of those directly affected. At that time, 5 offenders had been sentenced to jail, and 2 had re-offended over the course of 9 years.[44] The long-term preventive effects remain to be seen, but as John Braithwaite has observed, the rate of detection of sexual abuse by this method is striking: "When and where has the traditional criminal process succeeded in uncovering anything approaching 52 admissions of criminal responsibility for sexual abuse of children in a community of just 600?"[45]

The Hollow Water peacemaking circle process illustrates certain guiding principles of restorative justice. First, the participants' articulation of and commitment to a set of shared values sustains the circle. These include the protection of human dignity, individual and collective accountability, procedural equity, and the participation of all stakeholders. Cultivation of these values serves justice by nurturing the well-being of all members of society as persons who flourish only in relationship to one another.[46]

Because of its relational quality, practitioners frequently describe the restorative justice approach as an alternative to the adversarial mode characteristic of the Anglo/Western communal justice system in which each side, driven at least in part by fear of vulnerability, seeks to gain advantage at the other's expense.[47] Restorative justice measures, by contrast, attempt to disarm the fear and distrust that spring from and contribute to systemic violence. In the Hollow Water case, for example, community members believe that the circle process fosters long-term healing more effectively than traditional prosecution and enforcement procedures because it breaks the silence surrounding sexual abuse instead of rewarding reticence.[48]

Upholding personal and communal values in the dialogical process of the circle engenders respectful engagement, a second guiding principle of restorative practices.[49] "If I had to put restorative justice into one word," writes Howard Zehr, "I would choose respect: respect for all, even those who are different from us, even those who seem to be our enemies. . . . If we pursue justice as respect, we will do justice restoratively."[50]

Thirdly, to cultivate a climate of respect, restorative justice practices invite all those directly harmed by a situation of injustice to participate in righting the wrong done. Toward that end, they typically employ a consensus model of decision-making that entails attentiveness to the needs of all parties concerned.[51] While the interests of those gathered may conflict, the energy of the process is generative rather than divisive, as participants strive toward a decision that represents the collective wisdom of the group. Even when the outcome falls short of consensus, restorative justice practices reflect procedural equity. Respecting the view of every stakeholder forges stronger communal relationships. As signs of the radical interdependence of all within God's creation, these relational ties may free their subjects to embody the kind of peace that they seek, the *shalom* of right relationship.

Fourthly, a hermeneutic of peace guides discernment regarding the specific requirements of justice. The peace of *shalom* sheds the light of truth on systemic manifestations of wrongly ordered relationships. In the Hollow Water case, judicial authorities and the local community might have relied upon the traditional criminal justice system to prosecute youth for relatively minor offenses like vandalism. Had the process been so narrowly circumscribed, however, it likely would not have revealed the profound systemic disorder of multigenerational sexual abuse of which the youths' minor offenses were symptomatic.

Using the hermeneutical lens of peace—understood as right relationship—community members were able to address layers of violence almost imperceptible from the perspective of state-centered justice. Whereas the Anglo/Western system of justice tends to cast the state as the victim of crime, the circle process in Hollow Water shifted the focus to the particular stakeholders involved, affording community members the opportunity to grasp the full scope of victimization confronting them and to participate directly in naming and attempting to heal the harm done.[52] The Holistic Circle Healing Program has called a community profoundly fragmented by moral and social disorder to grow toward the integrity of *shalom*.

The Hollow Water community experience demonstrates a fifth principle of restorative justice: limiting recourse to retributive measures in order that other possibilities for securing justice might emerge. Whether restorative justice involves recourse to retributive measures remains a contested issue. Charles Barton argues that restorative practices often do justify punishment based on the retributive notion of just desert: The offender receives a punishment corresponding with his or her wrongful behavior.[53] As Howard Zehr acknowledges, restorative and retributive approaches to justice share an interest in vindication through reciprocity:

> Both retributive and restorative theories of justice acknowledge a basic moral intuition that a balance has been thrown off by the wrongdoing. Consequently, the victim deserves something and the offender owes something. Both [theories] argue that there must be a proportional relationship between the act and the response. Where they differ is on the currency that will right the balance or acknowledge that reciprocity.[54]

While retribution involves the infliction of pain in vindicating justice, a restorative account allows the hermeneutic of peace to elicit transformative means of addressing the harm done. With *shalom* as the moral horizon guiding work for justice, the restorative principles of direct, inclusive participation and respectful engagement give shape to specific practices. They call the offender to affirm his or her own human dignity as well as the victim's by acknowledging responsibility, making restitution, and attending to the causes of his or her behavior with the support of the surrounding community. While holding offenders morally accountable, restorative justice measures provide greater flexibility in determining what specific action steps might draw all concerned into right relationship.

The affected community determines whether and what kind of punitive measures appear warranted by a given offense. In the peacemaking circle process, for example, a jail sentence is one option available to the sentencing circle, but it would be considered a last resort. In some cases, an offender who has acknowledged guilt and has agreed to participate in the circle process may still face a mandatory minimum jail sentence. In this event, the community makes a commitment to accompany an offender who serves prison time as part of the circle process. As one Yukon community elder put it, "'How you send them away, determines how they come back. If you send them away with hate, anger—that's how they come back, full of hate and anger. Send them away with love—that's how they come back.'"[55] The *shalom* of right relationship flows from and leads to unflinching love of God and neighbor, particularly those alienated or excluded from the community by love's absence.

The action of loving a community into the wholeness of peace points to a sixth principle implicit in restorative justice practices, though it has not gained attention in the literature to date: The peace of right relationship entails making an option for the poor. While consensual decision-making and the circle practice of passing a talking piece do address power disparities among participants in a given community, such procedural equity does not necessarily require that the community grapple with structural violations of distributive justice. In order to restore the dignity of right relationship in situations of conflict, it is not enough for those at the center of societal power structures to communicate more effectively with those on the periphery. Rather, the entire community must opt for the poor by adopting the vantage point of those on the margins of social, economic, political, and cultural power structures in order to name and then transform systemic injustice.

Only through the option for the poor can restorative measures ensure the dignified participation of all those affected by systemic injustice. Poverty robs humans of their ability to participate fully in shaping their society. More than a mere absence of adequate income, it functions as a kind of capability deprivation, as the Nobel-winning economist Amartya Sen has shown.[56] Those lacking sufficient education, nutrition, shelter, health care, and political freedom find their possibilities to exercise agency on behalf of the common good truncated or foreclosed altogether. Sen observes, for example, that African American males living in U.S. inner cities enjoy a relatively higher level of income than males in certain regions of China and India, but their mortality rate is also significantly greater. Poverty strips them not only of capabilities but ultimately of life itself. Perhaps for this reason, Archbishop Oscar Romero identified social sin with the deaths of Salvadoran people wrought by political and socioeconomic structures of oppression and repression.[57]

Seen through the lens of capability deprivation, the truth of poverty as a form of violence emerges. Eight of the ten poorest countries have experienced significant armed conflict in recent years, reflecting the insidious cyclical relationship between extreme poverty and large-scale violence.[58] Schooled in the suffering caused by this phenomenon, Romero urged his people to opt for the poor as a constitutive dimension of their Christian faith. The vantage point of those on the periphery of societal power reveals the requirements of justice precisely in its felt absence.[59]

Conclusion:
Restorative Justice and Catholic Social Teaching

Guided by all of these principles, practices of restorative justice offer promising contributions to the tradition and culture of peace. But can they effectively address violations of justice at the international level? In a globalized, interdependent world, some forms of injustice unfold on multiple levels across the demarcations of nation-states, provinces, and villages. Admittedly, this makes it difficult to presume a cohesive community capable of applying restorative principles of justice.[60]

The hermeneutic of peace as *shalom* invites imaginative re-mapping of human interrelationship, following not the cartographer's lines of longitude and latitude but rather the web of life inscribed within creation, binding humanity and the entire cosmos together. Certain violations of justice inadvertently reveal these hidden strands of interrelationship. The rape and murder of four U.S. churchwomen in 1980 by Salvadoran forces trained at the School of the Americas served to raise the consciousness of U.S. Americans, calling attention to the insidious relationship that had long existed between U.S. taxpayers and the people of El Salvador, as well as the timeless ties of fidelity binding people of faith across the ephemeral boundaries of nation-states.

Precisely in this sort of galvanizing experience of brokenness, restorative practices of justice seek to build peace by creating space for new forms of community to take shape, transcending territorial stratifications and rendering the locus of restorative action more fluid. Zehr speaks of micro-communities of place and relationship, as distinguished from society, formed by those most directly affected by a specific experience of wrongdoing.[61] Consciences formed to identify individual complicity in structural injustice will draw people into such experiences of community. Those U.S. Americans who journeyed to El Salvador to witness for peace, organized protests of U.S. foreign policy in Central America, and welcomed Salvadorans fleeing persecution, sought to establish new forms of relationality faithful to the *shalom* of right relationship.

Driven by a similar desire, the U.S. bishops and the Holy See have adopted a restorative approach to justice in advocating for a presumption against war. They recognize that the human community "exists prior to the sovereign state and is a more appropriate point of reference for analyzing world politics," as Bryan Hehir has noted.[62] The entire conceptual framework of Catholic social teaching finds its basic orientation in this communal point of reference. Created out of love in the image of God as social beings, humans are called to enter into relationship, giving life to a multiplicity of communities as part of creation's journey toward the wholeness of peace in God. The integrity of God's gift of peace provides the ethical horizon for all works of peacemaking—interpersonal, societal, national, international, and cosmic.

As the U.S. bishops emphasized in their 1993 statement, *The Harvest of Justice Is Sown in Peace*, peacemaking requires disciplined practice of the "peaceable virtues" of faith and hope, courage and compassion, humility and kindness, patience and perseverance, civility and charity.[63] Ultimately, peace will spring from the virtuous practice of solidarity, which John Paul II describes as "a *firm and persevering determination* to commit oneself to the *common good*; that is to say, to the good of all and of each individual, because we are *all* really responsible *for all.*"[64]

Coming to appreciate the radical relationality of all creation in God is a fundamentally spiritual task, the fruit of grace. As the bishops acknowledged in their pastoral message following the events of September 11, 2001, "True peacemaking can be a matter of policy only if it is first a matter of the heart."[65] Only those who surrender in ongoing conversion to the peace of right relationship will be able to imagine and create restorative responses to grave offenses like terrorism.

The emergent Christian tradition of peace is taking shape around hearts and minds moved to practice solidarity with those on the world's margins. Pressed by the gradual distillation of internal debate about the conditions of *tranquillitatis ordinis*, this tradition is coming to a fuller understanding of the integrity of peace. Negatively put, peace is not possible at any cost; positively, it represents the fullness of *shalom*, in which right relationship serves as the measure of justice within the Christian religion of love.

Notes

1. John Courtney Murray, *We Hold These Truths: Catholic Reflections on the American Proposition* (New York: Sheed and Ward, 1960), 269.

2. U.S. Conference of Catholic Bishops, "Statement on Iraq," *Origins* 32, no. 24 (November 21, 2002): 406–8. The quote from *The Challenge of Peace*, §83. See also §70. This and other key church documents are available in David J. O'Brien and Thomas A. Shannon, eds., *Catholic Social Thought: The Documentary Heritage* (Maryknoll, NY: Orbis Books, 1992).

3. John L. Allen, Jr., "Pope's 'Answer to Rumsfeld' Pulls no Punches in Opposing War," *National Catholic Reporter*, February 14, 2003, 3–4. See also U.S. Conference of Catholic Bishops, *The Harvest of Justice*, I.B. Available December 12, 2006. www.usccb.org/sdwp/harvest.htm#theology.

4. John Paul II, "The International Situation Today," Address to the diplomatic corps accredited to the Vatican, *Origins* 32, no. 33 (January 30, 2003): 544.

5. John Paul II, "There is Still Room for Peace," Address before midday angelus, *L'Osservatore Romano*, March 17–18, 2003, 12.

6. On this point, see J. Bryan Hehir, "In Defense of Justice," *Commonweal* (March 10, 1991): 32–33.

7. See Augustine, *The City of God*, 14.15 and 19.6–7; and Roland Bainton's insight into Augustine's mournful acquiescence to the coercive power of the state in *Christian Attitudes Toward War and Peace: A Historical Survey and Critical Re-Evaluation* (Nashville: Abingdon Press, 1960), 98. See also John Howard Yoder, *When War is Unjust*, 153.

8. Thomas Aquinas, *Summa Theologiae*, II–II 40.1. See Lisa Sowle Cahill, "Christian Just War Tradition: Tensions and Development," in *The Return of the Just War*, vol. 2001/2, eds. María Pilar Aquino and Dietmar Mieth (London: SCM Press, 2001), 78–79; and Rowan Williams' response to George Weigel, "War and Statecraft: An Exchange," *First Things*, March 2004, 14–21. He links this passage to Aquinas' more general treatments of violence in *ST* I–II 6.4, II–II 66.8, and 175.1.

9. *ST* II–II 29.3, 4.

10. George Weigel, "Moral Clarity in a Time of War," *First Things* (January 2003): 21. See also his reply to Williams, "War and Statecraft. An Exchange."

11. James Turner. Johnson, *Morality & Contemporary Warfare* (New Haven, CT: Yale University Press, 1999), 35–36. See also James Turner Johnson, "Just War Theory: What's the Use," *Worldview* 19, no. 7–8 (1976): 41–47.

12. James Turner Johnson, "The Broken Tradition," *National Interest* 45 (Fall 1996): 27–36.

13. Augustine, *City of God* 19.6-7. As R. A. Markus has noted, the conception of order underlying Augustine's treatment of war in *City of God* reflected a growing appreciation toward the end of his life of "the precariousness of human order, the threat of dissolution and the permanent presence of chaos just beneath the surface . . ." R. A. Markus, "Saint Augustine's Views on the 'Just War,'" in *The Church and War*, vol. 20., ed. W. J. Sheils, Studies in Church History (Oxford, Oxfordshire: Published for the Ecclesiastical History Society by Basil Blackwell, 1983), 10.

14. Augustine, "Letter 138 to Marcellinus," in *Fathers of the Church, Vol. 11: St. Augustine Letters 131–164* (New York: Fathers of the Church, Inc., 1953), 46.

15. Christopher D. Marshall, *Beyond Retribution: A New Testament Vision for Justice, Crime, and Punishment* (Grand Rapids, MI: Wm. B. Eerdmans Pub., 2001), 48.

16. Heinrich Gross, "Peace," in *Encyclopedia of Biblical Theology: The Complete Sacramentum Verbi*, ed. Johannes Baptist Bauer (New York: Crossroad, 1981), 648.

17. See Perry B. Yoder, *Shalom: The Bible's Word for Salvation, Justice, and Peace* (Newton, KS: Faith and Life Press, 1987), 10–16; and Howard Zehr, *Changing Lenses* (Scottdale, PA: Harold Press, 1990) 130–32.

18. Marshall, *Beyond Retribution: A New Testament Vision for Justice, Crime, and Punishment*, 46–48.

19. Ibid., 49.

20. George Weigel, *Tranquillitas Ordinis: The Present Failure and Future Promise of American Catholic Thought on War and Peace* (New York: Oxford University Press, 1987), 184–85, 357–58.

21. George Weigel, "Moral Clarity in a Time of War," *First Things* 128 (January 2003): 24.

22. Augustine, *Letter 138*. In *Letter 189*, he called upon Boniface to be a peacemaker even while waging war. In calling attention to Augustine's emphasis on the importance of interior dispositions for right conduct in war, I do not intend to make any claims about the more complex issue of his overall theological conception of peace.

23. *ST* II–II 40.1 corpus.

24. John Paul II, "There is Still Room for Peace," 24.

25. John Paul II, "*Pacem in Terris*: A Permanent Commitment," World Day of Peace message, January 1, 2003, *Origins* 32, no. 29 (January 2, 2003): 486.

26. Ibid., 487.

27. Alasdair MacIntyre, *Whose Justice? Which Rationality?* (Notre Dame: University of Notre Dame Press, 1988), 12.

28. John E. Thiel, *Senses of Tradition: Continuity and Development in Catholic Faith* (New York: Oxford University Press, 2000), 149.

29. James Childress has suggested that pacifist and just war strands of thought represent two sub-traditions within the Christian tradition. See James F. Childress, "Contemporary Pacifism: Its Major Types and Possible Contributions to Discourse About War," in *The American Search for Peace: Moral Reasoning, Religious Hope, and National Security*, eds. George Weigel and John Langan (Washington, DC: Georgetown University Press, 1991), 127.

30. *The Challenge of Peace*, §93: "The category of comparative justice is destined to emphasize the presumption against war which stands at the beginning of just-war teaching. . . . [N]o state should act on the basis that it has 'absolute justice' on its side." Yoder noted that this addition to just war theory was misinterpreted by some and not appropriated by most theorists. See *When War is Unjust*, appendix V.

31. Sandra Harding, "Rethinking Standpoint Epistemology: What is 'Strong Objectivity,'" in *Feminist Epistemologies*, eds. Linda Alcoff and Elizabeth Potter, Thinking Gender Series (New York: Routledge, 1993), 54.

32. See Weigel, "Moral Clarity in a Time of War."

33. Weigel, *Tranquillitas Ordinis*, 378.

34. United Nations Commission on the Truth, *From Madness to Hope: The 12-Year War in El Salvador: Report of the Commission on the Truth for El Salvador* ([New York]: United Nations, Security Council, 1993), annex; and Priscilla B. Hayner, *Unspeakable Truths: Confronting State Terror and Atrocity*, preface by Timothy Garton Ash (New York: Routledge, 2000), 38–39. In his critique of *Tranquillitatis Ordinis*, David Hollenbach rightly raised concerns about Weigel's assessment of U.S. foreign policy in Central America; see "War and Peace in American Catholic Thought: A Heritage Abandoned?" *Theological Studies* 48 (1987): 723.

35. "CPT Mission Statement," http://cpt.org/publications/history.php.

36. Barry Stuart, "Circle Sentencing: Turning Swords Into Ploughshares," in *Restorative Justice: International Perspectives*, eds. Burt Galaway and Joe Hudson (Monsey, NY: Criminal Justice Press, 1996), 298; Leena Kurki, "Restorative and Community Justice in the United States," in *Crime and Justice: A Review of Research*, vol. 27 (Chicago: University of Chicago Press, 2000), 281.

37. L. Thomas Winfree, Jr., "Peacemaking and Community Harmony: Lessons (and Admonitions) from the Navajo Peacemaking Courts," in *Restorative Justice: Theoretical Foundations*, eds. Elmar G. M. Weitekamp and Hans-Jürgen Kerner (Cullompton: Willan Publishing, 2002), 290–91.

38. Stuart, "Circle Sentencing," 195.

39. Kurki, "Restorative and Community Justice in the United States," 280–81.

40. Barry Stuart, "Guiding Principles for Peacemaking Circles," in *Restorative Community Justice: Repairing Harm and Transforming Communities*, eds. S. Gordon Bazemore and Mara Schiff (Cincinnati, OH: Anderson Pub., 2001), 220–23, 228–29; Kay Pranis, "Peacemaking Circles," *Corrections Today* 59, no. 7 (December 1997): 72–76.

41. Stuart, "Guiding Principles," 226.

42. Kay Pranis, "Restorative Justice, Social Justice, and the Empowerment of Marginalized Populations," 292–93; Ibid., 228.

43. Rupert Ross, *Return to the Teachings: Exploring Aboriginal Justice* (Toronto: Penguin Books, 1996), 39.

44. Curt Taylor Griffiths and Ron Hamilton, "Sanctioning and Healing: Restorative Justice in Canadian Aboriginal Communities," in *Restorative Justice: International Perspectives*, eds. Burt Galaway and Joe Hudson (Monsey, NY: Criminal Justice Press, 1996), 182–83.

45. John Braithwaite, *Restorative Justice & Responsive Regulation*, Studies in Crime and Public Policy (New York: Oxford University Press, 2002), 25. It is tempting to measure the success of circle sentencing efforts by the outcome for the offenders. Stuart points to data that indicate a lower recidivism rate for offenders who have participated in the circle process and that both the gravity and frequency of their offenses have been reduced (Stuart, "Circle Sentencing," 293). Kurki, on the other hand, has noted the absence of any rigorous evaluation of restorative justice outcomes (Kurki, "Restorative and Community Justice in the United States," 241).

46. Pranis, "Restorative Justice, Social Justice," 288–89.

47. Stuart, "Circle Sentencing," 224.

48. Ross, *Return to the Teachings*, 38.

49. Stuart, "Guiding Principles," 225.

50. Howard Zehr, *The Little Book of Restorative Justice* (Intercourse, PA: Good Books, 2002), 36.

51. See Pranis, "Restorative Justice, Social Justice," 291.

52. On the historical development of state-centered justice, see Howard Zehr, *Changing Lenses*, 114–24.

53. Charles Barton, "Empowerment and Retribution in Criminal Justice," in *Restorative Justice: Philosophy to Practice*, eds. Heather Strang and John Braithwaite (Burlington, VT: Ashgate, 2000), 56–57. Barton's clarification sheds light on objections to the use of retributive measures under the guise of restorative justice. See Kathleen Daly, "Revisiting the Relationship Between Retributive and Restorative Justice," in *Restorative Justice: Philosophy to Practice*, 33–54; and Conrad Brunk, "Restorative Justice and the Philosophical Theories of Criminal Punishment," in *The Spiritual Roots of Restorative Justice*, ed. Michael L. Hadley, SUNY Series in Religious Studies (Albany: State University of New York Press, 2001), 47–48.

54. Howard Zehr, "Journey to Belonging," in *Restorative Justice: Theoretical Foundations*, 29. On this point, he refers to the work of Charles K. B. Barton, *Getting Even: Revenge as a Form of Justice* (Chicago, IL: Open Court, 1999) as well as Brunk. Zehr also addresses this issue in *The Little Book of Restorative Justice*, 58–59.

55. Stuart, "Circle Sentencing," 298. Also see Howard Zehr, *The Little Book of Restorative Justice*, 13.

56. Amartya Kumar Sen, *Development as Freedom* (New York: Anchor books, 2000), 23. Martha Nussbaum traces some implications of Sen's argument in her essay, "Human Capabilities, Female Human Beings," in *Women, Culture, and Development: A Study of Human Capabilities*, eds. Martha Craven Nussbaum and Jonathan Glover, Studies in Development Economics. (New York: Oxford University Press, 1995), 61–104.

57. See Oscar A. Romero, "The Political Dimension of the Faith from the Perspective of the Option for the Poor," Louvain Address, 2 February 1980 in *Voice of the Voiceless: The Four Pastoral Letters and Other Statements*, trans. Michael J. Walsh (Maryknoll, NY: Orbis Books, 1985), 177–87.

58. Frances Stewart, "Root Causes of Violent Conflicts in Developing Countries," *British Medical Journal* 324 (February 9, 2002): 342.

59. Rama Mani discusses the requirements of distributive justice in conflict situations in Rama Mani, *Beyond Retribution: Seeking Justice in the Shadows of War* (Cambridge, UK; Malden, MA: Polity Press; Blackwell Publishers Inc., 2002), 9.

60. Johnstone is highly critical of McCold's efforts to delineate the boundaries of "the community" that undertakes restorative justice, but in the end, he offers no constructive proposal, concluding that "the issue seems inherently contestable." See Gerry Johnstone, *Restorative Justice: Ideas, Values, Debates* (Cullompton: Willan Pub., 2002), 155; and Paul McCold, "Restorative Justice and the Role of the Community," in *Restorative Justice: International Perspectives*, eds. Burt Galaway and Joe Hudson (Monsey, NY: Criminal Justice Press, 1996), 85–101.

61. Howard Zehr, *The Little Book of Restorative Justice*, 28. Paul McCold develops this approach further in "Restorative Justice and the Role of the Community," 91–92.

62. J. Bryan Hehir, "What is the International Community: The Limits of Loyalty," *Foreign Policy* (September/October 2002): 38. Rowan Williams articulates a similar concern for the priority of human community over the interests of particular nation-states in his response to Weigel (Williams and Weigel, "War and Statecraft").

63. U.S. Conference of Catholic Bishops, *The Harvest of Justice is Sown in Peace*, I.A.1. Available December 12, 2006. www.usccb.org/sdwp/harvest.htm#theology.

64. Pope John Paul II, *Sollicitudo Rei Socialis [On Social Concern]*, encyclical letter (1987), §38, emphasis in the original. Available in O'Brien and Shannon, *Catholic Social Thought*.

65. U.S. Conference of Catholic Bishops, "Living with Faith and Hope After September 11," statement, November 14, 2001, *Origins* 31, no. 25 (November 29, 2001): 417.

Chapter 7

Community Policing as a Paradigm for International Relations

Tobias Winright

More than two decades ago, the Pinellas County Sheriff's Department on the Gulf coast of Florida across the bay from the city of Tampa hired me as a correctional officer to work at their maximum-security jail. My mother, who was a homicide detective, and my stepfather, who was a patrol sergeant, both worked for this law enforcement agency and suggested that I apply for a job there. As the first person in my immediate family to attend college, I lacked adequate financial backing, so I applied to several police departments hoping for a job to help pay my way through school. When the sheriff's department hired me, I was one of their youngest officers, having just turned nineteen years old. Somehow for the next four years, I attended classes full-time by day at the university and worked full-time mostly during the midnight shift at the sheriff's department. There I often witnessed and dealt with human nature at its worst.

I neither truly enjoyed that job, nor did I delight in the frequent hostility and conflict accompanying it. I preferred my academic studies and looked forward to the day when I would graduate from the university and be able to quit law enforcement in order to pursue graduate study in theology and ethics. To be sure, during my stint in law enforcement, I struggled as a practicing Christian over ethical issues that surfaced in this job, especially with regard to the use of force. I first began to wrestle with the issue of whether I should use force, especially lethal force, as I interviewed with various police departments, which all asked me some form of the following question: "Would you really, if necessary, shoot someone?" At the time I said yes and thus joined one of these departments. However, I had little idea then how to justify such use of force from a Christian moral perspective. Hence, this question continued to concern me during my years in uniform and on through my subsequent graduate studies in moral theology.

Imagine my interest, then, when after the dreadful terrorist attacks on the towers of the World Trade Center and on the Pentagon on September 11, 2001, a number of Christian ethicists proposed a "police" model for responding to and dealing with terrorism. Of course, most theologians writing about how to address terrorism and evaluate the U.S. "war on terror" have drawn upon either pacifism or just-war thinking, the traditional Christian ethical perspectives on political violence. Yet, interestingly, *both* pacifist and just-war Christian ethicists also have alluded to the possible relevance and legitimacy of a "police" rather than a "war" approach to dealing with terrorists.

On the one hand, a number of pacifists, who generally oppose all forms of violence and war, have found themselves supporting some sort of limited police action that would seek out, apprehend, and bring those terrorists responsible to justice. Rather than regarding the terrorist attack as an act of war, these pacifists view it as a crime against humanity that requires a policing and judicial response that corresponds to its criminal nature. Accordingly, Judith McDaniel, director of peacebuilding at the American Friends Service Committee, has written, "We need to talk about the events of 11 September as crimes against humanity and not as war. . . . This was a criminal act. And if you think of this as a criminal act, you're looking for justice in the context of law, whether that would be international law, or the World Court or the United Nations."[1]

On the other hand, many just-war thinkers also have advocated a police approach as a more effective and moral way to deal with terrorism. For example, leading just-war theorist James Childress criticized the Bush administration's invocation of the war metaphor for responding to and dealing with terrorism, noting, "Other usable metaphors were available. One alternative conceptualization was police action in pursuit of criminals."[2] Likewise, Jean Porter criticized the administration's quick employment of the war or military model, and she implied instead a law enforcement approach: "Like many others, I am troubled by the easy invocation of war, with its misleading implication that we are engaged in hostilities with whole nations, and not with independent groups of terrorists."[3]

These pacifist and just-war invocations of a police approach are welcome developments in the Christian ethics of war and peace, but they are equally curious given that little prior work by Christian ethicists exists on the topic of policing itself. In his classic work on just-war theory over thirty years ago, Ralph Potter observed, "Seldom have American Christian scholars addressed themselves seriously to the task of helping public officers reflect upon the mode of reasoning appropriate to their office that would guide them in determining when they should act, how they should act, and why."[4] Potter firmly believed that police officers need ethical guidance to help them to understand and evaluate carefully and critically the use of force in a way that coheres with moral principles. His concern echoed that of Francis J. Connell, C.Ss.R., who earlier in the twentieth century worried that although "Catholics receive abundant instructions on their duties as private individuals," the Catholic who occupies "some position of public authority" gets less help; Connell went on to highlight this problem with an interesting question: "What course of action should a Catholic police officer follow if he is told to 'shoot to kill' any malefactor he discovers in the act of robbery?"[5]

No Christian ethicist devoted thoughtful attention to the concerns raised by Connell and Potter until 1982 when Edward A. Malloy, C.S.C. published his slim volume, *The Ethics of Law Enforcement and Criminal Punishment*, which included as its first chapter a brief treatment of "Ethics and the Use of Force: An Analysis of the Role of the Police Profession." Indeed, Malloy observed that while much theological attention has been given to whether, when, or how Christians morally should participate in war, "there is a noticeable deficiency in applying such analysis to the domestic context of crime and punishment," with particular focus on policing.[6] Drawing analogically upon "the legacy of just war theory to formulate certain propositions applicable to situations where police use of force may be necessary," Malloy concluded that "the classic criteria for the justified use of violence are much easier to satisfy in the domestic context of police work than they are in the international setting of war."[7] Accordingly, he delineated how five criteria from the just-war tradition could be applied to policing, thereby yielding an ethical framework for justifying and evaluating police use of force within society. Interestingly, Malloy regarded his attempt at examining the ethics of policing and the use of force as a preliminary one that "might encourage other Christian ethicists to grapple with this problem of the control of, and response to, domestic violence."[8] Very few theological ethicists, however, have followed up on Malloy's invitation.

Hence a warm reception should greet Gerald Schlabach's exploration of how just policing in the international sphere could offer an area of convergence between pacifism and just war, thereby perhaps doing away with the division within the church caused by the issue of war. Given that so many Christian ethicists across the spectrum, from pacifism to just war, are today proposing a police approach for dealing with terrorism, it makes sense to consider in-depth what such an approach might look like and entail, especially with regard to the use of force. Moreover, because the above-mentioned works by theologians such as Malloy move from the direction of international conflict and just-war theory toward the domestic sphere and just policing, there remains room for Schlabach's thought experiment, which moves in the opposite direction, from the domestic sphere of just policing to the international sphere of just policing.

An important component in Schlabach's proposal for just policing is his suggestion that "community policing" might serve as a helpful paradigm for the international system. Indeed, he offers three main reasons why a community policing model would be fitting: "What makes it an appropriate model to extend by analogy into the sphere of international policing is the way that it integrates (1) the very sort of work on root causes of violence and conflict that pacifists have advocated as basic for achieving real peace with justice, (2) a continued but modified role for apprehending criminals, and (3) ample room for developing less-violent and non-violent tactics for even that apprehension."[9] The task of this chapter, therefore, is to provide additional background on the concept and practice of community policing in order to consider the prospects of Schlabach's proposal for extending such a model of policing to the international sphere. In other words, this chapter focuses on domestic community policing with a view toward the question: *What is it about community policing that makes it a promising model which might be extended into the international system?*

Models of Policing:
From Crime Fighter to Social Peacekeeper

In suggesting the suitability of a community policing paradigm, Schlabach implicitly recognizes that a more general call for a police approach begs the question of what model of policing is most congruent with just policing. Some models of policing may not cohere as closely with his understanding of just policing. Therefore, before exploring further what community policing *is*, it is necessary to examine what community policing *is not* by surveying other possible models of policing commonly found in the criminological literature. When we examine key features of four different models of policing, we find that only one seems fully consonant with Schlabach's understanding of community policing.

Only in the past thirty years or so have criminologists begun to examine police ethics in general, and the use of force in particular, with the aim of regulating and restraining police use of force. Indeed, many such scholars are attempting to formulate a model of policing that will provide a richer context and a stricter framework within which to judge when and how such force should be employed. One of the more recent philosophical contributions to this discussion is John Kleinig's book, *The Ethics of Policing.* A philosopher specializing in criminal justice ethics, he examines the moral foundations of policing and the specific problem of the use of force. Kleinig identifies various models of policing that are currently in circulation among criminologists, along with their correlative perspectives on the use of force, before offering his own recommendations on what he thinks would be the most ethical model of policing for today.

Indeed, there is a spectrum of policing models, which are vying to offer a normative framework for policing and the use of force, and which different philosophers, sociologists, and criminologists are advocating.[10] The two main models at opposite ends of the spectrum from each other are the "crime fighter" model and the "social peacekeeper" model. The former has been the primary paradigm in the United States and is generally synonymous with a military model. The latter has gradually been gaining acceptance more recently. Falling somewhere in between these two poles, two other models—the "emergency operator" and the "social enforcer"—also are competing in criminological circles as possible alternatives especially to the crime fighter model.

The primary model of policing that developed and prevailed among police institutions within the United States during much of the twentieth century has been the crime fighter model. As Kleinig notes, it is often referred to as the law enforcement or military model. According to Joycelyn Pollock-Byrne, police take "very seriously" their role as crime fighters, so much so that this forms and shapes their self-understanding.[11] Indeed, when referring to "real" police work, law enforcement officers generally have in mind crime fighting. Within this paradigm of policing, the use of force occupies a central position, for police officers believe they must be armed and ready to do battle with crime and criminals. Obviously, the political refrain in recent decades about winning "the war on crime" is consonant with the crime fighter approach, which is why Kleinig and others regard it as synonymous with a military model for policing. "The conception of the police as a quasi-military institution with a war-like mission," observes Egon Bittner, "plays an important part in the structuring of police work in modern American departments."[12]

Indeed, the popular book, *Shoot to Kill: Cops Who Have Used Deadly Force*, by former police officer Charles W. Sasser, evinces the extent to which the military metaphor has impacted the self-definition of the police in the United States. He writes that they are "soldiers in a strange war that will never end," risking their lives as a "final defense against the forces of darkness and evil" in the "continuing war against crime" while they patrol "the combat zone that is modern America."[13] Moreover, Sasser asserts, "It *is* a war out there," for police officers themselves frequently say, "It's a war out there, a war."[14] To support this view, Sasser notes that "several thousand American law enforcement officers" annually are assaulted "with everything from fists and broken street signs to knives and, of course, guns."[15] Police officers feel like they are always potentially in danger, and in order to deal effectively with such threats they want certain crime fighting tools, including weapons, equipment such as helmets and body armor, and the ability to use force when necessary.

Not only do American police tend to regard themselves as crime fighters in the war on crime, but as Jerome Skolnick and James Fyfe observe, the "military metaphor also colors the public's expectations of the police."[16] In this regard, political rhetoric of recent years about "getting tough on crime" has probably impacted the public's view. At the same time, Americans are likely influenced by popular depictions of policing on television and in movies, which focus more on crime fighting. Indeed, audiences of such television dramas and movies often see "heroic males regularly and successfully using lethal violence as a way of avenging wrongs," conveying the message that violence is a "way of life" in America for dealing with interpersonal conflict and social problems.[17] Police, too, are affected by such media portrayals of policing. "Fed on movies and television shows such as *Dirty Harry*, *Lethal Weapon*, and *Hill Street Blues*," new police officers, believes Fyfe, "are likely to believe that they are entering a world where death lurks around every corner, where every contact with a citizen may prove fatal."[18] Peter Scharf and Arnold Binder name these media depictions "the mythology of police work," especially with regard to viewing the gun as "the primary symbol of law enforcement," the "tool of the trade," and the "culturally defined essence of police work."[19] Accordingly, in this so-called war between law enforcement officers and suspected criminals, Robert Elias worries that the American public and its law enforcement personnel come to assume, through the influence of political rhetoric and media depictions, that "only superior firepower will ensure our security and win the day."[20]

The crime fighting or military model of policing has certain key characteristics. To begin, hierarchical departmental structures typically operating through a chain of command reflect this model, with divisions and squads consisting of captains, lieutenants, and sergeants. Furthermore, uniforms, badges, weapons, and a multitude of rules, regulations, and standard operating procedures mirror those of the military. Indeed, a demand for more and better technology and weaponry often accompanies departments that buy into the military model. According to Martin Edmonds, the "militarization" of the police and "their being armed with specialized equipment and weapons is an increasingly frequent phenomenon almost everywhere."[21] One clear example of this association of crime fighting with a military approach is the formation since 1974 of S.W.A.T. (Special Weapons and Tactics) teams in many American police departments, with their special gear, including helmets, semi-automatic assault rifles, tear gas, and flash grenades.

Another key trait of this paradigm is the emphasis on the centrality of coercive force as the most effective approach to policing. Indeed, it is because both institutions "are instruments of force" that the analogy often is assumed between the police and the military.[22] The use of force in policing, as in the military, is regarded as the "essential" or "inherent" ingredient in the profession, which is why a number of criminologists highlight that the police often are referred to as a law *enforcement* agency or as a police *force*.[23] Accordingly, this view of police as coercion specialists assumes "the *primacy* of force in coping with crime and criminals."[24] This model, therefore, reckons the use of force as the key characteristic of policing or, put differently, it regards coercive power as the *raison d'être* of policing.

However, other criminologists warn that the crime fighter or military model of policing may be the soil from which sprout the seeds of police brutality and excessive force. As one group of criminologists observes, the "belief that being a law enforcement officer is akin to the work of a soldier on the frontlines . . . [and] this pervasive sense that their mission is a dangerous one cannot help but affect the way that police officers deal with the public."[25] Apparently, there may be a tendency inherent in the use of such a martial metaphor that opens the door for police officers to yield to the temptation to employ excessive force or brutality. For as James Childress warns, metaphors "shape how we think, what we experience, and what we do by what they highlight and hide;" the war metaphor in particular "often fails to recognize the moral constraints on waging war."[26] That is, the controlling image of policing as warfare might dangerously tend to color police's perceptions of their work in ways that neglect or undermine the moral and legal guidelines for the use of force. Police fail to remember that the use of force in war also requires moral and legal principles for such force to be regarded as just. Rather than a just-war framework as an analogue for just policing, all too often American police and society appeal merely to a *war* metaphor, without the qualifier or adjective *just*, which in turn can lead to policing methods that may also fall short of what is just.

For one thing, the military or crime fighter model alienates the police from the public, often leading to the dehumanization of the very people that police are pledged to serve and protect. Everyone is viewed suspiciously and cynically as a potential "enemy," and a criminal suspect is especially regarded as such. In turn, this makes it easier, according to Paul Chevigny, for police "to abuse those who are the enemy, easier even to kill or torture them."[27] Here an "us versus them" attitude saturates the police's dealings with their fellow citizens, which a number of criminologists warn may encourage wrongdoing and unreasonable force. Thus, according to Bittner, the "quasi-military model implicitly extends the stamp of legitimacy to methods that would not be acceptable on moral and legal grounds."[28] Likewise, Skolnick and Fyfe assert that a "causal connection" exists between "the idea that cops are like soldiers in wars on crime" and the use of excessive force.[29] As a fairly recent example, they claim that the Rodney King beating should be considered a reflection of the predominant crime fighting philosophy of policing that the Los Angeles Police Department has exemplified in recent decades. Indeed, they believe that the war model of policing constitutes "a major cause of police violence and the violation of citizens' rights," and it "encourages police violence of the type that victimized Rodney King."[30]

It is therefore hard to imagine support of this model of policing either domestically or internationally by either pacifist or just-war Christians. Indeed, it should be noted that many of the psycho-social dynamics that Schlabach identifies as supposedly differentiating policing from war would actually continue to be found in the crime fighter approach to policing. That is, within the crime fighter paradigm, the phenomena Schlabach associates with war (the "rally-'round-the flag" phenomenon, the "blunt instrument" problem, etc.) also surface dangerously in policing that has a crime fighting mindset. Obviously, then, this model of policing would not be congruent with the just policing he proposes for the international sphere.

However, this is not the only model of policing available, and many criminologists who are critical of the crime fighter approach recommend other possible models. While continuing to emphasize the importance and legitimacy of the use of force, these other models devote more attention to the significance of other tasks in policing. For example, Howard Cohen suggests the "emergency operator" or "firefighter" model.[31] This approach highlights numerous other social and community services in which police are primarily involved. In her actual daily work, a police officer deals with a large array of problems and incidents, including, for example, intervening in domestic disputes, helping injured accident victims, dealing with people with mental illnesses, finding runaways, searching for lost children, informing people of the deaths of loved ones, directing traffic, and stopping suicide attempts. Indeed, it is now widely recognized that police spend the majority of their time (with estimates ranging from seventy to ninety percent) in these kinds of activities rather than using force in fighting crime. If this is the case, then, as Fyfe observes, "life in a patrol car has little in common with duty in a military combat zone."[32] The emergency operator model of policing therefore appears to be truer to the actual practices that typically occupy a police officer on routine duty, and the crime fighting model fails to do a police officer's work justice.

Yet, Cohen points out that there are, of course, other professionals who more competently provide many such social services (e.g., medical doctors, social workers, psychologists, marriage counselors, clergy, etc.). The police simply offer temporary *emergency* assistance therefore in place of these other professionals who cannot make it to the scene as quickly. As the first to arrive at many emergencies, the police may need to provide first aid or counseling, for example, because a medical doctor or a psychologist usually is not immediately present. Also, the danger may be too great for such professionals to intervene at the time.

In his treatment of Cohen's emergency operator model, Kleinig notes that *anyone* can act as an emergency stand-in; yet "the ubiquity and experience of the police in dealing with people will make them the most appropriate stand-ins where professionals are not available."[33] However, the authority of the police is both provisional and temporary in this model, so that their role or involvement in these social services is actually diminished rather than elevated in importance. They basically stop the bleeding, so to speak, until someone else more qualified can deal with the emergency. And their role in these emergencies seems to boil down both to their ability to respond quickly and, if necessary, forcefully. Therefore, contrary to his intentions, Cohen's model may perhaps end up reinforcing the claim that *real* police work consists in crime fighting.

Another alternative to the crime fighter model is the "social enforcer" model of policing advocated by Joseph Betz and Egon Bittner. Like Cohen, they observe that most of a police officer's time is spent with citizens who need some social service or assistance. Unlike Cohen, however, they do not equate police work with temporary social work, and they frankly admit that the use of force is the central feature of policing in their view. After all, if the police basically are social workers, then police could be done away with altogether, and all that would be needed would be more social workers. Instead, the police role is "to address all sorts of human problems when and insofar as the problems' solutions may require the use of force at the point of their occurrence."[34] In other words, police work involves responding to emergencies in which the use of force is always a potential requirement. Betz and Bittner thus supplement Cohen's understanding of policing, agreeing that they serve as emergency personnel while emphasizing that police also possess competency in doing so due to their authority to use force. Hence, in their social enforcer model of policing, the capacity to use force continues to lend "thematic unity" to all police activities, including "apprehending a criminal, driving the mayor to the airport, evicting a drunken person from a bar, directing traffic, controlling crowds, caring for lost children, administering first aid, and separating fighting relatives."[35]

Of course, the use of force in this model of policing is situated within a social framework that considers criminals as fellow citizens rather than as foreign enemies. Criminals are regarded as "an internal ill, not an external horde," for they instead "share the same social fabric."[36] This perspective thus should guard against the "us versus them" attitude commonly associated with the crime fighter model. Moreover, Betz and Bittner believe that this social enforcer model of policing requires more stringent rules governing and minimizing the use of force by police. Kleinig, however, is not so sure that this is enough.

For although the social enforcer model offers a helpful corrective to the crime fighter model of policing, especially by emphasizing other community service dimensions to police work, it nevertheless continues to locate the police capacity for the use of force at the center of policing. Indeed, on the one hand, Kleinig agrees that the crime fighter model cannot adequately rein in the use of force: "Unless and until police see themselves primarily as peacekeepers rather than as crime fighters," he writes, "fire-arms will tend to be used unnecessarily."[37] Yet, on the other hand, he has similar doubts about the social enforcer model of policing. Specifically, he believes that this model wrongly continues to focus "too directly on the coercive dimension of police authority" as its "distinguishing feature."[38]

Therefore, he argues that an alternative approach is needed "that acknowledges the nonnegotiable force at police disposal without trans-forming it into the police *raison d'être*."[39] Instead of seeing the use of force as the *primary characteristic* or as the *essence* of policing, Kleinig regards the use of force more as an *instrument* of policing. In his view, the "social peacekeeper" model of policing encompasses better most of the responsibilities and tasks of police in society, and in this model the fact that police are armed is merely "a contingent matter."[40] In this way, although there remains a place for the possibility of the use of force against an uncooperative or threatening suspect, "its instrumental or subservient character is emphasized."[41] Thus, the use of force by police is "a last (albeit sometimes necessary) resort rather than their dominant *modus operandi*."[42] Indeed, Kleinig suggests that had the Los Angeles police officers who participated in the beating of Rodney King under-stood themselves "primarily as social peacekeepers, for whom recourse to force constituted a last and regrettable option, events would almost certainly have turned out very differently."[43]

In addition, Kleinig regards this model as more faithful to the his-torical roots and practices of policing in England, with its emphasis on community service and peacekeeping. Indeed, though the *functional* origins of policing may be traced to ancient communal self-policing, modern policing began *institutionally* with Sir Robert Peel's establishment of the "New Police" of Metropolitan London in 1829. Due to increasing urban crime and riots, against which the earlier night watchmen and constables were ineffective with little or no enforcement capability, and against which the military was brutally effective with its excessive use of force, Peel organized the first modern police department. In his view, the institution of policing would do better than the watchmen and constables with regard to protecting the public and preventing crime, even though the police would continue to be relatively unarmed, with the exception perhaps of a truncheon. Moreover, in contrast to soldiers, the police would rely more on persuasion and would resort to using physical force only minimally, as a last resort. Indeed, according to David Ascoli, Peel "was stubborn to the point of obsession that his 'New Police' should be seen to be free of all taint of militarism," which is why they were required to wear "a quiet" uniform consisting of "a blue swallow-tail coat with white buttons" rather than the British military's red coat."[44] The primary object of this first police department, as explicitly reflected in its General Instructions from 1829, was the *prevention* of crime, and emphasis was placed on the use of persuasion, with physical force as a last resort and using only the minimum necessary for preventing or stopping a breach of the law.[45] Most importantly, in Peel's approach, the police would be citizens working in partnership with their community. A considerable part of their patrol duties, involving publicly walking regular beats in neighborhoods, also included traffic control, the prevention of cruelty to children and animals, finding missing persons, the care of the poor and destitute, extinguishing fires, the inspection of weights, bridges, and buildings, and even waking people up for work. As such, the London Metropolitan Police, according to Samuel Walker, "were *pro*active rather than *re*active."[46] Only within that overarching community peacekeeping framework were the New Police required occasionally to stop a crime in progress and to use force to apprehend criminals.

The approach advanced by Peel represents the historical roots of policing, encompassing an array of service and peacekeeping functions, in both England and America.[47] Kleinig's call for the social peacekeeper model of policing, therefore, attempts to reclaim key elements and practices of policing that were emphasized in the genesis and early years of policing. By situating policing within this social peacekeeping context, he believes that crime will be more effectively dealt with, and the use of force by police will less likely be excessive.

Characteristics of Community Policing

This social peacekeeper model resonates well with recent calls for community policing, and Kleinig occasionally notes the points of contact between them.[48] Many criminologists writing about community policing often observe that it is both a *philosophy* and a *strategy* of policing, which is why it seems appropriate to locate it within the philosophical model of social peacekeeping as delineated by Kleinig.[49]

One of the chief characteristics of community policing is that it involves a partnership between the police and the community. Put simply, it is more neighborhood-oriented. It seeks to foster a relationship of mutual trust, bonds of empathy, and a common purpose, rather than an adversarial "us versus them" mentality. Police and the citizens share a stake in the common good and welfare of their community.

In other words, the police are part of the community and therefore work in cooperation with the community. As such, many community policing programs establish decentralized sub-stations throughout the community, while encouraging police to purchase homes and reside in these neighborhoods. They get police out of their cars, walking beats, in order to get to know, listen to, and interact face-to-face with citizens. In addition, community policing programs promote the hiring of recruits who reflect or possess an understanding of the diverse communities that they will serve.

At the same time, as part of this partnership, community residents have a role to play in peacekeeping and crime prevention. Through neighborhood watch programs, safe houses, and other community service organizations, citizens share responsibility with police for the quality of life and common good of their community. Police officers also are encouraged to become involved in such community activities as coaching sports teams or participating in town and neighborhood meetings. Community agencies partner with police and citizens in this model. Thus together they can explore and possibly implement creative solutions to local problems that may give rise to crime.

Attached with this, community policing is more proactive than reactive, thereby involving a more preventive or problem-oriented approach to crime. That is, community policing seeks to identify, understand, and address the root causes of crime that may be found in the community. Both residents and police learn to identify the seedbeds from which criminal activity likely may sprout. Community policing attends to the wider social framework or patterns of activities that play a role in leading to crime. In this connection, a number of criminologists highlight James Q. Wilson's "broken windows" theory, wherein the key for police is both to repair the broken window as soon as possible and to discern and address what might cause someone to break that window in the first place. "Police do not simply dispose of each case," according to Steven R. Donziger, "they try to figure out why crime happened and how similar instances can be avoided."[50] Crime does not happen in a vacuum. Rather, it occurs within a community and may therefore be at least partly the result of problems within the community. Community police officers recognize this and work in cooperation with community members to prevent and solve their problems. Furthermore, the community policing model regards criminals as made and not born. Thus, the community and the police strive together to help any community members who are at risk of resorting to criminal activity. Also, when someone commits a crime, he or she will be treated as a fellow community member rather than some external enemy.

In this model, if force is necessary to apprehend the suspect, it should be in accordance with the governing criteria for the ethical use of force. Indeed, Kleinig provides the reminder that "any model of policing that fails to take into account their authority to employ force will be inadequate."[51] Accordingly, the community policing model accepts the ongoing existence of the need for the use of force by police in certain situations; however, it is the belief of criminologists who support community policing, such as Donziger, that "the number and magnitude of such crisis situations, at least in theory, should diminish because of prevention efforts made by community police officers."[52] In addition, community policing fosters and reinforces recent strides being made in the development and implementation of less-than-lethal techniques and weapons by which police may effectively apprehend resistant suspects, including tranquilizer darts, bean-bag projectiles, electrical stun guns, projectiles that cast a net over the suspect, and so on.[53] To be sure, such devices and methods also could be misused or abused; however, within a community policing paradigm less-than-lethal techniques and weapons should be used in ways more consonant with the view of the suspect as a fellow community member.

Conclusion:
Community Policing and the Problem of War

Community policing as a philosophy and as a strategy involves police and citizens cooperating as partners. It addresses the root causes of crime, situates police use of force to apprehend resistant or threatening suspects within a social peacekeeping framework and thus yields robust criteria governing such use of force. It provides further impetus for developing less-than-lethal methods and weapons for even when the use of force seems necessary. As such, pacifist Christians, especially in their work and experience with nonviolent resistance and peacemaking endeavors that attempt to curtail conflict at its source, should be able to contribute to and support community policing as extended by analogy to the international sphere. At the same time, just-war Christians, in their emphasis on the moral use of force as a last resort (after attempting nonviolent alternatives where possible and feasible) and consonant with other governing criteria, should also be able to contribute to and support community policing as extended by analogy to the international sphere.[54]

But what are the prospects of creating and implementing such an international community police institution. After all, currently existing international politics typically operates on the premise that nations are independent, sovereign, territorially-bounded entities. How realistic is this proposal for extending a just policing paradigm to the international arena? Among the various theories of international relations is there one that resonates well with an international community policing institution?

Over sixty years ago, during the early and dark years of World War II, the eminent scholar of police history and principles, Charles Reith, in his book, *Police Principles and the Problem of War*, anticipated and addressed such questions. Indeed, he called for an extension of police principles to the international level as a move toward the abolition of war. In the book's introduction, he wrote:

> What is needed urgently, at the moment, is not only understanding and appreciation of the values of our police conception and its history, but the practical vision of the possibilities of their lessons in the wider sphere of the rebuilding of a stricken world. The subject of this volume is the use that may be made of the "preventive" principle of police in solving the recurring wars among the nations.[55]

Simply put, Reith argued that just as during the early nineteenth century individual persons and parishes in London came to recognize realistically the need for a police institution that could prevent crime, enforce the laws, and protect the community, so too today ought individual nations recognize the practical need for an international police force that could prevent aggressive warfare, enforce international laws, and protect "the greatest community of all," the community of nations.[56]

Reith repeatedly emphasized "two facts" that he regarded as most essential: "Observance of international laws cannot be secured without provision of force for compelling it, and, if it is to be effective and enduring, the form which is established must be, in part, at least, of a preventive nature, and based securely on police principles."[57] To be sure, Reith appears to have in mind something akin to the social peacekeeping or community model of just policing. In addition, Reith's proposal resonates significantly with the school of international relations known as the liberal internationalist perspective, which is a more cosmopolitan viewpoint that focuses on multilateral cooperation, global institutions, and international law.[58] This school of thought would also, one would expect, support the creation of an international police force that attempts to work with people and various organizations in order to address problems before they give rise to conflict within the international community.

At the same time, Reith's proposal takes into consideration the concerns of the realist school of international relations with his recognition of the ongoing need for the use of force to enforce international law if rogue or recalcitrant nations pose a threat to other nations, ethnic groups, or international order.[59] The realist school warns against undue optimism about human nature and utopianism in international relations, and it thus continues to emphasize the ongoing potential need for the use of force by sovereign nations in order to defend themselves and their interests against hostile nations and groups. Because he did not underestimate the capacity for evil by nations and persons, Reith's proposal provided for an enforcement capacity by the international police. He emphasized the need for the provision of force in order to effectively ensure that nations comply with international law. Such force, however, would be governed by moral criteria, so that it would be the *force of law* rather than the *law of force*. Moreover, Reith did not call for the abolition of national sovereignty. Rather, just as individual citizens within society cede their right to defend themselves to the police (unless an attack by an aggressor is in progress, or such a threat is imminent, and no police are nearby to intervene), so too should individual nations qualify or cede their sovereignty, particularly with regard to the use of force, to the international police institution (unless an attack by an aggressor is in progress, or such a threat is imminent, and no international police are immediately able to intervene). Hence Reith's suggestion for an international police appears to account for some of the key concerns or emphases of both of the main schools of international relations today.

So what might such an extension of community policing possibly look like in the international arena? To begin, an international police would have to find its place within an overarching framework of international law. The police would be accountable to this law (and not considered "above the law"), and their role would be to prevent international crime and to apprehend or stop nations, individuals or groups suspected of posing a threat to persons, nations, and international order. Their role would not be to punish, for this would be the responsibility of the international court. In addition, while there would be an international police institution, presumably under the auspices of the United Nations, there also would be regional police "sub-stations" comprised mostly of personnel that reflect their "neighborhoods" (e.g., a European Union police force or a Caribbean police force). Additional police from outside of the region might be called upon when backup assistance is required; however, the regional police usually would be able to prevent crime and enforce the law in their corner of the international "community."

An international police institution, moreover, would partner and cooperate with "citizens" of the "community" such as non-governmental organizations, humanitarian aid groups, and other peacemaking entities in attempting to understand and address the root causes of crime and conflict. Like local community police who spend most of their time performing community services and tasks, perhaps an international police would normally be involved in programs, such as education, engineering, and constructing roads, or other services that contribute to the area's infrastructure and welfare. Accordingly, an international police institution would have other tasks and responsibilities (i.e., activities that are parallel to emergency assistance or social services provided by community police officers) that take up as much of their attention as intervening with force to apprehend "suspects." Furthermore, an international police institution would be authorized to use force if necessary but would also be at the forefront of research, development, and implementation of less-than-lethal technology and methods. The use of deadly force by international police, while permissible, definitely would be governed by clear criteria for when and how such force should be employed (e.g., proportionate force as a last resort when there is just cause).

Given that Reith's proposal for an international police was not fully accepted and implemented over sixty years ago, however, what are its prospects at this time? As Edward Le Roy Long notes, "Admittedly, the law enforcement model is not presently well developed on an international scale."[60]

Nevertheless, a confluence of several developments over the last few decades might indicate that the time is as ripe as ever for international just policing. For example, the International Criminal Court is a recent advance in this direction. It will try persons apprehended for human rights violations and crimes against humanity. An international police force would appear to be a logical corollary to such an entity. While some nations continue not to support it, most nations in recent years seem to approve of and back it.

Another example is the development of regional multilateral organizations, such as the European Union and the African Union, that promote cooperation between nations and are seeking to create new mechanisms for conflict prevention and resolution. In an article in the British Catholic magazine *The Tablet*, Denis MacShane praised recent expansions of the European Union, allowing more nations to become part of this regional cooperative venture: "It will boost peace, prosperity, and stability across the entire continent, helping to build a secure neighborhood and to tackle global threats such as terrorism and international crime."[61] For the past fifty years or so, especially during the Cold War era, nobody could have imagined this development as even a remote possibility. Now, however, former enemies cooperate for their common good. Perhaps this is a promising precedent for other regions around the world and for the global community of nations itself. Similarly, just as a New Police was organized nearly two centuries ago at a time when there were doubts, worries, and outright opposition by various individuals to such an institution, so too might an international police be created even though many individuals and individual nations currently express doubts, worries, and outright opposition to such an institution.

Another significant factor to consider is currently growing support for moving in this direction by various churches and religious leaders. In his Message for the 2003 World Day of Peace, Pope John Paul II reiterated the observation of Pope John XXIII in *Pacem in Terris* about "the obvious need for *a public authority, on the international level*, with effective capacity to advance the universal common good; an authority which [cannot] . . . be established by coercion but only by the consent of nations."[62] While pointing out that he is not calling for the creation of "a global super-state," the pontiff clearly believes that there is a need for an international institution, such as the United Nations, that can effectively prevent most conflict in its tracks by addressing its root causes. Still, as Archbishop Diarmuid Martin observes, "Enforcement procedures are still very weak and ambiguous."[63] Similarly, Phil Shiner asks, "Do the United Nations and international law still have muscles to flex when faced with conflicts such as the one in Iraq?"[64] Like Reith with regard to the League of Nations, Shiner laments the impotence of the United Nations in the face of terrorism and the way that various nations are taking it upon themselves to respond to it independently.

While not denying a nation's right of self-defense against attack, Shiner asserts that there also "must be mechanisms to enforce international law against those who ignore the resolutions of the U.N. General Assembly or Security Council."[65] In his view, the "war" approach to dealing with terrorism is not as effective as another approach: "The arms which have been most successful in the fight against terrorism right across the world have been primarily those of intelligence and international cooperation, of infiltration and of dismantling false ideologies, as well as, of course, development policies focused on the establishment of the infrastructures for democracy."[66] Shiner thus echoes key elements of the paradigm of community policing extended to the international level, which we have surveyed in this chapter. If he is right, then it is surely realistic to continue exploring, testing, and advocating for just policing in international affairs.

Notes

1. Quoted in Margot Patterson, "Experts Say Bombing is Risky Strategy," *National Catholic Reporter*, November 2, 2001, 4. Stanley Hauerwas made a similar suggestion (together with just-war proponent Paul J. Griffiths) in "War, Peace and Jean Bethke Elstain," *First Things* 136 (October 2003): 41–47. Also see William L. Hanson, "Police Power for Peace," *Friends Journal*, August 2004, 6–7, 34; along with the following, which Gerald Schlabach quotes on pp. 78–79 of the present book: Wallis, "Hard Questions for Peacemakers"; Wallis, "Interview with Stanley Hauerwas" (accessed May 25, 2004).

2. James F. Childress, "The Just-War Tradition and the Invasion of Iraq," Conference on Ethical Issues Raised by Pre-Emptive War (The Churches' Center for Theology and Public Policy, Wesley Theological Seminary, Washington DC, 2003), 4.

3. Jean Porter, in Peter Steinfels, et al., "What Kind of War?" *Commonweal* 128, no. 16 (September 28, 2001): 10; also see Steinfels, "What Kind of War?" 8; George Lopez, "After September 11: How Ethics Can Help," *America* 185, no. 10 (October 8, 2001): 20–24.

4. Ralph B. Potter, *War and Moral Discourse* (Richmond: John Knox Press, 1969), 60.

5. Francis J. Connell, *Morals in Politics and Professions: A Guide for Catholics in Public Life.* (Westminster, MD: Newman Press, 1946), v.

6. Edward A. Malloy, *The Ethics of Law Enforcement and Criminal Punishment* (Washington, DC: University Press of America, 1982), 2.

7. Ibid., 24.

8. Malloy, *The Ethics of Law Enforcement and Criminal Punishment*, ix. By "domestic violence" Malloy is not referring to spousal abuse within a household; rather, he means violence that occurs within a nation's borders, such as police use of force to apprehend a criminal suspect.

9. See chapter 5 of the present volume, pp. 94–95.

10. John Kleinig, *The Ethics of Policing*, Cambridge Studies in Philosophy and Public Policy (Cambridge: Cambridge University Press, 1996), 24. Similarly, David H. Bayley writes, "The 1990s are a watershed period in policing because very different paradigms are competing for the hearts and minds of police officers. . . ." (Bayley, *Police for the Future* [New York: Oxford University Press, 1994], 119).

11. Joycelyn M. Pollock, *Ethics in Crime and Justice: Dilemmas and Decisions*, Contemporary Issues in Crime and Justice Series (Pacific Grove, CA: Brooks/Cole Pub. Co., 1989), 73. Also see Kleinig, *The Ethics of Policing*, 24–25, 283, endnote 31.

12. Egon Bittner, *The Functions of the Police in Modern Society: A Review of Background Factors, Current Practices, and Possible Role Models.* (New York: J. Aronson, 1975), 52. Of course, as Michael S. Sherry makes clear, the military metaphor has impacted "every realm

of American life—politics and foreign policy, economics and technology, culture and social relations. . . ." (*In the Shadow of War: The United States Since the 1930's* [New Haven, CT: Yale University Press, 1995], x).

13. Charles W. Sasser, *Shoot to Kill: Cops Who Have Used Deadly Force* (New York: Pocket Books, 1994), vii.

14. Ibid., xv, 12. To be sure, Sasser attempts to qualify this description of policing, acknowledging that "it may not be war in a classical sense," but he maintains that "it is nonetheless *war*." Indeed, he asserts, "More important, the policeman sees it as war" (233). Kleinig, however, laments that "many police officers *like* to see themselves as crime fighters" in a "war" against crime (*The Ethics of Policing*, 25).

15. Sasser, *Shoot to Kill*, xv.

16. Jerome H. Skolnick and James J. Fyfe, *Above the Law: Police and the Excessive Use of Force* (New York: Free Press, 1993), 113. See Kleinig, *The Ethics of Policing*, 283, endnote 31.

17. Stuart A. Scheingold, *The Politics of Law and Order: Street Crime and Public Policy*, Longman Professional Studies in Law and Public Policy (New York: Longman, 1984), 63.

18. James J. Fyfe, "Training to Reduce Police-Civilian Violence," 175, in William A. Geller and Hans Toch, eds., *Police Violence: Understanding and Controlling Police Abuse of Force* (New Haven, CT: Yale University Press, 1996).

19. Peter Scharf and Arnold Binder, *The Badge and the Bullet: Police Use of Deadly Force* (New York: Praeger, 1983), 31, 32, and 38.

20. Robert Elias, "Taking Crime Seriously," *Peace Review* 6 (1994): 131.

21. Martin Edmonds, *Armed Services and Society* (Leicester: Leicester University Press, 1988), 7. See Sasser, *Shoot to Kill*, 136; Elias, "Taking Crime Seriously," 131; Kleinig, *The Ethics of Policing*, 283, endnote 31; Bayley, *Police for the Future*, 70; Bittner, *The Functions of the Police in Modern Society*, 53. Also, in a full chapter on "Cops as Soldiers," Skolnick and Fyfe list many examples of military jargon applied to policing, leading them to believe that most U.S. police departments have become "paramilitary" (Skolnick and Fyfe, *Above the Law*, 113–33).

22. Bittner, *The Functions of the Police in Modern Society*, 53.

23. Vance McLaughlin, *Police and the Use of Force: The Savannah Study*, foreword by Richard R.E. Kania (Westport, CT: Praeger, 1992), 1. Interestingly, McLaughlin acknowledges that police "seldom use force" in the "vast majority of police-citizen contacts," but he believes that force is central and "remains an ongoing concern for both police and public" (2). See also Scharf and Binder, *The Badge and the Bullet*, 38; Elias, "Taking Crime Seriously," 131.

24. Scheingold, *The Politics of Law and Order*, 101–2. In this vein, David Bayley asserts that "the defining task [in policing] is the application of physical force within a community" (David H. Bayley, *Patterns of Policing: A Comparative International Analysis*, Crime, Law, and Deviance Series. [New Brunswick, NJ: Rutgers University Press, 1985], 37). He acknowledges that police possess other responsibilities and that they do not always employ force in the performance of their duties, but he nevertheless emphasizes that the "unique characteristic of police is that they are authorized to use physical force to regulate interpersonal relations in communities" (103). Similarly, McLaughlin writes, "[Police] routinely use force to carry out their role as enforcers—the use of force is inherent in the profession" (McLaughlin, *Police and the Use of Force*, 1).

25. Victor E. Kappeler, Mark Blumberg, and Gary W. Potter, *The Mythology of Crime and Criminal Justice* (Prospect Heights, IL: Waveland Press, 1993), 131.

26. James F. Childress, *Practical Reasoning in Bioethics*, Medical Ethics Series (Bloomington, IN: Indiana University Press, 1997), 5, 7. Childress adds, however, that these "negative

or ambiguous implications of the war metaphor . . . can be avoided if . . . the metaphor is interpreted in accord with the limits set by the just-war tradition" (9).

27. Paul Chevigny, *Edge of the Knife: Police Violence in the Americas* (New York: New Press, distributed by Norton, 1995), 255–56. See also Elias, "Taking Crime Seriously," 131; Scheingold, *The Politics of Law and Order*, 101; Skolnick and Fyfe, *Above the Law*, 114.

28. Bittner, *The Functions of the Police in Modern Society*, 47–49. See also Kleinig, *The Ethics of Policing*, 24 and Joseph Betz, "Police Violence," 181–82, in Frederick Elliston and Michael Feldberg, eds., *Moral Issues in Police Work* (Totowa, NJ: Rowman & Allanheld, 1985). When police view the public as a whole cynically and suspiciously, according to Christopher Daskalos, "the chances of police misuse of force are greatly increased" and the temptation to use excessive force is "exacerbated" (Christopher Daskalos, "Current Issues in Policing," 67, in *The Past, Present, and the Future of American Criminal Justice*, ed. Brendan Maguire and Polly F. Radosh, [Dix Hills, NY: General Hall, 1996], 67.

29. Skolnick and Fyfe, *Above the Law*, xviii. To be sure, it would be helpful and more persuasive if empirical data supporting such a causal link could be provided.

30. Ibid., 12–13, 115–16. The 1991 report of the Christopher Commission (Independent Commission on the Los Angeles Police Department) corroborates this view when it suggests "a strongly enforcement-oriented agency can enhance the proclivity of aggressive officers to engage in proactive exercises that include uses of excessive force" (cited in William A. Geller and Hans Toch, "Understanding and Controlling Police Abuse of Force," 295, in Geller and Toch, *Police Violence: Understanding and Controlling Police Abuse of Force*).

31. Howard Cohen, "Authority: The Limits of Discretion," 27–41, in Elliston and Feldberg, *Moral Issues in Police Work*.

32. Fyfe, "Training to Reduce Police-Civilian Violence," 175. Bayley writes, "The paradox is that though police officers must prepare for war, they spend most of their time making peace in nonforceful ways" (Bayley, *Police for the Future*, 70). Also see Robert M. Fogelson, *Big-City Police*, An Urban Institute Study. (Cambridge, MA: Harvard University Press, 1977), 272; Brendan Maguire and Polly F. Radosh, "A Sociological Introduction to the American Criminal Justice System," 11, in Maguire and Radosh, *The Past, Present, and the Future of American Criminal Justice.*

33. Kleinig, *The Ethics of Policing*, 25.

34. Egon Bittner, "The Capacity to Use Force as the Core of the Police Role," 21, in Elliston and Feldberg, *Moral Issues in Police Work*; also see Egon Bittner, *Aspects of Police Work* (Boston: Northeastern University Press, 1990), 120–30; Betz, "Police Violence," 187.

35. Bittner, "The Capacity to Use Force," 18, 20-21; *The Functions of the Police in Modern Society*, 39, 42–44; *Aspects of Police Work*, 127–28.

36. Betz, "Police Violence," 186–87.

37. Kleinig, *The Ethics of Policing*, 117.

38. Ibid., 26–27, also see 24 and 96.

39. Ibid., 27.

40. Ibid., 293, endnote 3.

41. Ibid., 29.

42. Ibid., 29. In connection with this, Kleinig provides several criteria for governing and evaluating police use of force that bear a resemblance to the criteria of the just-war tradition (e.g., right intent, proportionality, etc.).

43. Ibid., 96.

44. David Ascoli, *The Queen's Peace: The Origins and Development of the Metropolitan Police, 1829–1979* (London: H. Hamilton, 1979), 89–90.

45. Ibid., 80, 85, 87; cf. Maguire and Radosh, "A Sociological Introduction to the American Criminal Justice System," 10–11. Also see Charles Reith, *A New Study of Police History* (Edinburgh: Oliver and Boyd, 1956), 140. The General Instructions of the London Metropolitan Police may be found in John Kleinig and Yurong Zhang, eds., *Professional Law Enforcement Codes: A Documentary Collection* (Westport, CT: Greenwood Press, 1993), 25–27.

46. Samuel Walker, *Popular Justice: A History of American Criminal Justice* (New York: Oxford: University Press, 1980), 60, emphasis in the original. Also see Stefan Petrow, *Policing Morals: The Metropolitan Police and the Home Office, 1870–1914* (New York: Oxford University Press, 1994), 39–41.

47. For additional works on the history of policing or on how policing in the United States came to follow and implement a crime fighter model, along with a more military approach, see Fogelson, *Big-City Police*; Roger Lane, *Policing the City: Boston, 1822–1885* (Cambridge, MA: Harvard University Press, 1967); Eric H. Monkkonen, *Police in Urban America, 1860–1920*, Interdisciplinary Perspectives on Modern History. (Cambridge [Eng.]: Cambridge University Press, 1981); Mark H. Moore and George L. Kelling, "'To Serve and Protect': Learning from Police History," *The Public Interest* 70 (Winter 1983): 49–65; Phillip Thurmond Smith, *Policing Victorian London: Political Policing, Public Order, and the London Metropolitan Police*, Contributions in Criminology and Penology, no. 7 (Westport, CT: Greenwood Press, 1985). For now, suffice to note that, according to Skolnick and Fyfe, this development was due to "some combination of American social and historical forces [which have] blended with the military model to produce a volatile mix" (Skolnick and Fyfe, *Above the Law*, 128).

48. Kleinig, *The Ethics of Policing*, 28, 78, 229–33.

49. For more on community policing, see Maya Harris West, principle author, *Community-Based Policing: A Force for Change*, A Report by PolicyLink in partnership with the Advancement Project (Oakland, CA: PolicyLink, 2001), Http://www.policylink.org/Research/Police/; Friedmann, *Community Policing: Comparative Perspectives and Prospects* (New York: St. Martin's Press, 1992); Gene Stephens, "Peace in the 'Hood,'" in James D. Sewell, ed., *Controversial Issues in Policing*, Controversial Issues Series (Boston: Allyn and Bacon, 1999); Gene Stephens, "The Future of Policing: From a War Model to a Peace Model," in Maguire and Radosh, *The Past, Present, and the Future of American Criminal Justice*; Steven A. Donziger, ed., *The Real War on Crime: The Report of the National Criminal Justice Commission* (New York: HarperPerennial, 1996), especially chapter seven, "Toward a New Model of Policing"; COPS Office, *What is Community Policing?* (Office of Community Oriented Policing Services, U.S. Department of Justice), Http://www.cops.usdoj.gov/print.asp?Item=36 (accessed 2 December 2006). A critical assessment of community policing may be found in William G. Doerner, "War on Crime," in Sewell, *Controversial Issues in Policing*. I wish to thank sociologist Dr. John McKeon for bringing to my attention some of these community policing resources.

50. Donziger, *The Real War on Crime*, 173.

51. Kleinig, *The Ethics of Policing*, 25.

52. Donziger, *The Real War on Crime*, 171.

53. Kleinig, *The Ethics of Policing*, 107. See also William C. Bailey, "Less-Than-Lethal Weapons and Police-Citizen Killings in U.S. Urban Areas," *Crime and Delinquency* 42 (October 1996): 535–36.

54. Of course, in this connection it depends on what type of pacifist and what type of just-war theory. Not all pacifists, such as those who espouse a form that involves passive non-resistance (e.g., Leo Tolstoy), would support any use of force by police, in a community model or otherwise. And, similarly, some versions of just-war theory may be more

restrained and governed by more robust ethical criteria than others. See Tobias Winright, "From Police Officers to Peace Officers"; and Tobias L. Winright, "Two Rival Versions of Just War Theory and the Presumption Against Harm in Policing."

55. Charles Reith, *Police Principles and the Problem of War* (London: Oxford University Press, 1940), viii.

56. Ibid., 1.

57. Ibid., 147.

58. See chapter 8 by Reina C. Neufeldt in the present book.

59. Reith believed that this was the flaw of the League of Nations; that is, it lacked enforcement capability. He hoped that a United Nations would rectify this; however, although many of its creators "insisted that the successor to the League of Nations must have enforcement powers . . . [and] must not only be able to help resolve international conflicts but also have a capacity for both deterrence and for military and economic coercion," this turned out not to be the case for what came to be the United Nations (Kalevi J. Holsti, *Peace and War: Armed Conflicts and International Order, 1648–1989*, Cambridge Studies in International Relations, vol. 14 [Cambridge: Cambridge University Press, 1991], 245; see also the rest of Chapter 10 in this work by Holsti, "Peace By Policing," 243–270). For a recent expression of this viewpoint, see Gabriel Moran, "Outlawing War: Reforming the Language of War is the First Step Toward Ending It," *National Catholic Reporter* 40, no. 3 (November 7, 2003): 14–15.

60. Edward Le Roy Long, *Facing Terrorism: Responding as Christians* (Louisville: Westminster John Knox Press, 2004), 51.

61. Denis MacShane, "A Day to be Proud," *The Tablet* 258 (May 1, 2004): 2.

62. John Paul II, "*Pacem in Terris*: A Permanent Commitment," World Day of Peace message, January 1, 2003, *America* 188, no. 4 (February 10, 2003): 19, emphasis in the original. The Anglican Archbishop of Canterbury, Rowan Williams, has called for something similar; see "War Leaders Will be 'Called to Account', Says Dr. Williams," *The Tablet* (October 18, 2003): 30–31.

63. Archbishop Diarmuid Martin, "Theological and Moral Perspectives on Today's Challenge of Peace," *Origins* 33, no. 26 (December 4, 2003): 448. This was a speech delivered on November 10, 2003 to the U.S. Catholic bishops at their fall meeting in Washington, DC.

64. Phil Shiner, "Viewpoint: Why Peace Needs Law," *The Tablet* 258 (January 24, 2004): 2.

65. Ibid. Former U.N. General Secretary, Boutros Boutros-Ghali, similarly called for an enforcement capacity in his *An Agenda for Peace, 1995*, second edition, with the new supplement and related U.N. documents (New York: United Nations, 1995), 28.

66. Shiner, 2.

Chapter 8

Just Policing and International Order: Is it Possible?

Reina C. Neufeldt

John Lennon sang about imagining a world where there were no countries, nothing to kill or die for, and where all the people lived in peace. I must admit that I find it hard to imagine a morning where I open the paper and do not find a story about casualties sustained in the "War on Terrorism," or deaths from fighting in Sudan or the Middle East. I am hardly alone with this problem of trying to imagine a world without violence and war—and I work on peacebuilding. Yet, if we cannot imagine a world without terrorism around the corner and without a single war occurring in one moment in time, then how can we achieve it?

For many, the imagination is something that belongs in our childhood; at worst it is what frustrated daydreamers like Walter Mitty rely on, or at best it is left to artists and inventors.[1] We bound ourselves by what we think is feasible, what we have seen work, what we have experienced. Yet the imagination is a powerful resource for pushing the boundaries of what is possible. Fortunately for those of us with limited imaginations, imagining is not necessarily a solo activity. Sometimes new technologies can help us all to imagine new possibilities. Benedict Anderson has argued that the printing press and regular newspapers meant that individuals could hear about, think about, and keep track of a community beyond a few local villages, which opened the door to imagine first nations and then nationalism.[2] Or, when the first rocket was built people could suddenly imagine traveling to the moon. In a similar way, the thought experiment for just policing involves imagining an international community and a method of maintaining security and order that goes beyond current formulations. This chapter explores technologies that can help us to imagine a world where community-based just policing maintains order. It then lays out a research agenda to help assess its viability.

Gerald Schlabach's argument for just policing in Chapter 4 is theologically driven. The argument negotiates a course between just war and pacifism, identifying state-sanctioned police action as a possible third way to deal with international security threats such as nuclear proliferation, aggression, terrorism, and so on.[3] The terrain for the argument in international relations is at least as rugged. Many arguments for global collective security mechanisms have been written off as idealistic and improbable. This will be explored further below but, briefly, states are typically understood as sovereign, independent, territorially bounded units that exist within a condition of anarchy. States make laws that protect the common good internally and protect "national interests" externally; sometime states are compared to billiard balls on a pool table because of the idea that they are self-contained units that are largely independent.[4] In order for just policing to be viable and functional it needs to address the challenges of the independent state system that suggests no state, particularly powerful states, will voluntarily allow one of its primary tools of power—military power—to be limited.

This chapter brings the concept of just policing into dialogue with the fundamentals of international relations. There is a focus on theory here because theories underpin how politicians and bureaucrats think about the state system and informs their choices and actions. The chapter begins by identifying the central assumptions of just policing that need to be held in order for it to function. The concept of just policing is then looked at through the more traditional international relations lenses of liberal internationalism and realism. We then put on two newer lenses that are products of more recent technologies, globalization and constructivism, and look again at the possibility of just policing. The final section starts to imagine the technology in practice in a move towards a just policing model in the international system and lays out a brief research agenda to explore the question further.

The Assumptions of Just Policing: Community, Common Good, and Order

We are talking here about utilizing the community policing model to deal with conflicts and security threats between states. Police forces usually deal with problems of order and law within states, while military forces deal with problems of order and threats between states, although in some conflict environments these roles overlap.[5] My point here is that the international community has used interim police forces and provided police training to states in order to bolster the rule of law and maintain order within a particular state.[6] However, in this book we are talking about applying a police model between states to see if it can be relevant for inter-state or international relations. There are some important differences in these contexts that need to be explored.

The just policing model contains certain assumptions about the nature of order and the community being policed. We need to articulate these and then see if they apply to states, or nation-states.[7] To briefly summarize, just policing seeks to secure the common good of the society within which the police operate according to the rule of law.[8] Police officers are embedded within the communities they police in order to ensure that they are accountable to the residents they are sworn to protect, relate to them as regular community members, and help prevent illegal behavior before it happens. From this description we can identify at least three key assumptions of the just policing model that need to be held if the model is going to work internationally. The first is that there is a community within which the police can be or are embedded within. The second is that there is general agreement on what constitutes the common good within that community. The third key assumption is that the community, including top officials, is interested in proactively pursuing the common good and maintaining order guided by the rule of law.[9]

These seem clear enough for local communities, but unfortunately we run into some problems when we look at the international system. The following section details problems as well as compatibilities with two leading areas of thought in the twentieth century, the liberal internationalist and realist perspectives.

International Relations:
Contested Notions of Community, Common Good, and Order

The state system we know today is a fairly recent invention. Its basic structure emerged in Europe after the Thirty Years War and was codified in the Treaty of Westphalia in 1648. Each state was to have a sovereign government that was viewed as equal to other legitimate, sovereign governments. The state system spread across the globe with European colonization. In the seventeenth and eighteenth centuries, nobility or their selected designees conducted state affairs quite privately, and economics and domestic politics were thought to be quite distinct enterprises from diplomacy. Then, in the nineteenth century diplomatic representatives engaged with each other more publicly according to emerging standards of behavior and formal bi-lateral and multi-lateral treaties became increasingly common and provided basic tenets for international law. Diplomacy was thought of as an art and not a science until the end of the nineteenth century, when it became the object of more careful scientific scrutiny and "political science."[10] International relations is a loosely designated area of research, study, and practice that focuses specifically on the interactions that occur between states; it emerged around the time that nuclear weapons raised the negative stakes of inter-state relations.[11] Two major, competing views of how the international system worked emerged in the twentieth century and dominated the field, particularly in America. These can be called realism and liberal internationalism.[12]

Liberal internationalism and realism continue to inform the decisions that government leaders make today. For example, as the United States government and others decided how to respond to North Korea's claims to be developing nuclear weapons, the decision makers weighed options according to their theories of how North Korea would respond to particular state actions.

I begin with liberal internationalism, which is also known as liberalism, or idealism, because it provides a good foundation for thinking about just policing.[13] Liberal internationalism draws on a long lineage of theological, political, economic, and legal thought and is rooted in the writings of Saint Augustine, Thomas Aquinas, Immanuel Kant, Hugo Grotius, and numerous others. Liberal internationalists argue that the international system consists of independent or sovereign but similarly minded units, called states, that are interested in cooperation and governed by law.[14] Natural law provided the original guiding framework for international law and has since become more codified in treaty law and so forth. Some of the elements of common interest are economic development, trade, basic human rights, peace, and order.[15] An early, vocal spokesman for liberal internationalism was U.S. President Woodrow Wilson. Wilson argued that national determination would produce representative democracies all interested in the same things: peace, respect for human rights, and prosperity. Cooperation is understood to be a normal feature of international relations in order to achieve shared interests rather than a marriage of convenience.[16] One of the strongest contemporary arguments for liberal internationalists today is that democracies and trading partners do not go to war against each other; this is called the democratic peace theory.[17]

Of course, international law and liberal internationalism do not preclude the use of force between sovereign states. Laws were developed to determine whether or not going to war was legitimate (*jus ad bellum*) and to guide how force is used during war (*jus in bello*). After World War II, the United Nations charter, which embodied many liberal internationalist ideals, was designed to prevent states from independently using force and to focus the power for use of force in the Security Council.[18] However, the Security Council was almost immediately frozen by cold war politics, and the other mechanism of collective security in the charter—a standing military force—never materialized. International peacekeeping therefore was developed as a rather creative tool of limited force to separate warring sides in order to create some political space in which peace would ideally be negotiated. The "traditional peacekeeping" model involved placing a lightly armed force in a buffer zone between belligerent parties. Traditional peacekeeping embodied liberal institutionalist values; it relied upon the cooperation of all parties and ensured the sovereign integrity of states while seeking politically negotiated solutions.[19]

When we look at the assumptions of just policing with our liberal internationalist lens, we see with clarity part of the vision we seek. There is support for the assumption of an international community, and the understanding that states are, by and large, interested in pursuing the common good and following international law. Some liberal institutionalists argue that we are on the brink of creating a world society with central, liberal, democratic governing institutions, such as the International Criminal Court.[20] Liberal internationalism gives us a good part of the vision we are looking for in the just policing model, as Winright also notes in Chapter 7.

There are shortcomings, however. Liberal internationalism has been unable to convincingly deal with the problem of aggressive and powerful states. There have been many occasions when collective action, cooperation, and the rule of law have failed. In the twentieth century the first global state institution, the League of Nations, was disbanded when collective action faltered in the face of Germany's belligerence in the lead-up to World War II. With the League's failure, the realist viewpoint came to the fore and the collective approach was critiqued as idealistic and utopian.[21] The United Nations, formed after World War II, reflected a significant adaptation to power politics with the big five, permanent members of the Security Council maintaining the power to veto any Security Council vote. Recently, the veto power was on display in the standoff between the United States and France when deciding whether or not to pursue further sanctions and weapons inspections versus military action in Iraq. The United States could veto any calls for further inspections. France could veto calls for a Security Council resolution approving immediate military action. Therefore a "Coalition of the Willing" invaded Iraq without a final resolution from the Security Council and little justification from within international law.[22]

Let us turn now to realism. Realism tends to dominate the field and popular understandings of international relations. "Realism" was built upon interpretations of the classic writings of Thucydides, Niccolò Machiavelli, Thomas Hobbes, and more recently Hans Morgenthau.[23] Power, particularly military power, is central to realism given that life is understood to be, as Hobbes said, "nasty, brutish, and short." States utilize power to ensure their own security and sovereignty, and pursue national interests in a system that is anarchical. National interests include things like homeland security, access to resources like oil and fresh water. Realists argue that states are rational, unitary actors using power to survive. War can therefore be understood as Clausewitz said, "the pursuit of politics by other means." It is not that states are inherently *bad*, but rather that they will use all means necessary to protect their interests. War is the internationally approved last resort to defend national interests between states.[24]

Neo-realist Kenneth Waltz developed an influential adaptation that highlighted the influence of the anarchical system on state actions. Waltz emphasized that the system of decentralized anarchy itself prevents independent, sovereign states from cooperating and creates a continuous dynamic of competition and threat.[25] The implication is that even if states want to cooperate, they will be inhibited because they do not really know and cannot depend on the other states to respect their own interests.[26] An army is in part to guarantee that another state will not invade. Anarchy does not mean disorder. Order in this system can be established by a balance of power, such as the one that existed between the U.S. and U.S.S.R. during the cold war. Or, one state can dominate, establish hegemony, and keep the others in line.[27] For example, many argue that there is currently a U.S. hegemony, given the U.S. military and economic strength.[28]

Now, if we look at the basic assumptions of just policing with our realist lens on we have a rather dim view of it. We find ourselves blocked at the very first assumption for just policing, namely that there is an international community. This assumption goes directly against the argument that the international system of sovereign actors is actually anarchic and has *no* community in any meaningful, cooperative sense. This clash over the issue of community is sometimes framed as the cosmopolitanism versus communitarianism debate, where cosmopolitans argue that states have universal moral obligations, while communitarians argue that such moral obligations are primarily to the members of each state.[29] Realists see very weak ties between states, and argue these are insufficient to hold states together in a community working towards a common good. Further, in realism, the rule of law has a very circumscribed role. Law is something that states agree to if it facilitates their national interest in a particular area. For example, states agree on shipping lanes or airport clearance procedures. However, in areas where they believe it may threaten their national interest, states will choose to stay outside of the law, ignore, or abrogate laws. States can choose to not sign on to specific legal mechanisms like the International Criminal Court, or can form bi-lateral treaties with countries to agree not to pursue war crimes against each other.

According to this view, if a police system ever emerged, it would likely be imposed by a hegemonic power. The powerful state actor or set of actors could impose a police force, somewhat akin to a military occupation, on the rest of the world. For example, the United States might become the "world's policeman" because of sheer military and economic power. Alternatively, states could agree to a policing system they all contribute forces to, as long as the most powerful states went along with it, but as soon as it threatened their interests they would pull out. These are both models of global policing, but certainly ones that are prone to abuses by the hegemonic power. Overall, it seems the realist lens identifies the challenges that power and politics present in the international system and which just policing will have to address in order to move from imagination into reality.

While realism is a dominant framework, it is important to note it has significant shortcomings in responding to the world's problems. First, and most problematic, is its inability to account for change in structures in the international system. For example, realists, like many others, were in a quandary at the end of the cold war when the Berlin Wall fell and the state system began to change. It was not predicted. Nor were there models to understand what would happen to the international system next.[30] Realism is also often criticized for being too simplistic in its narrow focus on states, power, and national interest. It does not account for sub-state groups like al Qaeda or for supra-state groups like the European Union.

In sum, when we look at just policing through our twentieth-century lenses we see both the challenges and the vision.[31] The concept of community and cooperation is contested in realism, with its formulation of power politics, sovereignty, and anarchy. However, we see the promise of cooperation and legal order in liberal institutionalism, which bridges the problems of sovereignty and anarchy. We now must look further to see if we have the technology that will both address the challenges of realism and help us build the metaphorical rocket to get us to our destination, which in this case is a believable vision of just policing.

Twenty-First-Century Lenses on Our Changing World

In the late 1980s and early 1990s the international system changed in dramatic and unexpected ways. The Berlin Wall fell. The balance of power between the United States and the Soviet Union was gone. Realists were stymied, and liberal institutionalists and others weren't much more capable of explaining these colossal shifts. Both schools of thought were criticized for underestimating and omitting the impact of a variety of other factors linked to change, such as the economy, gender, the environment, decision-making processes, culture, irrationality, domestic politics, and power.[32] Change became a central feature of the international system.

The bedrock concept of sovereignty also seemed to shift in the 1990s.[33] There were new demands for international humanitarian intervention within states like Somalia as they "failed" or others like the former Yugoslavia where internal conflict led to "ethnic cleansing." States also banded together to form tighter economic and political blocks like the European Union, and in the process voluntarily gave up some aspects of "sovereignty" to be part of these communities. The U.S.-led invasion of Iraq in 2003 highlighted that sovereign space was no longer the Holy Grail it was once thought to be. There were also changes in how we thought about threats. Terrorism, fresh water shortages, HIV/AIDS, and SARS would not respect state boundaries.[34] Uganda cannot be the only state trying to prevent the spread of HIV/AIDS. The United States cannot prevent terrorism by itself. Security threats crossed borders and required responses to do likewise.

Two very different ways of capturing change emerged in the late 1980s and early 1990s. The first, constructivism, was a theoretical approach vying with realism and liberal institutionalism for dominance as a grand theory in international relations. The second was the concept of globalization, which captured a wide variety of thinking about global change. These distinct areas of thought, which continue to develop, provided us with critical building blocks to think about our world and the process of change differently. Essentially they capture new technologies of thinking and action about change, states, and the state system. I look at both below.

Technologies of Change: Constructivism

Constructivism takes a new approach to the international system. Rather than assuming states are given entities, it focuses on how we actually make and sustain states and the international system. It looks at how actors and their actions follow rules that create and maintain the system of states that we currently live in. The international system is not static but a product of actors and their activities. States in turn are also influenced by the structures they create. For example, states work together to develop the institution of the United Nations, turning an idea into reality. Once the United Nations was formed, those same states had to react to it as a real entity that represented particular international norms and laws rather than just an idea. Constructivism also takes into account other forces and groups operating in the international system that affect change, like networks of non-governmental organizations. For example, the non-governmental organizations that banded together to ban anti-personnel landmines were an effective force in changing internationally agreed upon codes of conduct in war.[35]

The constructivist approach brings a focus on the rules and norms underlying the international system. Norms provide the framework within which states and other actors operate; they are like the rules of a game that guide what types of moves can be made with the game pieces.[36] Norms usually work together in sets. Sovereignty can therefore be understood to be the norm that emerges as a result of a whole set of norms around territorial borders, legitimate governance, and so forth. States follow particular practices like checking passports at borders that help reinforce the norm of territorial sovereignty. The constructivist lens helps us understand that norms change over time, and that states can proactively make changes, as well as be affected by them.[37] These norms are not external to states, as realism and liberal internationalism both suggest, but rather the product of use over time. Norms like anarchy or sovereignty seem permanent but actually can and do change over time, depending on which rules are used and which practices are repeated.[38] Martha Finnemore summarizes one process of change this way: "states are socialized to accept new norms, values, and perceptions of interest by international organizations."[39]

Constructivism also offers a thicker notion of the international community. States are seen as connected by a multiplicity of social interactions, roles, and expectations. Material forms of power, such as military force or financial capital, are also understood, framed, and acted upon based on a social understanding of what they mean—ideas and culture matter even when we talk about power.[40] For example, North Korea tried to claim loudly that it was restarting its nuclear weapons program at the same time that the U.S. was decrying WMD capabilities in Iraq. While the material capability in North Korea was greater, the United States government put a greater emphasis on the possible threat from Iraq based on a social interpretation of the actor making the threat and an interpretation of influence: the threat of Kim Jong Il and North Korea was minimized, while the threat of Saddam Hussein and Iraq was maximized.[41] These non-material factors significantly affected U.S. government action and how the American public interpreted each respective threat in addition to U.S. national interests. The multiple layers of socially mediated relationships put a spotlight on how much more tightly knit our social fabric at the international level than previously acknowledged. There is a community for just policing to be rooted in.

With our constructivist lens on we understand that states are agents within a structure that can both affect change in the structure and are affected by the structure. For just policing, this technology of how we think about the international system opens the door to move from some vague imagination of an end goal to more concrete possibilities of how to get there. We can see that security, concepts of community, global order, and national interest are norms that we can work at changing. Of course, there are many forces at work and so change is not a simple thing. Still, there are precedents. Just policing enters the realm of possibility when we see how the security norms can change.

Technologies of Change: Globalization

Constructivism provides us with a new technology of understanding change and relationships in the international system on a theoretical level. It is time to take a more focused look at technology in the more conventional sense, since it can also be brought to bear in our thinking about just policing. Modern technology helps us achieve all sorts of new things. It allows us to travel across distances faster, making the distances between Tokyo and New York, London and Cairo, and Toronto and Buenos Aires almost negligible.[42] We can visit, travel, and relocate to places around the globe with much greater ease than in any time in the past. It also takes far less time. Technology means that we can transfer information in the blink of an eye, watch re-runs of 1950s television shows, historical films, or live international newscasts from our living rooms. The production of many goods is now spread across multiple states. The world seems to get smaller and things seem more compressed.[43]

Globalization is a broad concept that focuses on the impact of modernization and modern technologies upon our lives. There is a very large literature on globalization that discusses what it is and how it affects our lives, economies, cultures, media, and ethnic identities.[44] Scholars argue in particular over what engine is driving the global change; for example, some argue it is economic liberalization, others media technologies, and yet others argue it is driven by a culture of individualism.[45] Most scholars recognize that globalization occurs because of a complex interplay of factors and technologies with a wide variety of push and pull factors as well as sites of resistance.

I bring globalization into this discussion because of two features it highlights in modern technology: (1) the idea that there are a growing number of interconnections around the globe, and (2) that these occur across geographic and political boundaries.[46] These two impacts show us how we can and do operate as a global community across territorial borders. Modern technology makes interconnections possible in a variety of ways. People with similar interests can meet and chat on the web, they can join listservs or specific interest groups. As long as their internet connection holds they can communicate and it doesn't matter where they sit. Connections are also made when people move, and increasingly people do move, whether they are politically forced or by choice. Interplay between people moving across spaces and coming into contact with more and more people with diverse backgrounds and cultural lenses gives people a window on parts of the world from which they were previously disconnected. Foreign locales become familiar. Diasporas maintain ties with their home but also bring knowledge of that home into their new setting.

These new technologies make all sorts of other communities possible. For example, active transnational advocacy networks, like the landmines case, utilize these technologies to create an effective social movement.[47] The interconnections that electronic media and global population flows offer us provide vibrant, interactive communities that exist across geographic space in ways that our global state system, with its rigid geographic boundaries, was never built to manage.[48] Globalization highlights the changes that modern technology brings to our world, changes that can reinforce a global community and affect our notion of sovereignty.

Putting Our Technology to Work

Before exploring further, let us revisit the central assumptions that just policing rests on in order to work. The assumptions are: (1) there is a community; (2) the community agrees on what the common good is; (3) the community is interested in maintaining order, which is rooted in the rule of law.[49] The greatest challenge for just policing, which our twentieth-century realist lens highlighted, was the argument that there is no community; rather, states are independent, sovereign units that often compete. Our other twentieth-century lens, liberal internationalism, supplied us with a vision of what a connected world might look like and provided a basis for understanding cooperation between states and the possibility of establishing some kind of global order. However, with both lenses we see that the borders between states are very well maintained, and police are used to ensure the rule of law and order within states, while militaries exist to ensure order and security internationally.

Constructivism and globalization lead us to understand the state in new ways, and affect this understanding of borders and sovereignty. With constructivism we see that the norms around what constitutes a nation, a community, and its security can and does change. We also see there are multiple connections between states and these connections point to a global milieu in which states are still important participants in the community but there are many other actors operating and connecting within that milieu. Globalization highlights how technologies create new connections and can reinforce other interconnections between peoples, institutions within and between states. Globalization seems to be diminishing boundaries between states. However, it is not clear how much globalization will alter sovereignty.[50] Will increased connections lead to the state disappearing entirely? Will the state stay the same? Will technology alter sovereignty in new ways that we have not imagined yet? There are no obvious answers.

Even without the answers we can see that constructivism and global-ization open up new space for us to imagine an operational just policing structure. Globalization suggests a fading of the state and an increas-ing connectedness. With this technology we begin to see what may be a reformulated international system that does not rely so much on the concept of sovereignty. The system may not be the cooperative cosmo-politan ideal of liberal internationalist thought, but rather something we have not yet fully imagined and grasped, one that entirely reframes the dilemma of competition and cooperation. When sovereignty is re-conceptualized—when the distinction between external order and war, and internal order and policing, loses force—we can begin to imagine how we can maintain security and order in new ways.[51]

Does this allow us to imagine a world where just community polic-ing is used to maintain order beyond the state? The future holds many possibilities. Let's imagine one possible scenario to get started.

Imagining Global Just Policing

In this scenario we start at the beginning of change, realizing that changing systems can take a very long time. In the beginning, a variety of governmental networks of police groups, as well non-governmental legal and human rights advocacy organizations and religious groups, form national and international networks to promote a new system to deal with security threats. It is a fairly rudimentary concept of just polic-ing. Over time, as more experts and local activists invest energy and time, the concept is developed further. As the concept is developed, broader coalitions of groups in the northern and southern hemisphere begin to work together. A few states and some international organizations, like the World Health Organization, start to support the idea as well. They provide some staffing and additional inputs into the concept. Their support is in part catalyzed by external pressure from advocacy groups, as well as a few individuals inside the bureaucracies who see this as a viable option to increasing security. A number of high-profile military generals also join the coalition to support the movement.

There are periods of time when it seems like there is a norm taking shape and moving forward. Then, there is counter-pressure and the various groups and actors feel like they are hitting a brick wall and going nowhere. However, these groups continue to work and build up new connections with other groups who support the effort. A number of significant multinational corporations join the movement when they decide that it means they will have more secure production lines and markets.

Gradually, the practice of how states deal with international security problems takes on characteristics that look more and more like community policing. The state system is changing and where military operations would have once been the standard intervening force, it makes more sense now to use regional and bolstered community police forces. Several governments decide to promote this norm in the international system and get it codified into law. They work to include it in U.N. meetings and Security Council resolutions. Advocates continue to support these efforts. The states do not disappear, but they realize that the distinction between external security threats and internal security threats are not two entirely different things. A large group of military professionals and police officers band together to develop models and protocols for international policing and demonstrate that it is possible as an intervention.

Finally, after five decades of hard work, an international convention is held to develop a treaty on just policing. States commit to reducing their militaries to levels that allow them to reinforce domestic policing and respond to additional domestic threats as required through the jointly defined just policing model. Wealthy states agree to provide additional support to poorer states. Protocols and accountability mechanisms are established. These states have populations that are highly interconnected: technologically, personally, socially, and economically. The tightness of these bonds means that there will be severe negative economic and political consequences domestically if a particular state leader wants to pull out. All states agree to sign the Just Policing Convention. They know they will encounter some challenges in maintaining it, but they are committed.

* * *

Bringing to bear the new technologies of globalization and constructivism, this imaginary scenario is not so far-fetched. We have seen new norms developed and solidified, such as in the landmines convention. We know that our financial transactions and physical movements are more profuse and integrated across the globe than ever. We can see the possibility of sovereignty fading and an opportunity for just policing in the new global arrangement that emerges. There are, however, a number of unanswered questions. For example, how would policing really work and what reformulations would be required? What are the comparative advantages of internal community police versus using more "neutral" outsiders sometimes to ease tensions? Will the connections and networks between peoples be enough to keep states accountable and prevent major abuses or aggression? I have laid out an initial conceptual basis for imagining just policing in the international system based on a shifting state system. With it, we can see at least part of the mechanics of the rocket that can get us to the moon. The next task is to test the machinery and ensure it will fly.

Notes

1. Mitty is a James Thurber character who endures a mundane existence by escaping into daydreams in the short story "The Secret Life of Walter Mitty."

2. Benedict R. O'G. Anderson, *Imagined Communities: Reflections on the Origin and Spread of Nationalism*, revised and extended ed. (London: Verso, 1991).

3. For the purposes of this paper security is defined as the assurance that a population is protected from foreseeable human-made threats to the survival and general well-being of the population. Threats might include nuclear proliferation, war (nuclear or conventional), shortages of food, water, shelter, and an absence of basic human rights.

4. Kenneth Neal Waltz, *Theory of International Politics*, Addison-Wesley Series in Political Science (Reading, MA: Addison-Wesley Pub. Co., 1979).

5. For example, in some cases a state will bring in the military to fight independence movements or insurgencies.

6. See the cases in Tor Tanke Holm and Espen Barth Eide, eds., *Peacebuilding and Police Reform*, The Cass Series on Peacekeeping, vol. 7 (London: Frank Cass, 2000) for examples of this type of police-related action.

7. The term "nation-state" was coined to capture the idea that a state was sovereign unit comprised of one nation or ethnic grouping and a legitimate internal political order. The view that nations and states must coincide continues to be debated. The term state is used in this article to de-link it from this automatic alignment.

8. See Schlabach, page 69 in the present book.

9. In a conversation Gerard Powers highlighted a related off-shoot of these three assumptions, which is the assumption that "outsiders" will be more prone to abuses than "insiders." This assumption is not explored in detail here but is included in the agenda for future research and is partly captured in the third assumption listed above, which is that insiders are for the rule of law and not corrupt or abusive.

10. Dougherty and Pfaltzgraff, for example, state: "The study of international relations consisted almost entirely of diplomatic history and international law, rather than of investigation into the processes of the international system." James E. Dougherty and Robert L. Pfaltzgraff, *Contending Theories of International Relations: A Comprehensive Survey* (New York: Longman, 1997), 11.

11. There are numerous arguments that the nature of the state is changing; for examples see Mathias Albert, David Jacobson, and Yosef Lapid, ed., *Identities, Borders, Orders: Rethinking International Relations Theory* (Minneapolis, MN: University of Minnesota Press, 2001); Michael J. Shapiro and Hayward R. Alker, ed., *Challenging Boundaries: Global Flows, Territorial Identities*, Borderlines, vol. 2 (Minneapolis, MN: University of Minnesota Press, 1996).

12. Examples of other bodies of thought are Marxism, Leninism or the English School (for an example see Hedley Bull, *The Anarchical Society: A Study of Order in World Politics* [New York: Columbia University Press, 1977]).

13. Some scholars make a distinction between liberalism and idealism, using idealism to refer to an approach that is driven by ideals and norms, and liberalism catching the rest. This distinction is not made here because there is a strong normative bias in the liberal institutional approach as well and the approaches contain similar overriding assumptions.

14. A liberal international understanding of decision-making with respect to North Korea leads to an entirely different set of actions. We would assume North Korea's actions would follow directly from the previous interaction with the United States. If the U.S. threatens escalation, North Korea threatens escalation, if the U.S. makes conciliatory gestures then North Korea makes conciliatory gestures—tit-for-tat cooperation. Liberal internationalists would pursue disarmament through a series of tit-for-tat cooperative steps with North Korea. For a more detailed examination see Leon V. Sigal, *Disarming Strangers: Nuclear Diplomacy with North Korea*, Princeton Studies in International History and Politics (Princeton, NJ: Princeton University Press, 1998).

15. For early works on world order see Richard A. Falk, "Toward a New World Order: Modest Methods and Drastic Visions," in *On the Creation of a Just World Order*, A Program of the World Order Models Project, ed. Saul H. Mendlovitz (New York: The Free Press, 1975), 211–23; Ernst B. Haas, *Beyond the Nation-State: Functionalism and International Organization* (Stanford, CA: Stanford University Press, 1964).

16. There are strains within liberal internationalism that agree with the idea that states are rational unitary actors, and others that disagree with this thesis and identify alternative forces that affect decision-making by politicians. For a snapshot of the debates between neorealism and neoliberalism, the 1980s derivatives of realism and liberal internationalism, see David A. Baldwin, *Neorealism and Neoliberalism: The Contemporary Debate*, New Directions in World Politics. (New York: Columbia University Press, 1993); Robert O. Keohane, *Neorealism and Its Critics* (New York: Columbia University Press, 1986); Kenneth A. Oye, ed., *Cooperation Under Anarchy* (Princeton, NJ: Princeton University Press, 1986).

17. See Bruce M. Russett and John R. Oneal, *Triangulating Peace: Democracy, Interdependence, and International Organizations* (New York: Norton, 2000).

18. Chapter I, Article 2.4 in the United Nations Charter states: "All Members shall refrain in their international relations from the threat or use of force against the territorial integrity or political independence of any state, or in any other manner inconsistent with the Purposes of the United Nations." (Accessed on-line at http://www.un.org/aboutun/charter/).

19. The various models of U.N. peacekeeping are presented and evaluated in John Hillen, *Blue Helmets: The Strategy of UN Military Operations* (Washington, DC: Brassey's, 2000).

20. For an overview of contemporary perspectives on international law and prospects for global order see Richard A. Falk, Lester Edwin J. Ruiz, and R.B.J. Walker, ed., *Reframing the International: Law, Culture, Politics* (New York: Routledge, 2002).

21. See Edward Hallett Carr, *The Twenty Years' Crisis, 1919–1939: An Introduction to the Study of International Relations* (New York: St. Martin's Press, 1940).

22. The argument the United States and the United Kingdom use to justify it revolves around a very expansive definition of "defense." For an overview of some of the basic arguments around the term defense see Christine D. Gray, *International Law and the Use of Force*, Foundations of Public International Law (Oxford: Oxford University Press, 2000).

23. Realism was solidified in the post-World War II work of Hans Joachim Morgenthau, *Politics Among Nations: The Struggle for Power and Peace*, rev. Kenneth W. Thompson (New York: McGraw-Hill, 1993).

24. Interestingly, this tenet is also enshrined in international law, an area that is typically seen as the bastion of liberal internationalism.

25. Kenneth Neal Waltz, *Man, the State, and War: A Theoretical Analysis* (New York: Columbia University Press, 1959); Waltz, *Theory of International Politics*.

26. If we analyze decision-making in the North Korea situation using realism we determine that North Korea wants to develop nuclear weapons in order to gain power in the region (and globally) to increase its ability to secure national interests. Utilizing this frame we then determine our actions within a "power game." That is, we engage in a series of interactions where we bring our power to bear and pressure the other country to do what we want them to do, e.g. not develop nuclear weapons. A version of this game is "chicken," where two states hurtle towards each other until one backs down.

27. See Robert Gilpin, *War and Change in World Politics* (Cambridge: Cambridge University Press, 1981).

28. Similarly, in the 1800s Great Britain dominated and largely policed the seas with its impressive naval fleet.

29. Cosmopolitans also argue that liberal democratic institutions can be extended to the global level. Communitarians counter argue that there is insufficient historical, cultural and customs internationally to hold a global democracy together. For a succinct summary of the debate see William Scheuerman, "Globalization," in *The Stanford Encyclopedia of Philosophy*, Fall 2002 ed., ed. Edward N. Zalta, Http://plato.stanford.edu/archives/fall2002/entries/globalization/.

30. See John Gerard Ruggie, "Continuity and Transformation in the World Polity: Toward a Neorealist Synthesis," in Keohane, *Neorealism and Its Critics*. See also post-cold war debates like that in Richard Ned Lebow and Thomas Risse-Kappen, ed., *International Relations: Theory and the End of the Cold War* (New York: Columbia University Press, 1995).

31. Interestingly, just policing maneuvers around one of the common logjams between realists and liberal internationalists, which is colliding worldviews on human nature (good or evil, competitive or cooperative, selfish or altruistic, and so on). Just policing instead suggests that most people are striving to be good members of their community but are not always so, and provides a mechanism to maintain order when they are not good community members.

32. An overview of these critiques can be found in Scott Burchill and Andrew Linklater, *Theories of International Relations*, with Richard Devetak, Matthew Paterson, and Jacqui True (New York: St. Martin's Press, 1996); Paul Kevin Wapner and Lester Edwin J. Ruiz, ed., *Principled World: Politics the Challenge of Normative International Relations* (Lanham, MD: Rowman & Littlefield, 2000).

33. For a closer and more critical look at variations in sovereignty over time see Stephen D. Krasner, *Sovereignty: Organized Hypocrisy* (Princeton, NJ: Princeton University Press, 1999); Stephen D. Krasner, ed., *Problematic Sovereignty: Contested Rules and Political Possibilities* (New York: Columbia University Press, 2001). For an interesting argument of the need to add considerations of hierarchy to international relations theory see David A. Lake, "The New Sovereignty in International Relations," *International Studies Review* 5, no. 3 (Fall 2003): 303–23.

34. Maryann K. Cusimano, ed., *Beyond Sovereignty: Issues for a Global Agenda* (Boston: Bedford/St. Martin's, 2000); Carla Koppell, *Preventing the Next Wave of Conflict: Under-*

standing Non-Traditional Threats to Global Security, with Anita Sharma (Washington, DC: Woodrow Wilson International Center for Scholars, 2003).

35. For a constructivist take on the landmines effort see Peter Howard and Reina Neufeldt, "Canada's Constructivist Foreign Policy: Building Norms for Peace," *Canadian Foreign Policy* 8, no. 1 (Fall 2000): 11–38.

36. They tease apart two general, interrelated types of norms: constitutive and regulative. Regulative norms are those that guide or regulate state behavior. An example would be a trade agreement between two states that is designed to limit the content and amount of goods moving across a border. Constitutive norms are those that guide how the system itself is set up or maintained. For example the norm that states are sovereign entities affects how states operate and interact. For additional discussion see Alexander Wendt, *Social Theory of International Politics,* Cambridge Studies in International Relations, vol. 67 (Cambridge, UK: Cambridge University Press, 1999).

37. Regime theory also focuses on cooperation around rules and norms in the international system but does not focus on the process of reciprocal construction as explicitly as constructivism. For a sampling of regime theory see Volker Rittberger, ed., *Regime Theory and International Relations,* with Peter Mayer (Oxford: Clarendon Press, 1993).

38. For example see Rey Koslowski and Friedrich V. Kratochwil, "Understanding Change in International Politics: The Soviet Empire's Demise and the International System," *International Organization* 48, no. 2 (Spring 1994): 215–48.

39. Martha Finnemore, *National Interests in International Society,* Cornell Studies in Political Economy. (Ithaca, NY: Cornell University Press, 1996).

40. Wendt, *Social Theory of International Politics.*

41. On North Korea see Peter Howard, "Why Not Invade North Korea? Threats, Language Games and U.S. Foreign Policy," *International Studies Quarterly* 48, no. 4 (Dec. 2004): 805–28.

42. For an exploration of the effect of globalization on connecting major cities across the globe see Saskia Sassen, *Cities in a World Economy,* Sociology for a New Century (Thousand Oaks, CA: Pine Forge Press, 2000).

43. The compression of space and time are examined closely in David Harvey, *The Condition of Postmodernity: An Enquiry Into the Origins of Cultural Change* (Oxford: Blackwell, 1989).

44. For example, Arjun Appadurai, an anthropologist, focuses on the cultural impact of globalization, identifies five "landscapes" of globalization: ethnoscapes, mediascapes, technoscapes, financescapes and ideoscapes in Arjun Appadurai, *Modernity at Large: Cultural Dimensions of Globalization,* Public Worlds, vol. 1 (Minneapolis, MN: University of Minnesota Press, 1996).

45. Examples of authors on globalization include Peter Dicken, *Global Shift: Reshaping the Global Economic Map in the 21st Century* (New York: Guilford Press, 2003); David Held, et al., *Global Transformations: Politics, Economics and Culture* (Stanford, CA: Stanford University Press, 1999); R. J. Holton, *Globalization and the Nation-State* (New York: St. Martin's Press, 1998); Fredric. Jameson and Masao Miyoshi, eds., *The Cultures of Globalization,* Post-Contemporary Interventions (Durham, NC: Duke University Press, 1998); James H. Mittelman, *The Globalization Syndrome: Transformation and Resistance* (Princeton, NJ: Princeton University Press, 2000); Leo Panitch, "Rethinking the Role of the State," in *Globalization: Critical Reflections,* ed. James H. Mittelman, International Political Economy Yearbook, vol. 9 (Boulder, Colo.: Lynne Rienner Publishers, 1996), 83–113; John Tomlinson, *Cultural Imperialism: A Critical Introduction* (London: Pinter Publishers, 1991).

46. Jan Aart Scholte, *Globalization: A Critical Introduction* (New York: Palgrave, 2000).

47. See Margaret E. Keck and Kathryn Sikkink, *Activists Beyond Borders: Advocacy Networks in International Politics* (Ithaca, NY: Cornell University Press, 1998).

48. An initial critique of territory in international relations appears in John Gerard Ruggie, "Territoriality and Beyond: Problematizing Modernity in International Relations," *International Organization* 47, no. 1 (Winter 1993): 139–74.

49. State actors have spent considerable time and energy defining elements of international law and basic parameters for the common good, such as the Universal Declaration of Human Rights or the Asian Human Rights Charter. We can debate whether or not this is really the common good, but a framework for thinking about it exists.

50. For musing on this subject see R.B.J. Walker, "After the Future: Enclosures, Connections, Politics," in *Reframing the International: Law, Culture, Politics*, eds. Richard A. Falk, Lester Edwin J. Ruiz, and R.B.J. Walker (New York: Routledge, 2002), 3–25.

51. A new area of debate has emerged in the U.S., where scholars such as Rogers Smith argue that the distinctions between external and internal security procedures have changed, but in ways that have eroded civil liberty protections for citizens. See Rogers Smith, "Civil Liberties in the Brave New World of Antiterrorism," *Radical History Review* 93 (Fall 2005): 170–85.

PART IV

Conclusions:
The Nearing Horizon

Chapter 9

The Doables:
Just Policing on the Ground

John Paul Lederach

I first bumped into the idea of the "doables" while in the Philippines in the late 1980s. A consortium of individuals, networks, and organizations who called themselves the Peace Advocates had proposed it. The ultimate goal of this loose coalition was to promote peace, an end to armed conflict through negotiations, and measures addressing the root injustices that perpetuated open conflicts. At the time there appeared to be small openings for ending the multiple armed conflicts in the country through negotiations, but those "peace processes" consistently faltered. The reason, it seems, was that they were so focused on a series of obstacles and intransigencies that they were incapable of delivering substantive responses to the immediate needs of those who were living at the edge of survival and suffering most. Thus, the Peace Advocates proposed an agenda of small steps that they believed to be available, accessible, and practical options of action, whether or not parties to the open war had or had not reached an agreement. These were the "doables."

This chapter will follow a roughly similar pathway in order to examine the "doables" of just policing. Guiding our inquiry will be three kinds of questions:

- What practices are readily *available* that connect to the framework of just policing? Here we are not looking for ideas, approaches, or actions that are new, and that some might therefore dismiss as marginal or unrealistic. We are not proposing a search for something wildly innovative that does not yet exist. Our inquiry suggests a search for what

175

already exists, what is within reach and practical. These are practices that could be implemented on a wider basis if placed in a context of legitimacy, support, and explicit investment.

- What is *accessible*? Initially inspired by the work of Marie Dugan,[1] I have described the principle of accessibility in other essays as an approach to social change that relies on alliances, connections, and action within identified points of "strategic" access.[2] The principle requires us to think not only about the purpose and content of the action, but about the *locus* of action that connects sets of people and activities who might not normally interact. Bringing them together creates a social space that increases the potential, impact, and outreach of any action beyond what might have initially been possible if they were not linked strategically. Accessibility pushes us to think about the "who" not just the "what" or content of an idea.

- What is *acceptable*? In the context of the present volume this question probably represents the greatest challenge. Bringing together a set of both pacifist and just war authors has tested the potential of "just policing" to serve as common ground between two traditions that have often preferred mutually exclusive expositions—or even mutual recriminations—around the theological correctness of their respective positions.

As he shares the task of concluding this volume, Drew Christiansen will explore the question of acceptability at greater length. Still, a chapter on the "doables" must begin to pose this question, at least, and a professional conciliator like myself must be inherently interested in whether two such distinct theological frames of reference can forge a common ground of action and strategy. My own framework is one of Anabaptist-Mennonite pacifism, but my professional work at conflict transformation, peacebuilding, and conciliation has often embedded me within contexts of deeply rooted and violent conflicts around the world.

As we proceed with each of these three inquiries, we will of course want to set our discussion of the "doables" in the context of what we have read so far, along with the challenges that are present in our contemporary world. If one lesson emerges most clearly from previous chapters, it is that just policing will require a shift in the guiding metaphor by which we think about war, peace, and social conflict.

The Metaphor Shift: From National to Human

The essays that come together in this volume represent a rich diversity. We have essays from authors who have explored just policing through very different professional lenses. Some are social theorists, while others are more given to a practitioner view; some write as theologians, while others work as ethicists. Second, we have people who in varying degrees find themselves spread across just war and pacifist traditions. They are fully capable of donning the lenses of the respective and quite diverse theological perspectives that give those traditions meaning and justification.

Reading through the preceding chapters challenged me with this question: What, if any, are the potential points of convergence or commonality that emerge across the breadth of this volume? What I discern here is a subtle but important shift of perspective. That shift, metaphoric in nature, builds from the image and understanding we have of *security*. Just policing, I propose, creates a point of convergence between the two traditions inasmuch as it presses upon us a metaphor shift from "national" to "human" security.

If we take seriously the work of George Lakoff and Mark Johnson on the role that metaphors play in social affairs[3] (and I think we should), metaphors are far more than poetic or rhetorical devices, and cannot be relegated to a marginal role in the construction of meaning. Metaphors are instrumental. In other words, they are central in how human beings frame what they experience *as* meaningful in the first place.[4] As Lakoff and Johnson put it in the provocative title of their book, we live by metaphors.

This volume, as much as anything else, engages a metaphor shift, the movement from one meaning structure to another. Just policing makes sense as a point of convergence between two very different theological traditions when understood as metaphor, a new framing of meaning. In the preceding chapters, I would argue, the discourse among the authors has provided a new point of reference for how we understand security, and how that concept affects faith, theology, and ethics in practical terms. In a single phrase: Just policing rises from the common acceptance that we are guided by the metaphor of *human* rather than *national* security. The implications are potentially far reaching.

First, some short definitions: Lakoff and Johnson suggest that metaphors create metaphoric concepts that are systematic in nature. In other words, metaphors create a conceptual system. As a metaphoric system, the assumption that "security is national" starts with the idea that safety and security result from defending the state and its borders against external enemies. "Our house" entails our national borders. "Our family" represents the symbolism of our entire national population. At the core of the metaphor is preparation and defense of the nation-state as an actor. Historically, defending the borders and family justified going out somewhere else in the world to stave off potential threats, such that "national defense" in many circumstances created actions abroad.[5]

Human security begins with a different metaphoric concept that reframes the *locus* of the meaning. "Security is human" places emphasis on the protection of individuals and local communities, and on how they are affected by whatever sources impact their safety, livelihood, and well-being. Those that use a broad definition of human security would argue that the greatest threats to security are a combination of internal and local violence, disease, hunger, and even natural disasters. Those with a narrower definition—one emerging more from the fields of conflict transformation and peacebuilding where the focus has been on human conflict and violence—place more emphasis on the protection of individuals. The Human Security Centre, a leader in this field, suggests precisely those words: "The traditional goal of 'national security' has been the defense of the *state* from external threats. The focus of human security, by contrast, is the protection of *individuals*."[6] As United Nations Secretary-General Kofi Annan has articulated it, human security is the "protection of communities and individuals from internal violence."[7] The switch in this metaphoric system recreates the location of security at local, community, family, and individual levels. The locus of national security is the state. The locus of human security is the community. This shift, I contend, is basic to how we understand and approach just policing.

Our Contemporary Context

As I was writing this chapter, the Human Security Centre's 2005 *Human Security Report*[8] splashed onto major newspapers. I say "splashed" because many papers reported the news with a rather sensational flair: Wars and violent conflicts are on the decline! On December 28, 2005, for example, *The Washington Post* ran a story under the headline, "Peace on Earth? Increasingly, Yes." *The Human Security Report 2005* had in fact pieced together some surprising observations by rigorous research done over more than a decade in cooperation with a series of international institutes located in Canada, the United States, Scandinavia, and Europe. Its research findings defy our prevailing, popularized myths about war, violence, and security. Among these findings were the following:[9]

- Genocides and politicides dropped by eighty percent between 1988 and 2001.
- The number of armed conflicts declined by forty percent since the early 1990s.
- Refugee populations dropped by forty-five percent in the same period.
- Military coups declined significantly in the last forty years.
- International terrorism was the only form of political violence that got worse, though even this trend is contested by different data findings.

These intriguing trends contrast with myths that often run in the opposite direction—a feeling that wars are more frequent, are getting more deadly, or that terrorism is the most important threat to human security. What accounts for these generally positive trends? The Human Security Centre notes a number of key factors.

At the broadest level, starting in the early 1990s, the end of the cold war made possible the decline of internal armed conflicts. In large part this happened because the United Nations, no longer caught in the paralyzing grip of the two-power bloc system, moved in far more vigorous, rigorous, and intensive ways to implement practices of conflict prevention and post-conflict peacebuilding. The report provides some impressive figures: a sixfold increase of preventative diplomacy missions; a fourfold increase of peacemaking efforts; a sevenfold increase of "friends" and "contact groups" who worked tirelessly; an elevenfold increase in economic sanctions placed against regimes; and a fourfold increase in peacekeeping. Accompanying these efforts was a far more direct investment of interest, energy, and commitment on the part of donor countries, multilateral cooperative organizations, and groups like the World Bank, regional banks, and literally thousands of non-governmental organizations or NGOs.

We can safely say that in the period between roughly 1990 and 2006 two things emerged that were unprecedented in earlier time periods. First, governments, bank bodies, and NGOs developed far more explicit, intentional, and sophisticated categories of action and implementation under the broad rubric of conflict transformation and peacebuilding than had ever existed before in their respective histories. These new ways of thinking and operating went hand in hand with existing forms of international relief and development. Second, this range of actors began to cooperate in ways that were not fully known in earlier time periods, thus creating a web of activity that went well beyond traditional notions of "international" state relations in reference to conflict, war, and post-war reconstruction. What has emerged from this cooperation and makes such a difference is what I would call a web of concerted action. As the report put it, "Not one of the peacebuilding and conflict prevention programs *on its own* had much of an impact on global security in this period. Taken together, however, their effect has been profound."[10]

It is when we contrast these research findings with dominant beliefs about security that we see a metaphoric shift underway. Recall that as a metaphoric concept, "national security" associates the needs of a population with the nation itself, as though the nation-state were a family to be protected. National security seeks to defend state borders and relies primarily—almost exclusively—on national defense and military systems. It fosters a patriotic "love of country" over against external threats generally and enemy nation-states especially. This conceptual system of meaning has so dominated discourse about security that it has stood nearly beyond question. The *Human Security Report* presses us to shift our assumptions and our guiding metaphors, however, when it summarizes a decade of research on international relations and national defense by noting that "secure states do not automatically mean secure peoples."[11]

As a point of convergence between just war and pacifist Christian traditions, just policing does more to extend this metaphoric shift than simply alter the meaning of the word *security*. More importantly, it shifts the very image, meaningfulness, and meaning structure of security by asking what guideposts and actions we ought to undertake and pursue in order to attain security. This shift conceptualizes security at the level of individuals and their communities on the one hand and the global community on the other. In the process we become more aware of a range of ways by which "policing" itself is understood. Tobias Winright has reviewed the literature on policing in Chapter 7 of this volume, highlighting and differentiating this range of approaches to policing. His work allows us to collate the metaphoric shift in our understanding of security with diverging assumptions about the nature of policing. Figures 1 and 2 may illustrate.

		"National" Security	"Human" Security
	Macro	Defense against external threats	Peacekeeping negotiated with local communities
		Main actor: a strong military	Transnational actors (U.N., N.G.O.s, multilateral)
Locus		International policing fronts for national self-interest	International policing protects human rights and fosters human security
	Micro	Militarization of policing Crime fighting as war The gun is primary symbol of security	Community policing Social peacekeeper Fabric of local relations is primary symbol of security

Figure 1: Metaphoric Concepts of Policing and Security

Figure 1 compares two ideas, the locus and the metaphors for security as they relate to policing. Locus refers to whether applications operate more at a micro level—perhaps more accurately, at a community level—or at a macro level of national and international systems. This is then cross-tabulated with our two metaphoric concepts of national and human security.

Within the national security approach, the metaphoric concept of "war" greatly influences local policing itself.[12] At both macro and micro levels security is sought as if it were a fight against an outside enemy; military-type strength and weaponry are considered central, and coercive enforcement becomes the key style of the approach.

On the side of human security, however, actors and approaches aim more at a model of social peacekeeping, embedded in developing local relationships where they envision policing as part of the community fabric. At the macro level this translates into a model of networking transnational actors in coordination with the local communities, where peacekeeping actually takes place. Ironically, international actors almost always conduct peacekeeping in someone else's local community. In today's world there are very few of what we might call border-based peacekeepers, in the sense that their role is to protect a national community from an external enemy. The human security model, therefore, must work much more carefully in negotiated ways with local communities.

The nature and impact of this metaphoric shift on our image of security may be much greater than initially appears, and will entail two important applications. First, in this shift, security moves away from an association of strength based on sanctioning armed power, toward an understanding of strength that is rooted in and rises from the context of holistic relationships. The nature of this shift, whether applied by community policing in a village or by international peacekeepers operating in another country, requires developing power *with* rather than power *over*.[13] Police and local communities must envision each other as belonging to the same shared local geography. Second, in this metaphoric shift, the *locus* of security increasingly is envisioned as local and networked-based rather than as national or interstate-national.

In a second way, Winright's review of policing models provides grist for our inquiry into practicalities. The models he identifies fall onto a typological spectrum, which in turn coincides with standard terms of debate concerning the use of coercive force. At one end are models whose "raison d'être" are defined by the use of coercive force; in other words, they are militaristic in nature. At the other end are models defined primarily by purposes of prevention and human security, relying much more on the instruments of nonviolence and persuasion than coercive or armed force. If we pushed our metaphoric concept to include the key symbols that guide it, we would see policing defined on one end by the centrality of the gun and on the other by the centrality of the word.

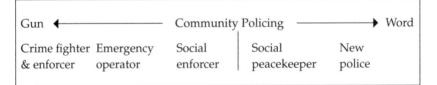

Figure 2: Spectrum of Policing Models

The spectrum in Figure 2 represents forms of power that run from "coercive" to "persuasive." Significant elements in our views on the meaningfulness of police and their source of power and identity stand out. On one end of the spectrum police identity develops through the metaphor of military armed and national defense, though police officers function in the very local communities from which they themselves come. On the other end of the spectrum a sense of embedded, family-like belonging in and with the community shapes police identity. This communal embeddedness shaped the early formation of police in Britain, as Winright describes them. From the color of clothes to a complete lack of weapons, great care was taken to make sure that these "New Police" would, in fact and function, not be confused or associated with the military.

On this spectrum, community policing emerges somewhere between the models of "social enforcer" and "social peacekeeper." As Winright describes these models, police do retain a coercive presence through the function of the gun, but do not rely on the gun as the defining component of their identity and work. Just policing in turn proposes a movement and space in which policing continues to shift away from a coercive, armed identity toward one that is embedded in local relationships and relies on nonviolent modalities for achieving the goals of local security.

Greater attention to what actually makes human beings secure (rather than nation-states) ought to disclose the "doables" and allow us to test them. What doables are available? What is accessible? What is acceptable?

What is Available?

A wide-ranging and comprehensive survey of the doables available for demonstrating and extending the potential of just policing could take us well beyond the reach of this chapter. Nevertheless, we may fruitfully explore several key "trends" that are most clearly relevant for the broader question of just policing. Three trends come to mind that offer concrete examples of practices that seem to fit closely with both community policing and its wider extension into just policing.

1. Community Policing in Post-Accord Settings

The first set of examples represents a trend toward community policing approaches in settings and countries that are emerging from long cycles of open violence and war. This is commonly known as the post-accord, or post-conflict, phase of peaceful transition. Observers typically speak of this as the "reconstruction" period following widespread violence, which comes in the immediate phase of implementing a signed peace agreement. Southern Africa, Northern Ireland, several countries in Central America, and the wider Balkans provide some of the most notable cases demonstrating the role of community policing in post-accord settings.[14] In all of these arenas policing represented a key challenge in the transformative process of moving from war to peace. In these settings the police function required more than simply providing local order. Policing had to face the challenge of reconstituting its core identity. I would describe this as a shift in identity that moved away from a model driven by the forces of war and toward a model driven by the forces of reconciliation.

One brief description is the case of Northern Ireland. In this context, the police force during the period of "the Troubles" was constituted and seen as one of the contending parties. The police force was overwhelmingly Protestant. They were engaged in an open war and heavily bunkered, literally and figuratively, in a mentality of military responses to sectarian violence. Policing was and still is a major component of the ongoing peace process. The police force has been working hard to transform itself toward a model of security that builds from and with the two main communities it must serve. This has come with intentional and explicit efforts to (1) diversify its staff, street patrols, and leadership; (2) develop greater capacity for respect and understanding of its diverse neighborhoods; (3) receive training in the areas of negotiation, cultural diversity, and community relations, often from experts in conflict resolution and mediation; and (4) re-constitute their role and the way that both communities perceive them. The goal is to be seen as being from and for the communities, rather than either partisans within the social and religious divide or an externally driven military presence. In all of these instances, the process of strategic transformation has moved local security toward the metaphor of community policing, from coercive to persuasive engagement. It is literally a transformative process that is creating a concrete example of just policing.

This example could be found over again in many settings of post-conflict transformation. I have personally seen similar efforts being undertaken in Central America, Somalia, and the Balkans.

2. Nonviolent Peacekeeping

A second trend emerges from increased efforts to develop and implement nonviolent approaches to peacekeeping, or to fulfill functions of peacekeeping nonviolently. This comes in numerous forms.

Forerunners here have arisen most often from within the pacifist-oriented community, in the efforts of Peace Brigades International, Witness for Peace, and Christian Peacemaker Teams. In these instances, NGOs, sometimes representing churches, have made concerted efforts for small but well-trained groups of people to provide active, international, and direct presence in zones of conflict. Their explicit and negotiated goals, among others, have been to accompany and protect vulnerable local populations, thereby solidifying zones of peace, increasing international awareness of human rights abuses, and contributing to local community reconciliation.

Building on this model but pursuing it with much greater connection to an international body and the legitimacy it offers have been the pilot efforts of Peaceforce. Peaceforce functions more explicitly as a nonviolent mobilized body for peacekeeping. Its approach, training, and deployment has developed in conjunction with the United Nations. Pilot initiatives are underway in Sri Lanka.

In fact, however, the military establishments in countries involved in peacekeeping missions are probably pursuing this model more actively than any other sector. The on-the-ground realities that confront military units on such missions require them to incorporate and build a much greater capacity for negotiation, peacebuilding, and conflict resolution, and to make these skills central rather than peripheral components of their work and objectives.[15] The skills and approaches that on-the-ground units find they need have not typically been part of their military preparedness. And yet many peacekeepers report that the key to their success lies in how well they relate to and work with communities. After all, absent such efforts and without such skills they are likely to see local conflicts explode into widely-spread violence.

One could argue that this increased interest in a new and quite different skill base actually constitutes a dynamic very close to our metaphor shift from national to human security. Though military units assigned to peacekeeping roles in potentially explosive situations represent external forces, more often than not the success of their peacekeeping efforts depends on how well they integrate, develop relationships with the community, and are able to engage in forms of conflict prevention and negotiation. Those efforts require adept skills of community building, language, and cultural intelligence. In many aspects, this too represents a trend toward a form of just policing as opposed to more traditional forms of military defense.

3. Community Peace Zones

Finally, a third trend emerges from intriguing examples of how local communities have directly engaged themselves in order to assure their own security, not as local militias but as active nonviolent negotiators with armed groups. Perhaps we can capture the essence of this phenomenon with the label of "building peace zones."

Some rather extraordinary examples exist in countries like Colombia, the Philippines, Nepal, and the Horn of Africa.[16] Communities that have been traversed and battered by the hard realities of violence, warlordism, armed groups, and militias have engaged nonviolently in actions to assure that certain areas—from whole communities to markets and schools—are respected as places where weapons and fighting will not be tolerated. The model is literally a form of human security in that communities are moving to protect themselves in their most intimate localities from violent atrocities.

A most intriguing example of this would be the Wajir story in Northeast Kenya. Initial efforts by a handful of women to create a safe market eventually translated into a wide community and regional process. That process included the brokering of ceasefires, the establishment of verification commissions, a program of disarmament, a newly transformed way of working with police, and the establishment of a permanent committee that works with local and national leaders on issues of security.[17]

In Wajir, the local community became the primary actor pursuing very concrete improvements in the ways their community was treated. These efforts strengthened the voice of those people most affected by the violence, and in substantial ways provided the moral fabric and ground rules of conduct. Ironically, in settings where there is a vacuum in the protection that state and local authorities typically provide, this activism fulfills many of the functions of policing.

What is Accessible?

The above trends demonstrate not only that "just policing" types of approaches and activities exist, but that they are growing and increasing in significant ways, even in more mainstream applications. Our inquiry about "doables" now turns to the question of accessibility. In raising the question of accessibility we mean to ask whether the ideas in this book and the examples in this chapter are simply the dreams of a few, somewhat off-the-wall idealists, or whether they would be scalable if the right set of people, organizations, and institutions would engage them more strategically and align their work and goals accordingly.

To address this question let us again recall the primary findings of *The Human Security Report 2005*. The major research finding of the Human Security Centre was not only that armed conflicts were on the decline, but that the primary reason for this was the concerted efforts of the U.N., donor governments, banking bodies, and NGOs. The key: Success was not due to any one group or effort, but to the sum total of the accumulated impact of cooperative efforts. This speaks directly to our inquiry into accessibility.

Accessibility as a principle poses questions not only about the content or approach to an idea; most importantly it addresses the "who" of the process. It seeks what I have sometimes called the "strategic who."[18] The strategic who is an approach to social change that asks, *Who, if they were to come together toward a common goal, would have an impact well beyond their numbers*? In this instance, it seems to me that our inquiry to a large degree is already answered: Human security increases in effectiveness *whenever* sets of people align their goals and efforts.

Community policing, for example, suggests that the effectiveness of efforts to provide safety and respond to a community does not lie with the size or amount of coercive force—primarily in the form of weapons—but rather in the fabric of relationships, cooperation, capacity for presence, prevention, and pro-active engagement from and with the community. It is a strategy that must embed itself and rise from relationship rather than impose itself externally. Applied to international settings, those involved in military peacekeeping operations seem to reach the same conclusion time and again. Overwhelming military strength may be able to physically "clear and clean" an area as a short-term strategy, though in places like Iraq there is significant debate about the capacity to accomplish even this. (Doubts have consistently arisen from a lack of security along the highway from Baghdad to the airport, or in any one of a number of local communities across Iraq.) In any case, overwhelming military campaigns have no capacity to assure a longer-term transformation of the context and people who need to engage in constructive change processes in their own communities.

Effective community policing and, I would argue, its parallel in international settings, relies more on the quality of relationships and the capacity to build from and with local populations. Such a task has far more to do with the creativity needed to address patterns of conflict and to forge strong preventative capacity from that base than it does the size or amount of weaponry. The key then is the degree to which coalitions of key actors can move together toward this common goal, human security.

In every example I have witnessed, the overall effectiveness of peacebuilding efforts came through cooperative and coordinated processes of transformation that included existing formal security institutions, local populations, and supporting governments, along with multilateral organizations and NGOs. This suggests that the ideas and approaches we need to implement and extend just policing models already exist but will need a far deeper understanding. Above all we must recognize that the strategy is not one that any single organization can conduct—whether a police department or a peacekeeping unit—but rather is only effective when a wide range of sectors in a locale or region pursue and achieve a *robust interdependence.*

So one conclusion we reach is that just policing is indeed doable because there are clear examples in which it has been carried out effectively. The other conclusion, in reference to accessibility is simply this observation: It is doable to the degree that a wider range of groups, organizations, and governments are willing to work with a far greater degree of interdependence, and are willing to include the local community receiving their good works, allowing it ample voice and participation.

What is Acceptable?

Our inquiry into acceptability enters the discourse between just war and pacifist traditions. In essence it poses this question: Would just policing, when seen from the perspective of examples of the "doables," be a point of convergence for both traditions?

Here the spectrum that Figure 2 lays out may offer some help. To look for a point of convergence obviously requires that we suspend any stubborn focus on remaining divergences, but also requires that we look for something other than agreement pure and simple. Rather, to look for convergence is to ask where practical and concrete examples are moving in the same direction and revealing a commonality of trends. I believe we find significant and substantial convergence between the two traditions when we identify trends such as the following in our concrete examples and practices:

- We find a shift toward human security as the guidepost, rather than national security. This is particularly true, I believe, because both traditions strongly endorse an ethos and ethic of human dignity. Almost beyond doubt, this commitment to human dignity is far more specific and present in the notion of human security than national security.
- We find a trend toward increasing institutional, local, and international capacity to assure prevention, accountability, and security through nonviolent means, particularly where nonviolent practices show themselves to be more effective and prudent at local levels.

- We find a move to include and build security with and for the populations most affected by a given situation. In other words, strategies of security increasingly include and respect those in the locality of actual implementation. This approach is consistent with both the Catholic principle of subsidiarity and the Mennonite practice of community discernment, to continue citing these two representative traditions.
- We find practices of interdependence that encourage a much wider and more effective cooperation between groups, organizations, and local communities. This kind of cooperative interdependence adheres closely to key premises that both traditions share about the nature of a good society, particularly when the focus of security is embedded in the fabric of real life communities and is assured by the quality of relationship, not the presence of firepower.

The most significant point of divergence still remains at the point where Christians in the two traditions debate whether just policing must require exclusively nonviolent methods, whether policing should or could disarm itself of weapons. Here the just war and pacifist traditions take divergent pathways.

On the one hand, the just war tradition would likely argue that self-preservation and the safety of innocent people through the use of coercion and armed force remains justifiable in extreme circumstances. Approached from this direction any emerging model of just policing would likely be something akin to local police bearing guns that they only rarely use, and then only as an ultimate and last point of response. Applied to international peacekeeping such a model would require far greater attention to the full range of alternatives and approaches available from the perspective of nonviolent strategy, but would retain the gun and coercion as background options available for last resort.

On the other hand, the pacifist tradition would likely insist that God has created human life and only God can take it away. Weapons and lethal force, therefore, are not admissible alternatives. This would argue for exclusively nonviolent means even if societies were fully to embrace just policing. One model here might be what has happened on numerous Mennonite university campuses that contract security services with groups that have the appearance of a quasi-police force but do not carry weapons.

Conclusion

To conclude we must return for a brief moment to the impact of practical examples themselves, which in the end are the concern of this chapter. Just policing creates a rich constructive exchange and learning for both just war and pacifist traditions. But it begins in real life situations that evolve and pose questions to people seeking to live out those traditions. As they then seek answers, they learn each other's lessons and notice trends that actually improve human security.

It has been my experience that our debates and disagreements often take place at too great a remove from the real life situations that many communities face around the world. Most just war and pacifist debates rage over those approaches to security that are based exclusively on the national security model of armed defense and its justified preparation, use, and deployment. But this diverts our attention away from on-the-ground realities and skews our debates. As the *Human Security Report 2005* states so well, "a new approach to security is needed because the analytical frameworks that have traditionally explained wars between states—and prescribed policies to prevent them—are largely irrelevant to violent conflicts *within* states. The latter now make up more than 95% of armed conflicts."[19]

Just policing, if it is to have relevance, must resituate the debate closer to affected communities and to the ongoing lessons we learn there about what really creates human security. The closer we come to that level, which is the gift of the "doables," the less distance we find between just war and pacifism. For both point toward a common concern: assuring the well-being of people and communities.

Notes

1. Marie Dugan, "A Nested Theory of Conflict," *A Leadership Journal: Women in Leadership, Sharing the Vision.* 1, no. 1 (July 1996): 9–19.

2. John Paul Lederach, *Building Peace: Sustainable Reconciliation in Divided Societies* (Washington, DC: United States Institute of Peace Press, 1997), 46–51; John Paul Lederach, *The Moral Imagination: The Art and Soul of Building Peace* (New York: Oxford University Press, 2005), 75–100.

3. George Lakoff and Mark Johnson, *Metaphors We Live By,* rev. ed. (Chicago: University of Chicago Press, 2003).

4. Ibid., ix.

5. Lakoff in particular has pursued the power metaphor as framing issues and meaning in reference to war and peace. Especially in the period following September 11, 2001, he has

written a series of articles on the topics of the Gulf Wars, terrorism, and political discourse in the United States. See George Lakoff, "Metaphor and War: The Metaphor System Used to Justify War in the Gulf," *Viet Nam Generation Journal* 3, no. 3 (November 1991), Http://www3.iath.virginia.edu/sixties/HTML_docs/Texts/Scholarly/Lakoff_Gulf_Metaphor_1.html; "Metaphors of Terror," in *The Days After: Essays Written in the Aftermath of September 11, 2001*, online collection (Chicago: University of Chicago Press, 2001), Http://www.press.uchicago.edu/News/daysafter.html; "Metaphor and War, Again," *AlterNet*, 18 March 2003, Http://www.alternet.org/story/15414/.

6. Human Security Centre, *Human Security Report 2005: War and Peace in the 21st Century* (New York: Oxford University Press, 2006), viii.

7. Ibid.

8. Ibid.

9. Ibid., 1.

10. Ibid., 9.

11. Ibid., viii.

12. See pages 134–38 in Tobias Winright's chapter, elsewhere in this volume.

13. Kenneth E. Boulding, *Three Faces of Power* (Newbury Park, CA: Sage Publications, 1990).

14. Charles Call and William Stanley, "Military and Police Reform After Civil Wars," in *Contemporary Peacemaking: Conflict, Violence and Peace Processes*, eds. John Darby and Roger MacGinty (New York: Palgrave Macmillan, 2003); Tor Tanke Holm and Espen Barth Eide, eds., *Peacebuilding and Police Reform*, Cass Series on Peacekeeping, no. 7 (Portland, OR: Frank Cass, 2000).

15. Recent planning documents from both the Pentagon and the State Department outline these concerns and goals. See for example the draft emerging in the State Department calling for the development of new approaches to peacekeeping and transformative diplomacy, *US Government Draft Planning Framework for Reconstruction, Stabilization, and Conflict Transformation*, United States Joint Forces Command J7 Pamphlet, Version 1.0 (Washington, DC: US Department of State, 2005), Http://www.dtic.mil/doctrine/training/crs_pam051205.pdf.

16. See Lederach, *Moral Imagination*; Steven Rood, *Forging Sustainable Peace in Mindanao: The Role of Civil Society*, Policy Studies, no. 17 (Washington, DC: East-West Center Washington, 2005).

17. Dekha Ibrahim and Jan Jenner, "Breaking the Cycle of Violence in Waji," in *Transforming Violence: Linking Local and Global Peacemaking*, eds. Robert Herr and Judy Zimmerman Herr (Scottdale, PA: Herald Press, 1998); Lederach, *Moral Imagination*, 10–13.

18. Cf. Lederach, *Moral Imagination*, 91–94. Chapters 8–10 of this book focus on the "who" of peacebuilding throughout.

19. *Human Security Report 2005*, 9.

Chapter 10

The Wider Horizon: Peacemaking, the Use of Force, and the Communion of Charisms

Drew Christiansen, S.J.

My friend Gerhard Beestermoeller was completing a lecture at Harvard's Center for the Study of World Religions on the future of just war in this age of terrorism. As he did so, Ralph Potter, emeritus professor of social ethics, turned and confided to me: just war should still be considered in the framework of Ernst Troeltsch's *Social Teachings of the Christian Churches*.[1] The German theologian and historian first published his massive survey in the early 1920s, and it remains as controversial as it is influential. Mennonites, for example, have chafed at the way Troeltsch's typology pigeonholes them, their ethic, and their stance toward culture.[2] But Potter was making another point, and an apt one.

Drawing on key passages in Thomas Aquinas and Immanuel Kant, Dr. Beestermoeller was making the sort of principle-laden, text-centered argument that is standard fare among philosophers and ethicists.[3] What we too often forget, Potter was suggesting, is that in Aquinas's Medieval setting, church thinking about war and peace was a pastoral task. And Aquinas represents but one example. As a pastoral task, Christian deliberation over war and peace has taken shape within the church's larger self-understanding or ecclesiology, within a larger set of doctrines especially about the church's relation to the world, in response to pastoral concerns for the moral formation and discipline of church members, and—in the case of mainline churches—in hope of offering moral guidance to public affairs. It is, therefore, much more than "a calculus," as

Father Bryan Hehir prefers to describe it, and more than a "decision-tool" for the use of force, as the late Paul Ramsey called it. The Christian approach to conflict (just war, nonviolence, peacebuilding, nonresistance, etc.) is a church-defining issue. And for that reason, at least since the Reformation, it has been a church-dividing issue, particularly splitting the magisterial churches from the Anabaptist churches.

In recent years, however, peacemaking has become a focus in explorations of church unity. In 2004 it became the very basis for a landmark report from the International Dialogue between Catholics and Mennonites, though key differences remain.[4] Gerald Schlabach's proposal is that just policing has the potential to overcome many remaining divisions between Catholics and Mennonites on nonviolence and the limited use of force.[5] If both churches, he believes, can move to accept policing rather than war as a possible model for keeping the peace (enforcing order in times of conflict), then the opportunity will increase for a common peace witness by these and other Christian communities.

The Ecclesial Horizon

Schlabach's proposal certainly implies changes in social norms, proscribing war *per se* as a sanctioned activity at least for Christians, while limiting and creating accountability for most other uses of force, but its implications apply first and foremost to the churches themselves. That is why he spends so much space, for example, explaining the pastoral implications of the switch from just war to just policing, particularly for the Catholic Church, which has been the principal carrier of the just war doctrine in Western culture.[6] Movement toward the just policing model is possible today because of changes in the life of both churches.

Nonviolence, Just War, and the Churches

In the course of the twentieth century, and especially since World War II, both churches have undergone dramatic changes. This may be more evident in the post-Vatican II Catholic Church than among Mennonites, thanks to the global impact of the Council, as well as the public role of recent popes and bishops' conferences like the United States Conference of Catholic Bishops.[7] As a participant in the International Mennonite-Catholic Dialogue, however, I became aware of gradual shifts in Mennonite life and thinking. These shifts distinguish today's Mennonites, at least in North America, from their progenitors in the Reformation. Their

approach to the Christian life also represents a departure from the re-
newed Anabaptist Vision popularized by Harold Bender in the mid-
twentieth century. Beginning with John Howard Yoder's challenge to
Bender's "Anabaptist Vision," there has been no lack of internal critique
of a supposedly primordial Mennonite ideal.[8] At the same time, other
Mennonite theologians have been exploring alternative ways to conceive
of the church's presence and witness in the world.[9]

In short, any shift along the Nonviolence/Just-War continuum from
either side depends on a background of lived engagements and evolving formulations of belief that provide a structure of plausibility for
accepting just policing as a church-uniting concept of political order. It
is that ecclesial and theological background that constitutes "the wider
horizon" of the just policing proposal. That wider horizon is the life of
the churches in the twenty-first century, particularly when we understand this life as the relation of the church community to the world and
the growing role of both churches in peacemaking.

Historic Disunity and Future Unity

The broader context for just policing in theology and church life brings
us, as Professor Potter suggested, to Ernst Troeltsch's classic formulation of religious types. In *The Social Teaching of the Christian Churches*,
Troeltsch distinguished three characteristic types of Christian religious
life: "church," "sect," and "mystic." While the terminology had roots in
church history, going back to the Book of Acts (24:5), Troeltsch, with his
interest in social teaching, identified a set of contrasting attitudes that
distinguish each type. One of the key axes on which Troeltsch contrasted
the historic types of religious communities was their attitude toward the
world. *Ad extra*, the "church" type took responsibility for the world; *ad
intra* it provided the means of salvation for people of very different social
backgrounds. By contrast, the "sect" held itself apart from the world;
it refused to take responsibility for public affairs. Internally, the "sect"
was a closed community, set apart from the world, and identified by its
distinctive, holy way of life. The "mystic," like today's New Ager, was
exclusively concerned with his or her own spiritual development; with
some exceptions, mystics had little to say to society.

The Catholic Church in its patristic and medieval forms, of course,
stands as the model for the "church" type, but Troeltsch applied the type
equally to what John Howard Yoder (following George H. Williams)
would later call "the magisterial Reformation"—that is the hierarchical

Lutheran, Calvinist, and Anglican churches.[10] By contrast, the Donatists are a classic example of the "sect" type; the fourth- and fifth-century North African Christians broke with Rome over the purity of their ministers and their refusal to collaborate with the imperial authorities. In the Reformation of the sixteenth century, the Anabaptists—including Mennonites—were examples of the "sect" type.

The earliest use of the word "sect" is found in the Latin Vulgate for Acts 24:5. "We have found this man . . . a ringleader of the sect of the Nazarenes (*secta Nazaraeorum*; in Greek, *Nazōraōn aireseōs*). The Code of Justinian likewise links sects and heresies. So, the ancient sources seem to favor the notion of sect as a breakaway or heretical group (Greek: *aireseōs*) or religious faction. Hence the pejorative weight of the term. While Troeltsch intended the types to be analytic, the term "sect" continued to carry the pejorative connotation of break-away groups that the imperial Roman church had established with its use of the term.

From the point of view of the groups in question, whether the Donatists or the Mennonites, the term was theologically problematic. After all, they regarded themselves, not the established church, as the bearers of the authentic tradition of the church that the official institution had corrupted. At issue was what constituted the true church. Whereas Catholics regard apostolic succession as the unbroken line of episcopal ordination, Mennonites use the term to refer to continuity of the apostolic way of life.

While the pejorative sense may still be found in some Catholic circles, official Catholicism avoids the term "sect." Today Catholics refer instead to "churches" and to "ecclesial communities;" the general practice of the Pontifical Council for Promoting Christian Unity is to refer to Christian communities with the term the communities themselves use. Technically, the Catholic practice is to speak of communities with apostolic (or episcopal) succession as "churches" and others as "ecclesial communities." The Pontifical Council, however, undertakes formal dialogues only with those communities it regards as churches.

The Plausibility of Just Policing

On many counts neither church fits its specified Troeltschian type any longer, and the narrowing of differences in recent decades makes theological movement toward agreement on just policing plausible for both communities. Still, key descriptors of the church-sect typology continue to be relevant for mapping both the distance that the two communities have traveled since the sixteenth century and that which remains for them to cover if just policing is to be accepted as a common teaching (and discipline). These key descriptors are: (1) ecclesiology, that is, the self-understanding of the church; (2) attitudes of the church to the world (politics, society, and culture); (3) conceptions of holiness; and (4) the range of communion or recognized membership in the church.

These terms still provide the deep background behind the just war/nonviolence/pacifism divide that underlies the just war/just policing alternatives. By "deep background" I mean the underlying beliefs that result in a church affirming a specific stance toward the legitimacy or illegitimacy of official use of force. (Thus, for example, traditionally Catholic acceptance of natural law resulted in accepting just-war thinking, whereas Mennonite emphasis on the Sermon on the Mount as the New Law led to its rejection.) By reviewing shifts in these key dimensions of church life, therefore, we should be better prepared to assess the possibility of convergence by Mennonites, Catholics, and others around the idea of just policing. For purposes of brevity, I will focus principally on church-world relations.

Both churches will face challenges simply to agree on an official concord, to say nothing of achieving full communion. There are particular pastoral hurdles Catholics must undertake to make just policing a point of agreement. Likewise, descriptors such as "church," "world," "holiness," and "communion" point to ecclesiological and theological issues that Mennonites must address before just policing can become a matter of concord between the two churches. But that is what it means for just policing to be a doctrinal and pastoral issue, rather than a mere academic exercise or a simple case of applied ethics on which moral theologians and theological ethicists may agree or not. All the elements are intertwined, and a shift in one will result in a shift for all. Still, my argument is that because of developments which have already taken place in both communities, further changes in the direction of just policing will not constitute infidelity to the gospel. Nor will ecumenical support by Catholics and Mennonites for a social-pastoral policy favoring just policing face an insuperable obstacle.

Just Policing: The Domestic Analogy

How realistic is it, in a political sense, to think of the control of international conflict as *policing* rather than *war*? Among Catholics the criticism I have heard leveled most often at Schlabach's just policing proposal is that to replace war with policing is basically confused. Joseph Capizzi of the Catholic University of America, in a response to Schlabach's initial essay on just policing, claims that he confuses genus and species.[11] J. Bryan Hehir, in an oral response to a presentation I once made on the combination of nonviolence and just war in current Catholic teaching, likewise insisted that the inclusion of both concepts in church teaching is logically "incoherent."[12]

Most, however, would not see the problem with just policing as a logical problem but rather as a practical one, namely, the disparity in authority and organization between the nation-state and international society. That is, the nation-state has the sovereign authority and organizational capacity needed to enforce the peace domestically, and to defend its people and interests from external threat by the use of force. In contrast, the international community, whether in the form of the United Nations or regional alliances, is dependent on the good will and resources of one or more nation-states to defend the common good, as the mounting of recent humanitarian interventions illustrates.[13] The inability of the U.N. Security Council to respond and the slowness of NATO to involve itself in stopping ethnic cleansing in Bosnia, as well as the U.N.'s failure so far to stop the killing in the Darfur region of Sudan, are clear examples of such weakness in the international community.

Walzer on the Domestic Analogy

While many theorists and analysts are reluctant to recognize the growth in potential for the exercise of international authority, not everyone is immune to the relevance of the analogy between war and policing. In his book *Just and Unjust Wars*, Michael Walzer makes considerable use of "the domestic analogy," that is, the similarity and dissimilarity between the state and the world community, in order to articulate his version of the just war tradition. Walzer writes: "When the analogy is made explicit, as it often is among lawyers, the world of states takes on the shape of a political society the character of which is entirely accessible through such notions as crime and punishment, self-defense, law enforcement, and so on."[14] The international community is like "a domestic society," he continues, "in that men and women live at peace within it (sometimes determining the conditions of their own existence, negotiating and bargaining with their neighbors). It is unlike domestic society in that every conflict threatens the structure as a whole with collapse . . . because there is no policeman."[15] For Walzer, as for most international theorists, the lack of authority (the policeman), and of organization (courts, prisons, etc.) results in a self-help world in which armed resistance and cooperation in resistance against aggression are a necessity. Thus, the warrant for war as an instrument of national self-defense emerges from the lack of effective organization by the international community.

Just Policing: An Emerging Reality

The world, however, is changing. Since Walzer first wrote, and despite adverse developments in the war on terror after 9/11, the international community itself has evolved. Humanitarian intervention, surely an extension of the domestic policing model and a contested idea only a decade ago, has become in some measure an accepted phenomenon. While utilized spottily, it is increasing in efficacy. In the Balkans the techniques of policing have evolved, and even in Congo a weak U.N. force has recently acted more aggressively, departing from the traditional peacekeeping or monitoring model to take up a stronger enforcement mode. In East Timor, the Australians undertook, with a U.N. mandate, a humanitarian intervention outside the traditional Western zone of interest.

Militaries themselves have changed as well, despite the aberrations of the war in Iraq and the war on terror. "Constabulary force" models of the military received growing attention in the 1980s, thus relating military strategy directly to the policing paradigm; meanwhile, the development of an array of non-lethal weapons suggested the possibility of a yet-untried shift to constabulary style deployments.[16] The evolution of the military "mission" during the Clinton administration—with policing activities in Haiti, Bosnia, and Kosovo, and logistical support for the Australian intervention in East Timor—approximated the constabulary model, even though some leaders, like Colin Powell, continued to argue for exclusive adherence to the warrior model.[17] Even Donald Rumsfeld's Defense Department, following the insurgency in Iraq, now recognizes the need for a new, multi-functional military, less arrayed for all-out war, and more prepared for police-like duties. At the same time, following the nonviolent revolutions in the Philippines and Eastern Europe in the 1980s, recent years have seen a new wave of nonviolent revolutions in Bolivia, Georgia, Ukraine, and Lebanon, showing the increasing salience of active nonviolence and a decreased need for the deployment of outright force.

Admittedly, as Walzer wrote of international community, "the whole thing [is] shaky because it lacks the rivets of authority," but the jerry-rigging has gotten a lot better. The international criminal court is up and running, even if the United States is not a participant. International tribunals in the Hague and Arusha try and convict war criminals, and the convicts are imprisoned. We can also discern in official proposals for U.N. reform the shape of further evolution in authority and organization towards a stronger, more authoritative international system. In addition, all sorts of social-political innovations have been put into practice that move the world away from war and toward nonviolent resolution of conflict: truth and reconciliation commissions, conflict resolution/transformation, peacemaker teams, human rights monitors, public acts of forgiveness, and so on.[18] There is, no doubt, a considerable distance to go, but the similarities between domestic society and the international order are stronger than thirty years ago. The U.N. reform attempts to formalize these gains and build upon them. Even as the Iraq war seemed to revive (ultra)realist understandings of international order, many of these other developments continued to unfold of their own momentum. If anything, the failures of the war-fighting strategy in Iraq have reinforced the case for more subtle, police-like models of enforcement.

Encountering the Spirit in the World

Just policing, therefore, is more thinkable and politically feasible today than during the cold war. Movement on the part of the churches can reinforce and, one would hope, improve the secular trends promoting the shift from warfare to international policing. This was the hope of the U.S. Catholic bishops in their 1993 pastoral statement, *The Harvest of Justice Is Sown in Peace*. After noting that the presupposition of their teaching on peace and war was that "In situations of conflict, [Christians'] constant commitment ought to be, as far as possible, to strive for justice through nonviolent means," the bishops went on to speak of civic obligations to build up nonviolent alternatives to armed conflict in public institutions.[19] They wrote:

> National leaders bear a moral obligation to see that nonviolent alternatives are seriously considered for dealing with conflicts. New styles of preventative diplomacy and conflict resolution ought to be explored, tried, improved and supported. As a nation we should promote research, education and training in nonviolent means of resisting evil.[20]

The bishops, of course, endorse something less than an absolute moral obligation. The duty of nonviolence is *prima facie*. As such, it is conditioned by the requirement that political and social actors resort to it repeatedly, even if not indefinitely. The bishops thus continue to legitimate recourse to just war as an exceptional measure, when those repeated attempts at nonviolent conflict resolution fail. For Mennonites and for many Catholic peace activists, this lack of moral rigor counts as a serious flaw in the teaching. Nonetheless, the stated duties are strong ones, and they are public obligations, binding on both political leaders and citizens.[21] For our purposes, however, the teaching on nonviolence in *The Harvest of Justice* illustrates how the churches can respond in a supportive way to peacemaking initiatives by secular social movements and para-church groups.

Of course, the motives for Catholic-Mennonite agreement on just policing are not solely or primarily political. They are also religious, with a view toward the integrity of their gospel witness and the unity of Christ's church. Still, secular progress toward nonviolent resolution of conflict, which includes just policing, is desirable for theological reasons as well. Catholic social teaching and the Second Vatican Council's understanding of the relationship between church and world give strong support to service of the world through peacemaking.[22] It also accords with the practice of active nonviolence by many Mennonites as well as currents of Mennonite theology that favor church-world engagement. Just as the war in Iraq provoked prophetic condemnation on the part of most churches, so the positive evolution of secular attitudes toward conflict ought to elicit greater willingness to encourage the spread of such secular developments.[23] The witness of Christian peacemaking, whether through grassroots work in zones of conflict or in advocacy with political institutions, will illuminate more fully the potential for nonviolent resolution of conflict in the world community.[24]

A more fundamental reason for supporting peace movements outside the church is the New Testament witness itself. "*Spiritus spirat ubi vult,*" "the Spirit blows where it wills," (John 3:8). God's freedom to effect his universal salvific will repeatedly challenges the disciples and even Jesus himself. Acknowledging the Spirit's work in the world can be a stumbling block for the churches as it was for the disciples. The perennial temptation of devoted church members is to believe that God works only in the church and to dismiss or challenge divine action beyond the recognizable boundaries of the community. Even in the New Testament, however, divine action takes place outside the formal boundaries of Israel, the prototype of the church. It takes place among the Samaritans, in the preaching of people other than the disciples, and in the outpouring of the Spirit on the Gentiles. Why should we too not be challenged by the Spirit's manifestation outside the church community? As we explore, in the words of the international dialogue report, how to be peacemakers together, both the Mennonite Church and the Catholic Church need to develop a more thoroughgoing understanding of God's action outside the church proper, along with the tools of discernment to guide them in responding to initiatives outside the church. Witness to peace is an ecumenical task; it is also a human one in which God is drawing together the one human family. When we focus too narrowly on the church as the locus of God's actions and our own integrity as the heart of our witness, we may miss the opportunity to share fully in God's unfolding plan for the one human family.[25]

The Two Churches Today: Rethinking Troeltsch

Far from being an ethical and policy initiative, then, just policing is the fruit of converging lines of development in the world and in the churches. These convergences strengthen the case for just policing. Underlying many of them are shifts in the churches' self-understandings or ecclesiology. Convergences around their understanding of church, and particularly the role the church plays in the world, I propose, make possible greater agreement between Catholics, Mennonites, and others on peacemaking. This may come to include the exceptional use of force as a part of just policing.

1. *Sacrament of Unity.* From the late sixteenth century until the Second Vatican Council (1963–5), the dominant theology of the church in Roman Catholicism was that of a *societas perfecta*, or complete society.[26] As formulated by the Jesuit Robert Bellarmine (1542–1621), the church paralleled political society in being a fully functioning institution, fitted with the authority, the organization, and the means to attain its end, the salvation of the faithful. Bellarmine, the premier Catholic political theorist of the time, adapted his model from that of political societies in the early modern period. As Avery Dulles has noted, this model of the church stressed the church's visible structure, especially the rights and powers of its officers.[27] The model conceived of the church along institutional lines, in terms of lines of authority, organizational structure, role responsibilities, and legal norms. Despite overemphasis on the church's institutional reality, Dulles has noted, this model was rarely advocated "in its purity," since other more holistic and biblically based models such as the Mystical Body of Christ always supplemented it.

The Second Vatican Council, however, set the institutional model aside and employed several alternate models for understanding the mystery of the church.[28] These included: the church as communion, the people of God, a pilgrim people, a servant (of the world). For peacemaking, the most important was the church as sacrament. *Lumen Gentium*, the council's Dogmatic Constitution on the Church, declared:

> "By her relationship with Christ, the Church is a kind of sacrament or sign of intimate union with God, and of the unity of all mankind. She is also an instrument for the achievement of such union and unity."[29]

The council's sacramental model of the role of the church in the world is of special relevance to the Catholic-Mennonite dialogue because the second part of the definition—the church as an instrument of the unity of the human family—brings the church's peacemaking role to the forefront of its symbolic and pastoral functions.[30]

The church-as-sacrament is a decidedly Catholic approach to peacemaking, of course. Where Mennonites tend to emphasize the avoidance, prevention, and correction of violent conflict, Catholics tend to emphasize the bonds that bring human beings together. The Catholic approach emphasizes positive peacemaking measures, by which I mean measures that are necessary for constructing the underlying conditions for peace, above and beyond the avoidance and resolution of violent conflict. Thus the council emphasized the church's unitive function as a particular service the church gives to society.[31] Specifically, the church's role is to foster "progress toward unity, healthy socialization, and civil and economic cooperation."[32] This is an example of a Catholic—in particular a Thomist—social sensibility, namely, that human beings are "social animals," reflecting in their created dynamics the law of love that underlies all reality.[33] Long before "interdependence" and "globalization" became familiar terms, the council underscored the rise, spread, and integration of organizations as a positive contribution to human well-being, and so to peace.

To be sure, the council urged Christians, "and upon all people to put aside, in the family spirit of the children of God, all conflict between nations and races and to build up the internal strength of just human associations."[34] One development of the post-conciliar teaching on peace, in fact, has been the realization that active nonviolence in the defense of justice, conflict resolution, and peacebuilding are necessary steps to promoting the unity of the human family. Promotion of the positive elements of peace need to be supplemented by nonviolent strategies for avoiding and resolving conflict.

Still, the institutional dimension of peacemaking and the role of socialization in establishing peace are among the distinctively Catholic contributions to the two churches' common vocation to peacemaking. In *The Harvest of Justice*, for example, the U.S. bishops identified nonviolence as a public obligation that needs to take form in public institutions.[35] Just policing would be the expression of a refined Catholic-Mennonite view of socialization in which the negative, violent elements in the international system would be addressed in organized, nonviolent, and less violent, preferably nonlethal, ways. Recent innovations already point in these directions. Some institutional mechanisms are already coming online (humanitarian intervention, war crimes tribunals, the International Criminal Court). Meanwhile, component activities appropriate to the just policing model such as human rights monitoring, peacekeeping, peace enforcement, and arrests of war criminals are all being refined.

Promoting church-based conflict resolution and peacemaking activities are necessary but insufficient expressions of the peacemaking role of the church. By themselves they fail to organize nonviolent practices in public ways. If the domestic (police) analogy is ever to be feasible in the international arena, the international community itself needs the authority, organization, and policing power to make it effective. Successive popes and the Holy See regard the growth of international organizations, international law, and the United Nations system as key elements of a culture of peace.[36]

To highlight the public, institutional, and international dimensions of peacemaking is not to evade the church's own responsibilities. Self-appropriation of the sacrament-of-unity model of ecclesiology continues to make demands on the Catholic Church. To outside observers local churches and episcopal conferences sometimes seem slow to take the Vatican's lead, but this impression often results from failures of communication rather than inaction. In the case of the United States Conference of Catholic Bishops (USCCB), for example, media attention focuses on moments of crisis, when policy formulation centers on the responsible exercise of power by the world's hyperpower. Long-term work on peacemaking institutions is less visible. The USCCB, along with Catholic Relief Services, was a founder of the Catholic Peacebuilding Network. Likewise, although Catholic lay organizations, ecclesial movements, and religious orders have had increasing interaction with international and transnational institutions, media neglect leaves the impression that the presence and impact is slight, especially for a body of some 1.2 billion souls. Of course, lay and religious groups working under the radar of media attention may be better able to pursue the development of alternative peacemaking institutions that then, as they mature, can be adopted by the wider church and finally the public.

Mennonites, through the Mennonite Central Committee (MCC), are already engaged both in advocacy with international organizations like the U.N. and in the development of novel peacemaking practices.[37] The latter would seem to have fairly wide acceptance within the church, but MCC activists are a subset of Mennonites worldwide. As Guatemalan Mennonite leader Mario Higueros explained to the International Catholic-Mennonite Dialogue, many Mennonites do not regard active peacemaking as part of their vocation. Rather, like many Evangelicals, they are primarily concerned with individual salvation in narrowly religious terms. The Mennonites' challenge, it seems to this Catholic, is twofold: First they must win acceptance among the church's peace party for a positive conception of peace that favors the development of (national and international) public institutions for fostering and maintaining peace. Second, they must develop a church-wide consensus around this broader understanding of peace. The 2004 Mennonite-Catholic dialogue report takes a step in this direction by endorsing a full-spectrum conception of peace, that includes the dimension of world order and thereby puts the idea into play for the one million Mennonites who belong to the Mennonite World Conference. While existing involvements with world organizations seems to offer tacit concurrence with the world-order side of peacemaking, and while theologians like Duane Friesen and Ted Grimsrud have created frameworks for this-worldly involvement, a friendly observer such as myself must wonder: Given the dispersal of authority among Mennonites, will church-wide agreement supporting public institutions for peacemaking be an exceedingly challenging task for Mennonites?

2. *The People of God.* In terms of popular religious language and liturgical practice, "people of God" may have become the most common image in Catholic usage in the years following the Second Vatican Council. Dulles has observed that the people-of-God model is "more democratic in tendency than the hierarchical [institutional] models." It "emphasizes the immediate relationship of all believers to the Holy Spirit, who directs the Church" and "the mutual subordination of the members toward one another. . ." In other words, it appears to be "more Protestant," less Roman, and less hierarchical.[38] For all these reasons, conceiving of the church as the people of God—and even more, treating it as such—brings the Catholic Church closer to the Mennonite understanding of "the be-

lievers church," though hierarchy would still create some distance for Mennonites to cover to a common ecclesiology on this point.

Another potential difficulty for rapprochement here is the question of what constitutes peoplehood. Is it a positive mission affirming the dynamics of unity in the world, as in the vision of Vatican II, or is it a culture-critical role in which the church's stand toward the world is essentially prophetic? For complex theological reasons, John Howard Yoder opted for the latter role and dismissed the former.[39] As much as the rejection of violence, the affirmation of positive moral developments in the world remains a point of division between what I would call the Catholic and Mennonite temperaments. Catholics are disposed to find good in the unfolding of the secular world, even to the point of admitting that the church learns from the world.[40] The risk, of course, is that the church will be co-opted, mistaken, or deceived. As I have already pointed out, Mennonites and Catholics with a Mennonite disposition tend to resist affirming any worldly progress as involving a spark of divine inspiration, though not everyone is as reluctant to affirm such developments as Yoder was. Duane Friesen has attempted to develop a middle position in which "the church's calling is not to withdraw from culture, but to seek the shalom, the peace and well-being, of the city where we dwell."[41] Still, the mission of the people of God is one supposition of the just policing proposal that needs further elucidation in both churches and in the dialogue between them.

In the forty years since Vatican II, the Catholic Church's progress in adopting the people-of-God model has hardly moved in a straight line, particularly with respect to the church's internal organization. Still, one way in which it has developed is in the constancy of the teaching on the duty to read and respond to "the signs of the times." To take seriously the signs of the times is to nurture a gospel-based morality that exceeds any rule-book Christian ethics. It is to promote communal discernment about evolving social questions, with the gospel and Catholic social teaching as the primary sources for communal reflection.

For Mennonites accustomed to communal discernment, the signs-of-the-times methodology should offer little practical difficulty.[42] In the Catholic Church, however, what tends to remain a challenge is to make the practice of reading the signs of the times "church-wide and parish-deep," as Gerald Schlabach describes it. In the years since the council, reading the signs of the times has largely been a function of the magisterium (hierarchical teaching authority), along with religious congregations and lay ecclesial movements like Focolare and the Community of

Sant'Egidio. Parishes infrequently function as communities of moral discernment. Furthermore, restorationist and neo-orthodox currents in the Catholic Church emphasize the church's immutable teaching in a way that discourages historical consciousness and hardly invites the faithful throughout the church to read the signs of the times for themselves.

All the same, the method is an integral part of the Catholic social teaching and the prescribed way for the whole church and particularly lay people to witness to the gospel in today's world. Furthermore, the definition of the parish as "a community of communities and movements" by the Synod for America (1997–99) suggests a broader and more dynamic understanding of the local Catholic congregation that could foster communal discernment and public witness. In this schema, sub-communities and movements are expected to provide initiative and models for discernment on the parish and diocesan level.

In the context of the people-of-God ecclesiology, we can also better appreciate the conviction of the International Catholic-Mennonite Dialogue, and of the church authorities who approved its first quinquennial report, that the two churches share a common vocation to be peacemakers. Joined in the one church of Christ, both communities possess a shared, historic mission to promote peace nonviolently. They participate in the vocation of the one church of Christ to be "an instrument of [God's] peace." Both our ecumenical relationship and our unity within the one church of Christ are realized in peacemaking.

Again, on the Catholic side, living out this model of church requires making that identity as a peacemaker church-wide and parish-deep. On this point, Catholics face a number of issues. While the justice dimension of peace has taken hold of large segments of the church, the sacramental role of the church as sign and instrument of the unity of the human family, and thus peace, is yet to be appropriated in many segments of the church. Following Vatican II, a number of liturgical changes were made in keeping with this commitment, but they remain optional and much less utilized than they might be. Popes, many bishops, church agencies, and ecclesial movements have certainly made peacemaking part of their own vocation, but it is still not a part of the self-understanding of the average Catholic. The council, Pope John Paul II, and the U.S. bishops have recognized and endorsed nonviolence as the basic Christian option for social change and conflict resolution. But the teaching on nonviolence, while integrated into official teaching, remains largely unappropriated in the larger church. Furthermore, a multi-author study on nonviolence commissioned in the 1990s by the Pontifical Council for Justice and Peace, for example, was never released. Nonetheless, John Paul II regarded the adoption of nonviolence and the rejection of war as one of the key signs of the times favoring a culture of life.[43]

For Mennonites, the question once again is whether and how the church, or parts of it, can legitimately discern the signs of the times with other Christians and people of goodwill. Legitimacy refers here, in Mennonite terms, to fidelity to the Scriptures and to the discipleship tradition of apostolic life. Communal discernment is a traditional part of congregational life for Mennonites, so the issue is whether that process can be extended to embrace others who are not members of that local community, beginning with Catholic Christians. Discernment with men and women of goodwill will be an even harder test.

3. *Church as Servant.* Church-as-servant, in some ways, may be the most problematic Vatican II model for the Catholic-Mennonite relationship. Servanthood itself is not foreign to Mennonite spirituality. The image of Christ as servant is fundamental; Mennonites would share with Catholics the ideal of "the suffering servant." What many Mennonites should find strange is the Catholic notion that the servant-church serves the world. Vatican II is quite clear that service of the world (the world in a positive, non-pejorative sense) is close to the heart of the church's mission.[44] In Christian experience, after all, suffering and effectiveness are not mutually exclusive realities.

Implicit in this conception of the church-as-servant, however, seems to be that one can expect success and progress, for example, in securing human rights or improving peaceable ties among people. For some Mennonites, this almost presents a scandal. Yoder, for example, explicates suffering as essential to the service that marks the church. This seems to imply, moreover, that it is un-Christlike to expect success in that service. The Catholic model does not turn its back on suffering, indeed it regards suffering as normal. But neither does it regard Christian suffering as any less Christ-like if it comes as an integral part of efforts to change the world.[45]

4. *A Community of Disciples.* The fourth approach to church is that of a community of disciples. With respect to the Catholic side of the Catholic-Mennonite dialogue, perhaps the most important development in the Second Vatican Council was its articulation of "the universal call to holiness."[46] This is the affirmation that all Catholics have a duty to live a holy, Christian life. Implied in this teaching is the rejection of the medieval notion of different states of life in the church (lay, clergy, and religious), so that laypeople were expected only to meet minimal moral

standards (the Ten Commandments, the natural law), whereas others, especially religious, were committed to living the evangelical counsels. The counsels of poverty, chastity, and obedience, of course, have been key features of Christian holiness and following of Christ for Catholics, just as nonviolence has been for Mennonites. Since the universal call to holiness involves all church members, however, it must issue in expressions of Christian discipleship that range widely. Nonviolence, while strongly endorsed by the late Pope John Paul II, is still a central commitment only for small groups of Catholics, such as Catholic Workers and some members of Pax Christi, though its influence over Catholic minds and hearts continues to spread.[47] Active peacemaking is a commitment for a range of groups including the Community of Sant'Egidio and Focolare (two growing lay movements begun in Italy) and for umbrella groups like the Catholic Peacebuilding Network, begun in the United States with international ties.

In addition, as in the past, a great variety of Christian virtues form the basis of different styles of Christian living, care of the sick and infirm, for example, or preaching and evangelization. In the modern Catholic imagination, though charity is regarded as the first among the virtues, concern for the poor probably holds the position that nonviolence, broadly speaking, holds in the Mennonite mind. In the last few decades, moreover, the pursuit of justice for the oppressed and the defense of human rights, as expressions of that concern, have been dominant themes in church teaching and practice. Each plays a prominent role in shaping the positive Catholic conception of peace. The variety of traditional callings found in the Catholic Church today—lay and clergy, active and contemplative—can and do co-exist in a single Christian community. Among the "active" charisms, then, standard vocations such as preaching, education, and health care can surely co-exist with newer ones such as nonviolence, working for justice, and defending human rights.

A Catholic co-existence of callings is not so far from Mennonite experience as may first appear. Active participation in the community of disciples is certainly central to the Mennonite model of church. Discipleship or *nachfolge* (following after Christ) is the predominant way they speak of the moral requirements of church membership, and conscious commitment to a distinctively Christian way of life is essential to the adult baptism that incorporates men and women fully into the church. Yet, even among Mennonites there are wide differences on the principal virtue of Christian nonviolence. Some continue to maintain the traditional pacifist position of non-resistance; others now understand their commitment to be to active nonviolence, and still others have developed a specialized, even professional commitment to conflict resolution or transformation and peacebuilding. So, even in the Mennonite community, following the gentle and peaceful Christ already expresses itself in a variety of manifestations or callings.

Individual Mennonite communities, of course, would encourage one or another of these approaches, and some would accept a wide range of them. As I understand it, however, there is such diversity among Mennonites and a dispersal of authority through individual congregations that there is at present no official acceptance of the range of callings one would find among Catholic communities. In the Catholic Church, after all, the hierarchy officially authorizes the particular charisms of individual communities (religious orders, secular institutes, and lay movements) as legitimate expressions of the universal call to holiness. It is the acceptance of such a range of callings as genuine expressions of a Christlike life that would make just policing a legitimate calling for members of both churches and allow common agreement between them on the question.

Conclusion: Just Policing and the Communion of Charism

A final model of the church is that of a communion. Here too a resolution to differences over just policing might be found. The model of the church as a communion of disciples has New Testament roots in the term *koinonia* or community, and in biblical metaphors of the Mystical Body of Christ and the People of God. It has both spiritual and sociological dimensions.[48] On the spiritual side, the church is an expression of the union of the faithful in the grace of the Spirit. On the sociological side, it consists of the unity in Christ of those who participate in a variety of gifts or charisms. All contribute to the building up of the one Body of Christ. Their respective gifts all are services building up the common good. One way to think of the possibility that just policing might become a work that unites the Catholic and Mennonite churches is to treat it as a charism within the communion of the church. To do so, of course, will require an effort that openly strives to prevent practitioners from sliding into unjust war and militarism. But, the question is, can the two churches recognize it as a point along a continuum with non-resistance and active nonviolence?

For Catholics, of course, the acceptance of just policing would seem to be a lesser problem, since it accepts both humanitarian intervention and, in exceptional circumstances, just war. What would seem to be required would be further specification of humanitarian intervention, of a strong Catholic preference for international policing generally, and of requirements for Christian participation in such policing. For Mennonites, however, the step from peacebuilding to just policing may be a very long one indeed, since just policing will inevitably entail some limited force.

Some (Mennonite partners in particular) will certainly demand the Catholic Church reject just war outright. I do not see that happening soon for two reasons. First, it is such a long tradition to renounce. Secondly, whenever people examine the morality of the use of force, the just-war principles reappear. They are applicable to policing, including international policing, and one may find them implicit even in Gandhi's rules for conduct of nonviolent campaigns.[49] At the same time, a practical rejection of just war cannot be ruled out. There is a current in Vatican thinking that has played with this possibility for some time. As early as the end of the first Gulf War, the semi-official Vatican journal *Civiltà Cattolica* ran a long editorial contending that the usefulness of the just war doctrine had come to an end.[50] Already the president of the Pontifical Council for Justice and Peace, in fact, has declared that the just war has gone the route of the death penalty. That is, it may be permissible in principle, but in practice it is no longer applicable. Short of renunciation of just war, however, what one must expect of the Catholic Church is a rigorous moral training of those Catholics who participate in just policing (and in genuinely just war as long as it is permitted), plainer criticism of unjust use of military force by political authorities, and outright public condemnation (not simple questioning) of unjust wars. As Gerald Schlabach has insisted, the real issue for the vast community of the Catholic Church, is how to make just policing a truly Christian charism and not simply the baptism of the warrior ethos.

For Mennonites, recognition of just policing would mean accepting as members of their communion those who, as part of their Christian commitment, would participate in policing missions. At a minimum, it would mean not excluding them from communion.[51] For Mennonites as for Catholics, it would entail defining the limits of just policing and the role of the Christian police officer, while assuring that proper training and discipline are provided to see that policing is a tool of peace rather than a step toward war.

Notes

1. Ernst Troeltsch, *The Social Teaching of the Christian Churches*, trans. Olive Wyon, introd. by Richard Niebuhr, reprint, 1981 (New York; Chicago: Macmillan; University of Chicago Press, 1931).

2. The complaint applies also to the better known work of H. Richard Niebuhr, *Christ and Culture*, Harper Torchbooks/Cloister Library (New York: Harper and Row, 1956), which refined Troeltsch's typology in some ways, but retained its basic approach.

3. Gerhard Beestermoeller, "Just War: A Peacemaking or War Driving Force?" Unpublished paper delivered at the Harvard Center for the Study of World Religions, February 14, 2005.

4. Mennonite World Conference and Pontifical Council for Promoting Church Unity, "Called Together to be Peacemakers" (available at http://www.mwc-cmm.org/MWC/dialogue, and http://bridgefolk.net/theology). See also Marlin Miller and Barbara Nelson Gingrich, eds., *The Church's Peace Witness* (Grand Rapids, MI: Wm. B. Eerdmans, 1994), and Jeffrey Gros and John D. Rempel, ed., *The Fragmentation of the Church and Its Unity in Peacemaking* (Grand Rapids, MI: Wm. B. Eerdmans Pub. Co., 2001).

5. See pages 3 and 19 in the present volume, or Gerald W. Schlabach, "Just Policing: How War Could Cease to be a Church-Dividing Issue," in *Just Policing: Mennonite-Catholic Theological Colloquium 2002*, ed. Ivan J. Kauffman, Bridgefolk Series, no. 2 (Kitchener, Ontario: Pandora Press, 2004), 19–75.

6. Schlabach, "Just Policing," 49–54.

7. For a Mennonite interpretation of these Catholic developments, see John Howard Yoder, *The Priestly Kingdom: Social Ethics as Gospel* (Notre Dame, IN: University of Notre Dame Press, 1984), 5–6.

8. Harold S. Bender's seminal essay, "The Anabaptist Vision," has been reprinted numerous times, but first appeared in *Church History* 13 (March 1944): 3–24 and *Mennonite Quarterly Review* 18 (April 1944): 67–88. For surveys of modern Mennonite history, see Paul Toews, *Mennonites in American Society, 1930–1970: Modernity and the Persistence of Religious Community*, The Mennonite Experience in America, vol. 4 (Scottdale, PA: Herald Press, 1996); Leo Driedger and Donald B. Kraybill, *Mennonite Peacemaking: From Quietism to Activism* (Scottdale, PA: Herald Press, 1994).

9. For constructive Mennonite theological proposals, see Ted Grimsrud, "Anabaptist Faith and American Democracy," *Mennonite Quarterly Review* 78, no. 3 (July 2004): 341–62; Duane K. Friesen, *Artists, Citizens, Philosophers: Seeking the Peace of the City: An Anabaptist Theology of Culture*, foreword by Glen Stassen (Scottdale, PA: Herald Press, 2000); John Howard Yoder, *For the Nations*; Glen H. Stassen, et al., *Authentic Transformation: A New Vision of Christ and Culture* (Nashville: Abingdon Press, 1996).

10. John Howard Yoder, *The Royal Priesthood: Essays Ecclesiological and Ecumenical*, ed., with an introduction by Michael G. Cartwright, foreword by Richard J. Mouw (Grand Rapids, MI: Wm. B. Eerdmans, 1994), 269, n. 6.

11. Joseph E. Capizzi, "War Remains Church Dividing," in *Just Policing: Mennonite-Catholic Theological Colloquium 2002*, ed. Ivan J. Kauffman, Bridgefolk Series, no. 2 (Kitchener, Ontario: Pandora Press, 2004), 76.

12. Hehir made his remarks in a concluding response at a symposium on three Catholic traditions on war and peace (Traditional Just War-so-called, contemporary Just War, and Pacifism), sponsored by the Jesuit Conference at Georgetown University, December 1, 2004. See Dolores R. Leckey, ed., *Just War, Lasting Peace: What Christian Traditions Can Teach Us*, forthcoming (Maryknoll, NY: Orbis Press, 2006). It seems to me Hehir may have been

conflating nonviolence with pacifism. In any case, the combination of nonviolence and just war is the official Catholic position, articulated in U.S. Conference of Catholic Bishops, *The Harvest of Justice is Sown in Peace*, as well as the final report of the international dialogue between Mennonites and Catholics, "Called Together to be Peacemakers," approved for publication by the Vatican's Congregation for the Doctrine of the Faith under the auspices of the Pontifical Council for Promoting Christian Unity.

13. It is because of this lack of effective international authority that the Second Vatican Council permitted the conditional (i.e., just) use of war within the international sphere; see *Gaudium et spes*, §79.

14. Michael Walzer, *Just and Unjust Wars: A Moral Argument with Historical Illustrations* (New York: Basic, 1977), 58.

15. Ibid., 58–59.

16. On the constabulary model of military service, see Sir John Winthrop Hackett, "Today and Tomorrow," in *War, Morality, and the Military Profession*, ed. Malham M. Wakin (Boulder, CO: Westview Press, 1986), 91–105.

17. Dana Priest, *The Mission: Waging War and Keeping Peace with America's Military* (New York: W.W. Norton, 2004).

18. Among others, see Hayner, *Unspeakable Truths*; Desmond Tutu, *No Future Without Forgiveness* (New York: Doubleday, 1999); Cynthia Sampson and John Paul Lederach, ed., *From the Ground up: Mennonite Contributions to International Peacebuilding* (Oxford: Oxford University Press, 2000); William Bole, Drew Christiansen, and Robert T. Hennemeyer, *Forgiveness in International Politics: An Alternative Road to Peace* (Washington, DC: United States Conference of Catholic Bishops, 2004).

19. USCCB, *The Harvest of Justice is Sown in Peace*, I.B. Available December 12, 2006. www.usccb.org/sdwp/harvest.htm#theology.

20. Ibid., I.B.1.

21. According to *The Harvest of Justice*, such public obligations to nonviolence raise the threshold for the use of force. Also see John Howard Yoder, *When War is Unjust*, 71–75. Yoder made the same point in correspondence with the ad-hoc committee, headed by Cardinal Joseph Bernardin, that drafted *The Harvest of Justice*.

22. *Gaudium et spes*, §42.

23. In *The Priestly Kingdom*, 42–43, John Yoder took a more negative position, arguing for a hermeneutic of suspicion toward natural revelation, claiming the church ought to be culture-critical. Yoder certainly went too far when he wrote, "The real test of the accessibility of a common moral language . . . must not then be the times when we find ourselves agreeing with 'men of goodwill' (especially if they not be western humanists), it must be the capacity of this line of reasoning to illuminate meaningful conversations with Idi Amin or Khomeini or Chairman Mao." If there ever was a dismissive argument *ad absurdum*, this is certainly it. Yoder seems especially perverse in rejecting dialogue with Western humanists and others whose universal values are derived from the Christian moral heritage itself (Ibid).

24. *Gaudium et spes*, §§15–16, 20–23.

25. For a Mennonite theology of discernment of the elements of the world with which Christians can identify, see Thomas N. Finger, *Christian Theology: An Eschatological Approach*, vol. 2 (Scottdale, PA: Herald Press, 1989), 271–96; also Grimsrud, "Anabaptist Faith and American Democracy." Friesen's proposals in *Artists, Citizens, Philosophers*, though constructive, seem to this author to be too derivative of the primary church experience and insufficiently attentive to what the world gives to the church. What John Howard Yoder proposed in "How H. Richard Niebuhr Reasoned: A Critique of *Christ and Culture*," in *Authentic*

Transformation, 31–89, was that Christians discern various elements of culture separately, but his proposal remains inchoate and is undercut by Yoder's estimate of contemporary culture as fallen too low to be capable of transformation in a Christian context.

26. In the context of the Perfect Society model, "Catholic" meant Roman Catholic. Today Catholic embraces the Eastern Catholic churches and so has a broader meaning.

27. Avery Robert Dulles, *Models of the Church* (Garden City, NY: Doubleday, 1974), 31.

28. On models and mystery, see Dulles, *Models of the Church*, 178–92.

29. *Lumen Gentium* §1.

30. Yoder proposes a Mennonite sacramental view of the church in "The Kingdom as Social Ethic," in *The Priestly Kingdom*, 93. He cites the Catholic usage, though he prefers to focus on specific "ordinances"—the traditional Mennonite term for the sacraments—rather than on the church itself as sacrament. The Catholic meaning of the church as a sacrament of union with God and the unity of the human family finds its complement in the image of the church as servant, with emphasis on its role in promoting the unity of the humanity.

31. On the unitive dynamism of the human community promoted by the church, see *Gaudium et spes*, §§24 and 42.

32. Ibid., §42.

33. Ibid., §24.

34. Ibid., §42.

35. See *The Harvest of Justice*, I.B.1; *Compendium*, 494–96; David Smock, ed., *Catholic Contributions to International Peace*, Special Report, no. 69 (Washington DC: United States Institute for Peace, 2001), Http://www.usip.org/pubs/specialreports/sr69.pdf, which includes a summary of Drew Christiansen, "Catholic Peacemaking: From *Pacem in Terris* to *Centesimus Annus.*"

36. See John Paul II, *"Pacem in Terris:* A Permanent Commitment," World Day of Peace message, January 1, 2003; and *Compendium*, §§433–45.

37. For multiple examples of Mennonite peacemaking, see Sampson and Lederach, *From the Ground Up*.

38. Dulles, *Models of the Church*, 49.

39. John Howard Yoder, *The Priestly Kingdom*, 15–45.

40. On the church learning from the world, even from its persecutors, see *Gaudium et spes*, §44.

41. Friesen, *Artists, Citizens, Philosophers*, 16.

42. For Mennonites, it is collaboration with those whom Catholic teaching calls "men and women of goodwill"—conscientious unbelievers—that may pose more of a problem.

43. See John Paul II, *Evangelium vitae*, §27, and *Centesimus Annus*, §§23, 25 and especially 52.

44. *Lumen Gentium [Dogmatic Constitution on the Church]* (1964), §§3 and 92; *Gaudium et spes*, §§40–45.

45. On the role of suffering in the nonviolent transformation of the world, see John Paul II, *Centesimus Annus*, §§23 and especially 25. Also see John Paul II, *Sollicitudo Rei Socialis [On Social Concern]*, §§25 and 40. For a contrast in the latter encyclical with John Yoder's evaluation of contemporary culture, see §29: "*all is not negative* in the contemporary world, nor would it be, for the heavenly Father's providence watches over our daily cares. . . ."

46. *Lumen Gentium*, §§39–42.

47. On nonviolence, see *Centesimus Annus*, §§23, 25 and 52.

48. Dulles, *Models of the Church*, 42–57; *Lumen Gentium*, §§4, 7–9, 12–14, 18, 30.

49. Joan V. Bondurant, *Conquest of Violence: The Gandhian Philosophy of Conflict* (Berkeley: University of California Press, 1969), 38–41.

50. For an English translation, see *Civiltà Cattolica*, "Modern War and the Christian Conscience," trans. Peter Heinegg, in *But Was It Just? Reflections on the Morality of the Persian Gulf War*, eds. Jean Bethke Elshtain and David E. DeCosse (New York: Doubleday, 1992), 107–25.

51. Yet another "minimum" might be possible if Mennonites believe that the unambiguous witness of their peacemaking vocation must continue to require nonviolent standards of membership. This alternative would be to conceive of their identity, both as a Christian community and as individuals, in ways that are analogous to that of religious orders. In other words, communion in Christ's church would not be at stake, but obedient participation in the community's charism of consistent nonviolence would be. To be sure, such a polity would not be without its own challenges. Mennonites would have to recognize non-pacifist Christians and churches as legitimate, which many have done implicitly but not officially, nor with explicit theological justification. At most, Mennonites extend a kind of tacit communion with other Christians by working within the ecclesiology of Protestant denominationalism, which offers a loose functional equivalent of Roman catholicity, and through "open communion" in the practice of the Lord's Supper.—Editor, with encouragement from Christiansen.

Bibliography

Abuza, Zachary. "Al Qaeda's Southeast Asian Network." *Contemporary Southeast Asia* 24, no. 3 (December 2002).

Albert, Mathias, David Jacobson, and Yosef Lapid, eds. *Identities, Borders, Orders: Rethinking International Relations Theory*. Minneapolis, MN: University of Minnesota Press, 2001.

Allen, John L., Jr. "Pope's 'Answer to Rumsfeld' Pulls no Punches in Opposing War." *National Catholic Reporter*, February 14, 2003, 3–4.

American Friends Service Committee (AFSC). "International Legal Remedies in Response to the Attacks of September 11th, 2001," 2001. Http://www.wcc-coe.org/wcc/behindthenews/analysis20.html.

Anderson, Benedict R. O'G. *Imagined Communities: Reflections on the Origin and Spread of Nationalism*. Revised and extended ed. London; New York: Verso, 1991.

Appadurai, Arjun. *Modernity at Large: Cultural Dimensions of Globalization*. Public Worlds, Vol. 1. Minneapolis, MN: University of Minnesota Press, 1996.

Aquinas, Thomas. *Summa Theologiae*. Latin text and English translation. Blackfriars Edition. New York: McGraw-Hill, 1964.

Ascoli, David. *The Queen's Peace: The Origins and Development of the Metropolitan Police, 1829–1979*. London: H. Hamilton, 1979.

Augustine. *The City of God*. Translated by Henry Bettenson. Introduction by David Knowles. Harmondsworth, Middlesex, England: Penguin, 1972.

Bailey, William C. "Less-Than-Lethal Weapons and Police-Citizen Killings in U.S. Urban Areas." *Crime and Delinquency* 42 (October 1996): 535–36.

Bainton, Roland H. *Christian Attitudes Toward War and Peace: A Historical Survey and Critical Re-Evaluation*. Nashville: Abingdon Press, 1960.

Baldwin, David A. *Neorealism and Neoliberalism: The Contemporary Debate*. New Directions in World Politics. New York: Columbia University Press, 1993.

Barber, Benjamin R. *Jihad Vs. Mcworld*. New York: Random House, 1995.

Barton, Charles. "Empowerment and Retribution in Criminal Justice." In *Restorative Justice: Philosophy to Practice*, Edited by Heather Strang and John Braithwaite, 55–76. Burlington, VT: Ashgate, 2000.

———. *Getting Even: Revenge as a Form of Justice*. Chicago, IL: Open Court, 1999.

Bayley, David H. *Patterns of Policing: A Comparative International Analysis.* Crime, Law, and Deviance Series. New Brunswick, NJ: Rutgers University Press, 1985.

———. *Police for the Future.* Studies in Crime and Public Policy. New York: Oxford University Press, 1994.

Bender, Harold S. "The Anabaptist Vision." *Church History* 13 (March 1944): 3–24; *Mennonite Quarterly Review* 18 (April 1944): 67–88.

Bittner, Egon. *Aspects of Police Work.* Boston: Northeastern University Press, 1990.

———. *The Functions of the Police in Modern Society: A Review of Background Factors, Current Practices, and Possible Role Models.* New York: J. Aronson, 1975.

Blinken, Anthony J. "Winning the War of Ideas." In *The Battle for Hearts and Minds: Using Soft Power to Undermine Terrorist Networks.* Edited by Alexander T. Lennon. A Washington Quarterly Reader. Cambridge, MA: MIT Press, 2003.

Bole, William, Drew Christiansen, and Robert T. Hennemeyer. *Forgiveness in International Politics: An Alternative Road to Peace.* Washington, DC: United States Conference of Catholic Bishops, 2004.

Bondurant, Joan V. *Conquest of Violence: The Gandhian Philosophy of Conflict.* Berkeley: University of California Press, 1969.

Boulding, Kenneth E. *Three Faces of Power.* Newbury Park, CA: Sage Publications, 1990.

Boutros-Ghali, Boutros. *An Agenda for Peace, 1995.* Second edition, with the new supplement and related U.N. documents. New York: United Nations, 1995.

Braithwaite, John. *Restorative Justice & Responsive Regulation.* Studies in Crime and Public Policy. Oxford: Oxford University Press, 2002.

Brunk, Conrad. "Restorative Justice and the Philosophical Theories of Criminal Punishment." In *The Spiritual Roots of Restorative Justice,* edited by Michael L. Hadley. SUNY Series in Religious Studies, 31–56. Albany: State University of New York Press, 2001.

Bull, Hedley. *The Anarchical Society: A Study of Order in World Politics.* New York: Columbia University Press, 1977.

Burchill, Scott, and Andrew Linklater. *Theories of International Relations.* With Richard Devetak, Matthew Paterson, and Jacqui True. New York: St. Martin's Press, 1996.

Cady, Duane L. *From Warism to Pacifism: A Moral Continuum.* Philadelphia: Temple University Press, 1989.

Cahill, Lisa Sowle. "Christian Just War Tradition: Tensions and Development." In *The Return of the Just War,* Vol. 2001/2, edited by María Pilar Aquino and Dietmar Mieth, 74–82. London: SCM Press, 2001.

———. "Just Peacemaking: Theory, Practice, and Prospects." *Journal of the Society of Christian Ethics* 23, no. 1 (2003): 195–212.

Call, Charles, and William Stanley. "Military and Police Reform After Civil Wars." In *Contemporary Peacemaking: Conflict, Violence and Peace Processes,* edited by John Darby and Roger MacGinty. New York: Palgrave Macmillan, 2003.

Calvin, John. *The Institutes of the Christian Religion.* Vol. 2. Edited by John T. McNeill. Translated by Ford Lewis Battles. The Library of Christian Classics, vol. 21. Philadelphia: Westminster Press, 1960.

Capizzi, Joseph E. "War Remains Church Dividing." In *Just Policing: Mennonite-Catholic Theological Colloquium 2002*, edited by Ivan J. Kauffman. Bridgefolk Series, no. 2, 76–88. Kitchener, Ontario: Pandora Press, 2004.

Carr, Edward Hallett. *The Twenty Years' Crisis, 1919–1939: An Introduction to the Study of International Relations*. New York: St. Martin's Press, 1940.

Chacko, James, and Stephen E. Nancoo, eds. *Community Policing in Canada*. Edited by James Chacko. Toronto: Canadian Scholar's Press, 1993.

Chevigny, Paul. *Edge of the Knife: Police Violence in the Americas*. New York: New Press, distributed by Norton, 1995.

Childress, James F. "Answering That of God in Every Man: An Interpretation of Fox's Religious Thought." *Quaker Religious Thought* 15, no. 3 (1974): 2–41.

———. "Contemporary Pacifism: Its Major Types and Possible Contributions to Discourse About War." In *The American Search for Peace: Moral Reasoning, Religious Hope, and National Security*, edited by George Weigel and John Langan, 109–31. Washington, DC: Georgetown University Press, 1991.

———. "Just-War Criteria." In *Moral Responsibility in Conflicts: Essays on Nonviolence, War, and Conscience*, 63–94. Baton Rouge: Louisiana State University Press, 1982.

———. "The Just-War Tradition and the Invasion of Iraq." Conference on Ethical Issues Raised by Pre-Emptive War. The Churches' Center for Theology and Public Policy, Wesley Theological Seminary, Washington DC, 2003. Http://www.cctpp.org/childresspaper.htm.

———. *Practical Reasoning in Bioethics*. Medical Ethics Series. Bloomington: Indiana University Press, 1997.

Christiansen, Drew, S.J. "Peacemaking and the Use of Force: Behind the Pope's Stringent Just-War Teaching." *America* 180, no. 17 (May 15, 1999): 13–18.

———. "What is a Peace Church?: A Roman Catholic Perspective." Paper presented at the International Mennonite-Roman Catholic Dialogue. Karlsruhe, Germany, 2000.

Civiltà Cattolica. "Modern War and the Christian Conscience." Translated by Peter Heinegg. In *But Was It Just? Reflections on the Morality of the Persian Gulf War*, edited by Jean Bethke Elshtain and David E. DeCosse, 107–25. New York: Doubleday, 1992.

Commission on International Affairs in Church of Norway Council on Ecumenical and International Relations. *Vulnerability and Security: Current Challenges in Security Policy from an Ethical and Theological Perspective*, 2002. http://www.kirken.no/english/engelsk.cfm?artid=5850.

Connell, Francis J. *Morals in Politics and Professions: A Guide for Catholics in Public Life*. Westminster, MD: Newman Press, 1946.

COPS Office. *What is Community Policing?* Office of Community Oriented Policing Services, U.S. Department of Justice. http://www.cops.usdoj.gov/print.asp?Item=36.

Cornell, Svante E. "The Kurdish Question in Turkish Politics." *Orbis* 45, no. 1 (Winter 2001).

Cronin, Audrey Kurth, and James M. Ludes. *Attacking Terrorism: Elements of a Grand Strategy*. Washington, DC: Georgetown University Press, 2004.

Cusimano, Maryann K., ed. *Beyond Sovereignty: Issues for a Global Agenda*. Boston: Bedford/St. Martin's, 2000.

Daly, Kathleen. "Revisiting the Relationship Between Retributive and Restorative Justice." In *Restorative Justice: Philosophy to Practice*, edited by Heather Strang and John Braithwaite, 33–54. Aldershot Burlington, VT: Ashgate, 2000.

Dart, John. "U.S. Bishops Split on War's Morality." *Los Angeles Times*, February 26, 1991, A-11.

de Wijk, Rob. "The Limits of Military Power." In *The Battle for Hearts and Minds: Using Soft Power to Undermine Terrorist Networks*, edited by Alexander T. Lennon. A Washington Quarterly Reader. Cambridge, MA: MIT Press, 2003.

Dicken, Peter. *Global Shift: Reshaping the Global Economic Map in the 21st Century*. New York: Guilford Press, 2003.

Dickey, Christopher, and John Barry. "Has the War Made Us Safer?" With Gameela Ismail. *Newsweek*, April 12, 2004, 24–26.

Donziger, Steven A., ed. *The Real War on Crime: The Report of the National Criminal Justice Commission*. New York: HarperPerennial, 1996.

Dougherty, James E., and Robert L. Pfaltzgraff. *Contending Theories of International Relations: A Comprehensive Survey*. New York: Longman, 1997.

Dörries, Hermann. *Constantine the Great*. New York: Harper & Row, 1972.

Driedger, Leo, and Donald B. Kraybill. *Mennonite Peacemaking: From Quietism to Activism*. Scottdale, PA: Herald Press, 1994.

Dugan, Marie. "A Nested Theory of Conflict." *A Leadership Journal: Women in Leadership, Sharing the Vision*. 1, no. 1 (July 1996): 9–19.

Dulles, Avery Robert. *Models of the Church*. Garden City, NY: Doubleday, 1974.

Durnbaugh, Donald F. *The Believers' Church*. New York: Macmillan, 1968.

Edmonds, Martin. *Armed Services and Society*. Leicester: Leicester University Press, 1988.

Elias, Robert. "Taking Crime Seriously." *Peace Review* 6 (1994).

Elliston, Frederick, and Michael Feldberg, eds. *Moral Issues in Police Work*. Totowa, NJ: Rowman & Allanheld, 1985.

Falk, Richard A. "Toward a New World Order: Modest Methods and Drastic Visions." In *On the Creation of a Just World Order*. A Program of the World Order Models Project, edited by Saul H. Mendlovitz, 211–23. New York: The Free Press, 1975.

Falk, Richard A., Lester Edwin J. Ruiz, and R.B.J. Walker, eds. *Reframing the International: Law, Culture, Politics*. New York: Routledge, 2002.

Finger, Thomas N. *Christian Theology: An Eschatological Approach*. Vol. 2. Scottdale, PA: Herald Press, 1989.

Finnemore, Martha. *National Interests in International Society*. Cornell Studies in Political Economy. Ithaca, NY: Cornell University Press, 1996.

Fletcher, Richard A. *The Barbarian Conversion: From Paganism to Christianity*. New York: H. Holt and Co., 1998.

Fogelson, Robert M. *Big-City Police*. An Urban Institute Study. Cambridge, MA: Harvard University Press, 1977.

Ford, John C., S.J. "The Morality of Obliteration Bombing." *Theological Studies* 5 (September 1944): 261–309.

Freeman Adams, Christopher. "Fighting Crime by Building Moral Communities." *The Christian Century* 111, no. 27 (October 5, 1994): 894–96.

Friedmann, Robert R. *Community Policing: Comparative Perspectives and Prospects.* New York: St. Martin's Press, 1992.

Friesen, Duane K. *Artists, Citizens, Philosophers: Seeking the Peace of the City: An Anabaptist Theology of Culture.* With a foreword by Glen Stassen. Scottdale, PA: Herald Press, 2000.

———. *Christian Peacemaking & International Conflict: A Realist Pacifist Perspective.* With a foreword by Stanley Hauerwas. Christian Peace Shelf Selection. Scottdale, PA: Herald Press, 1986.

———. "Encourage Grassroots Peacemaking Groups and Voluntary Associations." In *Just Peacemaking: Ten Practices for Abolishing War,* edited by Glen Stassen, 176–88. Cleveland: Pilgrim Press, 1998.

———. "Naming What Happened and How We Respond." *Peace Office Newsletter* 32, no. 1 (April-June 2002): 7.

Friesen, Duane K., and Gerald W. Schlabach, eds. *At Peace and Unafraid: Public Order, Security and the Wisdom of the Cross.* Scottdale, PA: Herald Press, 2005.

Gaffigan, Stephen J., and the Community Policing Consortium. *Understanding Community Policing: A Framework for Action.* Washington, DC: Bureau of Justice Assistance, 1994.

Geller, William A., and Hans Toch, eds. *Police Violence: Understanding and Controlling Police Abuse of Force.* New Haven, CT: Yale University Press, 1996.

Gilbert, Paul. *New Terror, New Wars.* Washington, DC: Georgetown University Press, 2003.

Gilpin, Robert. *War and Change in World Politics.* Cambridge: Cambridge University Press, 1981.

Gottwald, Norman K. *All the Kingdoms of the Earth: Israelite Prophecy and International Relations in the Ancient Near East.* New York: Harper & Row, 1964.

Grant, Michael. *Constantine the Great: The Man and His Times.* New York: Scribner's Maxwell Macmillan International, 1994.

Gray, Christine D. *International Law and the Use of Force.* Foundations of Public International Law. Oxford: Oxford University Press, 2000.

Greene, Jack R., and Stephen D. Mastrofski. *Community Policing: Rhetoric or Reality.* Edited by Jack R. Greene. New York: Praeger, 1988.

Gregory, Brad S. *Salvation at Stake: Christian Martyrdom in Early Modern Europe.* Harvard Historical Studies, vol. 134. Cambridge, MA: Harvard University Press, 1999.

Griffiths, Curt Taylor, and Ron Hamilton. "Sanctioning and Healing: Restorative Justice in Canadian Aboriginal Communities." In *Restorative Justice: International Perspectives,* edited by Burt Galaway and Joe Hudson, 175–91. Monsey, NY: Criminal Justice Press, 1996.

Grimsrud, Ted. "Anabaptist Faith and American Democracy." *Mennonite Quarterly Review* 78, no. 3 (July 2004): 341–62.

Gros, Jeffrey, and John D. Rempel, eds. *The Fragmentation of the Church and Its Unity in Peacemaking.* Grand Rapids, MI: Wm. B. Eerdmans Pub. Co., 2001.

Gross, Heinrich. "Peace." In *Encyclopedia of Biblical Theology: The Complete Sacramentum Verbi,* edited by Johannes Baptist Bauer. New York: Crossroad, 1981.

Haas, Ernst B. *Beyond the Nation-State: Functionalism and International Organization.* Stanford, CA: Stanford University Press, 1964.

Hackett, Sir John Winthrop. "Today and Tomorrow." In *War, Morality, and the Military Profession,* edited by Malham M. Wakin, 91–105. Boulder, CO: Westview Press, 1986.

Hanson, William L. "Police Power for Peace." *Friends Journal* (August 2004): 6–7, 34.

Harding, Sandra. "Rethinking Standpoint Epistemology: What is 'Strong Objectivity.'" In *Feminist Epistemologies,* edited by Linda Alcoff and Elizabeth Potter. Thinking Gender Series, 49–82. New York: Routledge, 1993.

Harvey, David. *The Condition of Postmodernity: An Enquiry Into the Origins of Cultural Change.* Oxford, England: Blackwell, 1989.

Hauerwas, Stanley, and Paul J. Griffiths. "War, Peace and Jean Bethke Elstain." *First Things* 136 (October 2003): 41–47.

Hayner, Priscilla B. *Unspeakable Truths: Confronting State Terror and Atrocity.* With a preface by Timothy Garton Ash. New York: Routledge, 2000.

Hedges, Chris. *War is a Force That Gives Us Meaning.* New York: Public Affairs, 2002.

Hehir, J. Bryan. "In Defense of Justice." *Commonweal* (March 10, 1991): 32–33.

———. "The Moral Calculus of War." *Commonweal* 118, no. 4 (February 22, 1991): 125–26.

———. "What is the International Community: The Limits of Loyalty." *Foreign Policy* (September/October 2002): 38–39.

Held, David, Anthony McGrew, David Goldblatt, and Jonathan Perraton. *Global Transformations: Politics, Economics and Culture.* Stanford, CA: Stanford University Press, 1999.

Hershberger, Guy F. *War, Peace, and Nonresistance.* 3rd ed. Christian Peace Shelf Selection. Scottdale, PA: Herald Press, 1969.

———. *The Way of the Cross in Human Relations.* Scottdale, PA: Herald Press, 1958.

Hillen, John. *Blue Helmets: The Strategy of UN Military Operations.* Washington, DC: Brassey's, 2000.

Hoffman, Bruce. "The Logic of Suicide Terrorism." *Atlantic Monthly* 291, no. 5 (June 2003).

Hollenbach, David. "War and Peace in American Catholic Thought: A Heritage Abandoned?" *Theological Studies* 48 (1987): 711–26.

Holm, Tor Tanke, and Espen Barth Eide, eds. *Peacebuilding and Police Reform.* Cass Series on Peacekeeping, no. 7. London: Frank Cass, 2000.

———, eds. *Peacebuilding and Police Reform.* The Cass Series on Peacekeeping, vol. 7. London: Frank Cass, 2000.

Holsti, Kalevi J. *Peace and War: Armed Conflicts and International Order, 1648–1989.* Cambridge Studies in International Relations, vol. 14. Cambridge New York: Cambridge University Press, 1991.

Holton, R. J. *Globalization and the Nation-State.* New York: St. Martin's Press, 1998.

Howard, Peter. "Why not Invade Iraq! Threats, Language Games and U.S. Foreign Policy." Forthcoming. *International Studies Quarterly.*

————. and Reina Neufeldt. "Canada's Constructivist Foreign Policy: Building Norms for Peace." *Canadian Foreign Policy* 8, no. 1 (Fall 2000): 11–38.

Howitt, Arnold M., and Robyn L. Pangi, eds. *Countering Terrorism: Dimensions of Preparedness*. BCSIA Studies in International Security. Cambridge, MA: MIT Press, 2003.

Human Security Centre. *Human Security Report 2005: War and Peace in the 21st Century*. New York: Oxford University Press, 2006.

Ibrahim, Dekha, and Jan Jenner. "Breaking the Cycle of Violence in Waji." In *Transforming Violence: Linking Local and Global Peacemaking*, edited by Robert Herr and Judy Zimmerman Herr. Scottdale, PA: Herald Press, 1998.

Jameson, Fredric, and Masao Miyoshi, eds. *The Cultures of Globalization*. Post-Contemporary Interventions. Durham, NC: Duke University Press, 1998.

John Paul II, Pope. *Centesimus Annus* [On the Hundredth Anniversary of *Rerum Novarum*]. Encyclical letter, 1991. Available December 12, 2006. www.vatican .va/holy_father/john_paul_ii/encyclicals/documents/hf_jp-ii_enc_ 01051991_centesimus-annus_en.html.

————. *Evangelium vitae* [The gospel of life]. Encyclical letter, 1995.

————. "The International Situation Today." Address to the diplomatic corps accredited to the Vatican. *Origins* 32, no. 33 (January 30, 2003): 543–45.

————. "*Pacem in Terris*: A Permanent Commitment." World Day of Peace message, January 1, 2003. *Origins* 32, no. 29 (January 2, 2003): 484–87; *America* 188, no. 4 (February 10, 2003).

————. *Sollicitudo Rei Socialis* [On Social Concern]. Encyclical letter, 1987.

————. "There is Still Room for Peace." Address before midday angelus. *L'Osservatore Romano*, March 17–18, 2003, 1, 12.

Johnson, James Turner. "The Broken Tradition." *National Interest* 45 (Fall 1996): 27–36.

————. "Just War Theory: What's the Use." *Worldview* 19, no. 7–8 (1976): 41–47.

————. *Morality & Contemporary Warfare*. New Haven: Yale University Press, 1999.

Johnstone, Gerry. *Restorative Justice: Ideas, Values, Debates*. Cullompton: Willan Pub., 2002.

Kappeler, Victor E., Mark. Blumberg, and Gary W. Potter. *The Mythology of Crime and Criminal Justice*. Prospect Heights, IL: Waveland Press, 1993.

Kauffman, Ivan J., ed. *Just Policing: Mennonite-Catholic Theological Colloquium 2002*. Bridgefolk Series, no. 2. Kitchener, Ontario: Pandora Press, 2004.

Keck, Margaret E., and Kathryn Sikkink. *Activists Beyond Borders: Advocacy Networks in International Politics*. Ithaca, NY: Cornell University Press, 1998.

Keohane, Robert O. *Neorealism and Its Critics*. New York: Columbia University Press, 1986.

Kleinig, John. *The Ethics of Policing*. Cambridge Studies in Philosophy and Public Policy. Cambridge New York: Cambridge University Press, 1996.

————, and Yurong Zhang, eds. *Professional Law Enforcement Codes; a Documentary Collection*. Westport, CT: Greenwood Press, 1993.

Koppell, Carla. *Preventing the Next Wave of Conflict: Understanding Non-Traditional Threats to Global Security*. With Anita Sharma. Washington, DC: Woodrow Wilson International Center for Scholars, 2003.

Koslowski, Rey, and Friedrich V. Kratochwil. "Understanding Change in International Politics: The Soviet Empire's Demise and the International System." *International Organization* 48, no. 2 (Spring 1994): 215–48.

Krasner, Stephen D., ed. *Problematic Sovereignty: Contested Rules and Political Possibilities*. New York: Columbia University Press, 2001.

———. *Sovereignty: Organized Hypocrisy*. Princeton, NJ: Princeton University Press, 1999.

Kurki, Leena. "Restorative and Community Justice in the United States." In *Crime and Justice: A Review of Research*, Vol. 27, 235–303. Chicago: University of Chicago Press, 2000.

Lake, David A. "The New Sovereignty in International Relations." *International Studies Review* 5, no. 3 (Fall 2003): 303–23.

Lakoff, George. "Metaphor and War, Again." *AlterNet*, 18 March 2003. Http://www.alternet.org/story/15414/.

———. "Metaphor and War: The Metaphor System Used to Justify War in the Gulf." *Viet Nam Generation Journal* 3, no. 3 (November 1991). Http://www3.iath.virginia.edu/sixties/HTML_docs/Texts/Scholarly/Lakoff_Gulf_Metaphor_1.html.

———. "Metaphors of Terror." In *The Days After: Essays Written in the Aftermath of September 11, 2001*. Online collection. Chicago: University of Chicago Press, 2001. Http://www.press.uchicago.edu/News/daysafter.html.

———, and Mark Johnson. *Metaphors We Live By*. Rev. ed. Chicago: University of Chicago Press, 2003.

Lane, Roger. *Policing the City: Boston, 1822–1885*. Cambridge: Harvard University Press, 1967.

Laqueur, Walter. *The New Terrorism: Fanaticism and the Arms of Mass Destruction*. New York: Oxford University Press, 1999.

Lebow, Richard Ned, and Thomas Risse-Kappen, eds. *International Relations: Theory and the End of the Cold War*. New York: Columbia University Press, 1995.

Leckey, Dolores R., ed. *Just War, Lasting Peace: What Christian Traditions Can Teach Us*. Forthcoming. Maryknoll, NY: Orbis Press, 2006.

Lederach, John Paul. *Building Peace: Sustainable Reconciliation in Divided Societies*. Washington, DC: United States Institute of Peace Press, 1997.

———. "The Challenge of Terrorism: A Traveling Essay," 2001. Http://www.mediate.com/articles/terror911.cfm.

———. *The Moral Imagination: The Art and Soul of Building Peace*. New York: Oxford University Press, 2005.

———. "Quo Vadis? Reframing Terror from the Perspective of Conflict Resolution." Town Hall Meeting. University of California, Irvine, 2001. Http://www.nd.edu/%7Ekrocinst/sept11/ledquo.html.

Lennon, Alexander T., ed. *The Battle for Hearts and Minds: Using Soft Power to Undermine Terrorist Networks*. A Washington Quarterly Reader. Cambridge, MA: MIT Press, 2003.

Littell, Franklin Hamlin. *The Origins of Sectarian Protestantism: A Study of the Anabaptist View of the Church*. New York: Macmillan, 1964.

Long, Edward Le Roy. *Facing Terrorism: Responding as Christians*. Louisville: Westminster John Knox Press, 2004.

Lopez, George. "After September 11: How Ethics Can Help." *America* 185, no. 10 (October 8, 2001): 20–24.

Luther, Martin. "Whether Soldiers, Too, Can be Saved." 1526. Translated by Charles M. Jacobs, and Robert C. Schultz in *The Christian in Society III*. Vol. 46 of *Luther's Works*, edited by Robert C. Schultz, Helmut T. Lehmann, gen. ed., 87–137. Philadelphia: Fortress Press, 1967.

Machel, Graça. *The Impact of War on Children*. A review of progress since the 1996 United Nations Report on the impact of armed conflict on children. New York: Palgrave, 2001.

MacIntyre, Alasdair. *After Virtue: A Study in Moral Theory*. 2nd ed. Notre Dame, IN: University of Notre Dame Press, 1984.

———. "The Privatization of Good: An Inaugural Lecture." *The Review of Politics* 32 (1990): 344–61.

———. *Three Rival Versions of Moral Enquiry: Encyclopedia, Genealogy, and Tradition*. The Gifford Lectures 1988. Notre Dame, IN: University of Notre Dame Press, 1990.

———. *Whose Justice? Which Rationality?* Notre Dame, IN: University of Notre Dame Press, 1988.

MacShane, Denis. "A Day to be Proud." *The Tablet* 258 (May 1, 2004): 2.

Maguire, Brendan, and Polly F. Radosh, eds. *The Past, Present, and the Future of American Criminal Justice*. Dix Hills, NY: General Hall, 1996.

Malloy, Edward A. *The Ethics of Law Enforcement and Criminal Punishment*. Washington, DC: University Press of America, 1982.

Mani, Rama. *Beyond Retribution: Seeking Justice in the Shadows of War*. Cambridge, UK: Blackwell Publishers Inc., 2002.

Markus, R. A. "Saint Augustine's Views on the 'Just War.'" In *The Church and War*, Vol. 20, edited by W. J. Sheils. Studies in Church History, 1–13. Oxford, Oxfordshire: Published for the Ecclesiastical History Society by Basil Blackwell, 1983.

Marsh, Charles. "Wayward Christian Soldiers." *New York Times*, January 20, 2006.

Marshall, Christopher D. *Beyond Retribution: A New Testament Vision for Justice, Crime, and Punishment*. Grand Rapids, MI: Wm. B. Eerdmans Pub., 2001.

Martin, Archbishop Diarmuid. "Theological and Moral Perspectives on Today's Challenge of Peace." *Origins* 33, no. 26 (December 4, 2003): 448.

Martineau, James. "The 'Police Analogy.'" Excerpt from *National Duties and Other Sermons and Addresses*, 1903 in *War and the Christian Conscience: From Augustine to Martin Luther King, Jr.*, compiled by Albert Marrin, 119–24. Chicago: Henry Regnery Company, 1971.

McCold, Paul. "Restorative Justice and the Role of the Community." In *Restorative Justice: International Perspectives*, edited by Burt Galaway and Joe Hudson, 85–101. Monsey, NY: Criminal Justice Press, 1996.

McLaughlin, Vance. *Police and the Use of Force: The Savannah Study*. With a foreword by Richard R.E. Kania. Westport, CT: Praeger, 1992.

Mennonite World Conference, and Pontifical Council for Promoting Church Unity. "Called Together to be Peacemakers: Report of the International Dialogue Between the Catholic Church and Mennonite World Conference, 1998–2003." *Information Service* 2003-II/III, no. 113 (2004): 111–48.

Miller, Marlin, and Barbara Nelson Gingrich, eds. *The Church's Peace Witness.* Grand Rapids, MI: Wm. B. Eerdmans, 1994.

Miller, Richard B. "Aquinas and the Presumption Against Killing and War." *Journal of Religion* 82, no. 2 (April 2002): 173–204.

Mittelman, James H. *The Globalization Syndrome: Transformation and Resistance.* Princeton, NJ: Princeton University Press, 2000.

Monkkonen, Eric H. *Police in Urban America, 1860–1920.* Interdisciplinary Perspectives on Modern History. Cambridge [Eng.]: Cambridge University Press, 1981.

Moore, Mark H., and George L. Kelling. "'To Serve and Protect': Learning from Police History." *The Public Interest* 70 (Winter 1983): 49–65.

Moran, Gabriel. "Outlawing War: Reforming the Language of War is the First Step Toward Ending It." *National Catholic Reporter* 40, no. 3 (November 7, 2003): 14–15.

Morgenthau, Hans Joachim. *Politics Among Nations: The Struggle for Power and Peace.* Revised by Kenneth W. Thompson. New York: McGraw-Hill, 1993.

Mueller, John E. *War, Presidents, and Public Opinion.* New York: Wiley, 1973.

Murray, John Courtney. *We Hold These Truths: Catholic Reflections on the American Proposition.* New York: Sheed and Ward, 1960.

Musto, Ronald G. *The Catholic Peace Tradition.* Maryknoll, NY: Orbis Books, 1986.

Niebuhr, H. Richard. *Christ and Culture.* Harper Torchbooks/Cloister Library. New York: Harper and Row, 1956.

Niebuhr, Reinhold. *The Essential Reinhold Niebuhr: Selected Essays and Addresses.* Edited by Robert McAfee Brown. New Haven: Yale University Press, 1986.

———. *Human Nature.* Vol. 1 of *The Nature and Destiny of Man.* 1941. The Scribner Lyceum Editions Library. New York: Scribner's, 1964.

———. "The Limits of Military Power." *New Leader* (May 30, 1955): 16ff.

———. *Moral Man and Immoral Society.* Reprint ed. The Scribner Lyceum Editions Library. New York: Scribner's, 1960.

———. *Reinhold Niebuhr: Theologian of Public Life.* Edited by Larry L. Rasmussen. Minneapolis: Fortress Press, 1991.

———. "Why the Christian Church is not Pacifist." In *Christianity and Power Politics*, 1–32. New York: Charles Scibner's Sons, 1940.

Nussbaum, Martha Craven. "Human Capabilities, Female Human Beings." In *Women, Culture, and Development: A Study of Human Capabilities*, edited by Martha Craven Nussbaum and Jonathan Glover. Studies in Development Economics, 61–104. Oxford: Clarendon Press, 1995.

O'Brien, David J., and Thomas A. Shannon, eds. *Catholic Social Thought: The Documentary Heritage.* Maryknoll, NY: Orbis Books, 1992.

Office of the Coordinator for Reconstruction and Stabilization (S/CRS), U.S. Department of State, and US Joint Forces Command Joint Warfighting Center (JWFC). *US Government Draft Planning Framework for Reconstruction, Stabilization, and Conflict Transformation.* United States Joint Forces Command J7 Pamphlet, Version 1.0. Washington, DC: US Department of State, 2005. Http://www.dtic.mil/doctrine/training/crs_pam051205.pdf.

Oye, Kenneth A., ed. *Cooperation Under Anarchy*. Princeton, NJ: Princeton University Press, 1986.

Panitch, Leo. "Rethinking the Role of the State." In *Globalization: Critical Reflections*, edited by James H. Mittelman. International Political Economy Yearbook, vol. 9, 83–113. Boulder, CO: Lynne Rienner Publishers, 1996.

Pape, Robert. "The Strategic Logic of Suicide Terrorism." *American Political Science Review* 97, no. 3 (August 2003).

Peak, Kenneth J., and Ronald W. Glensor. *Community Policing and Problem Solving: Strategies and Practices*. Englewood Cliffs, NJ: Prentice Hall, 1996.

Petrow, Stefan. *Policing Morals the Metropolitan Police and the Home Office, 1870–1914*. Oxford: Clarendon Press, 1994.

Pollock, Joycelyn M. *Ethics in Crime and Justice: Dilemmas and Decisions*. Contemporary Issues in Crime and Justice Series. Pacific Grove, CA: Brooks/Cole Pub. Co., 1989.

Pontifical Council for Justice and Peace. *Compendium of the Social Doctrine of the Church*. USCCB Publishing no. 5–692. Cittá del Vaticano; Washington, DC: Libreria Editrice Vaticana; [distributed by the] United States Conference of Catholic Bishops, 2004.

Potter, Ralph B. *War and Moral Discourse*. Richmond: John Knox Press, 1969.

Pranis, Kay. "Peacemaking Circles." *Corrections Today* 59, no. 7 (December 1997): 72–75.

———. "Restorative Justice, Social Justice, and the Empowerment of Marginalized Populations." In *Restorative Community Justice: Repairing Harm and Transforming Communities*, edited by S. Gordon Bazemore and Mara Schiff, 287–306. Cincinnati, OH: Anderson Pub., 2001.

Priest, Dana. *The Mission: Waging War and Keeping Peace with America's Military*. New York: W.W. Norton, 2004.

Radu, Michael. "The Rise and Fall of the PKK." *Orbis* 45, no. 1 (Winter 2001).

———. "Terrorism After the Cold War: Trends and Challenges." *Orbis* 46, no. 2 (Spring 2002).

Ramsey, Paul. *War and the Christian Conscience: How Shall Modern War be Conducted Justly?* Published for the Lilly Endowment Research Program in Christianity and Politics. Durham, NC: Duke University Press, 1961.

Reith, Charles. *A New Study of Police History*. Edinburgh: Oliver and Boyd, 1956.

———. *Police Principles and the Problem of War*. London: Oxford University Press, 1940.

Rittberger, Volker, ed. *Regime Theory and International Relations*. With Peter Mayer. Oxford: Clarendon Press, 1993.

Romero, Oscar A. "The Political Dimension of the Faith from the Perspective of the Option for the Poor." Louvain Address, 2 February 1980 in *Voice of the Voiceless: The Four Pastoral Letters and Other Statements*, translated by Michael J. Walsh, 177–87. Maryknoll, NY: Orbis Books, 1985.

Rood, Steven. *Forging Sustainable Peace in Mindanao: The Role of Civil Society*. Policy Studies, no. 17. Washington, DC: East-West Center Washington, 2005.

Ross, Rupert. *Return to the Teachings: Exploring Aboriginal Justice*. Toronto: Penguin Books, 1996.

Ruggie, John Gerard. "Territoriality and Beyond: Problematizing Modernity in International Relations." *International Organization* 47, no. 1 (Winter 1993): 139–74.

Russell, Frederick H. *The Just War in the Middle Ages*. Cambridge Studies in Medieval Life and Thought, 3d Ser., Vol. 8. Cambridge: Cambridge University Press, 1975.

Russett, Bruce M., and John R. Oneal. *Triangulating Peace: Democracy, Interdependence, and International Organizations*. New York: Norton, 2000.

Sampson, Cynthia, and John Paul Lederach, eds. *From the Ground up: Mennonite Contributions to International Peacebuilding*. Oxford New York: Oxford University Press, 2000.

Sandlin, Lee. "Are we Finally Losing the War? / Losing the War." Two-part series. *Chicago Reader*, March 1997.

Sassen, Saskia. *Cities in a World Economy*. Sociology for a New Century. Thousand Oaks, CA: Pine Forge Press, 2000.

Sasser, Charles W. *Shoot to Kill: Cops Who Have Used Deadly Force*. New York, NY: Pocket Books, 1994.

Save the Children. *Mothers & Children in War & Conflict*. State of the World's Mothers 2002. Westport, CT: Save the Children USA, 2002.

———. *Protecting Children in Emergencies: Escalating Threats to Children Must be Addressed*. Policy Brief, vol. 1, no. 1. Westport, CT: Save the Children USA, 2005.

Scharf, Peter, and Arnold Binder. *The Badge and the Bullet: Police Use of Deadly Force*. New York: Praeger, 1983.

Scheingold, Stuart A. *The Politics of Law and Order: Street Crime and Public Policy*. Longman Professional Studies in Law and Public Policy. New York: Longman, 1984.

Schell, Jonathan. "No More Unto the Breach." Two-part series. *Harper's* (March and April 2003): 33–46, 41–55.

———. *The Unconquerable World: Power, Nonviolence, and the Will of the People*. New York: Metropolitan Books, 2003.

Scheuerman, William. "Globalization." In *The Stanford Encyclopedia of Philosophy*. Fall 2002 ed., edited by Edward N. Zalta. Http://plato.stanford.edu/archives/fall2002/entries/globalization/.

Schlabach, Gerald W. "Deuteronomic or Constantinian: What is the Most Basic Problem for Christian Social Ethics?" In *The Wisdom of the Cross: Essays in Honor of John Howard Yoder*, edited by Stanley Hauerwas, Chris K. Huebner, Harry Huebner, and Mark Thiessen Nation, 449–71. Grand Rapids: Eerdmans, 1999.

———. "Just Policing and the Christian Call to Nonviolence." In *At Peace and Unafraid: Public Order, Security and the Wisdom of the Cross*, edited by Duane K. Friesen and Gerald W. Schlabach, 405–22. Scottdale, PA: Herald Press, 2005.

———. "Just Policing: How War Could Cease to be a Church-Dividing Issue." In *Just Policing: Mennonite-Catholic Theological Colloquium 2002*, edited by Ivan J. Kauffman. Bridgefolk Series, no. 2, 19–75. Kitchener, Ontario: Pandora Press, 2004.

———. "Just Policing: How War Could Cease to be a Church-Dividing Issue." Forthcoming. *Journal of Ecumenical Studies* (2006).

———. "Just Policing, Not War." *America* 189, no. 1 (July 7–14, 2003): 19–21.

Scholte, Jan Aart. *Globalization: A Critical Introduction*. Basingstoke: Palgrave, 2000.

Schroeder, Paul W. "Work with Emerging Cooperative Forces Within the International System." In *Just Peacemaking: Ten Practices for Abolishing War*, edited by Glen Stassen, 133–46. Pilgrim Press, 1998.

Sen, Amartya Kumar. *Development as Freedom*. New York: Anchor Books, 2000.

Sewell, James D., ed. *Controversial Issues in Policing*. Controversial Issues Series. Boston: Allyn and Bacon, 1999.

Shapiro, Michael J., and Hayward R. Alker, eds. *Challenging Boundaries: Global Flows, Territorial Identities*. Borderlines, vol. 2. Minneapolis, MN: University of Minnesota Press, 1996.

Sharp, Gene. *Making Europe Unconquerable: The Potential of Civilian-Based Deterrence and Defence*. Cambridge, MA: Ballinger Pub. Co., 1985.

———. *The Politics of Nonviolent Action*. 3 vols. Edited by Marina Finkelstein. Boston: Extending Horizons, 1973.

———. *Social Power and Political Freedom*. Extending Horizons Books. Boston: P. Sargent Publishers, 1980.

Sharp, Gene, and Bruce Jenkins. *Civilian-Based Defense: A Post-Military Weapons System*. Princeton, NJ: Princeton University Press, 1990.

Sherry, Michael S. *In the Shadow of War: The United States Since the 1930's*. New Haven: Yale University Press, 1995.

Shiner, Phil. "Viewpoint: Why Peace Needs Law." *The Tablet* 258 (January 24, 2004): 2.

Sigal, Leon V. *Disarming Strangers: Nuclear Diplomacy with North Korea*. Princeton Studies in International History and Politics. Princeton: Princeton University Press, 1998.

Skolnick, Jerome H., and James J. Fyfe. *Above the Law: Police and the Excessive Use of Force*. New York: Free Press, 1993.

Smith, Michael Joseph. "Strengthen the United Nations and International Efforts for Cooperation and Human Rights." In *Just Peacemaking: Ten Practices for Abolishing War*, edited by Glen Stassen, 146–55. Pilgrim Press, 1998.

Smith, Phillip Thurmond. *Policing Victorian London: Political Policing, Public Order, and the London Metropolitan Police*. Contributions in Criminology and Penology, no. 7. Westport, CT: Greenwood Press, 1985.

Smith, Rogers. "Civil Liberties in the Brave New World of Antiterrorism." *Radical History Review* 93 (Fall 2005): 170–85.

Smock, David, ed. *Catholic Contributions to International Peace*. Special Report, no. 69. Washington DC: United States Institute for Peace, 2001. Http://www.usip.org/pubs/specialreports/sr69.pdf.

Stassen, Glen, ed. *Just Peacemaking: Ten Practices for Abolishing War*. Cleveland: Pilgrim Press, 1998.

———. *Just Peacemaking: Transforming Initiatives for Justice and Peace*. Louisville, KY: Westminster/John Knox Press, 1992.

———. "Turning Attention to Just Peacemaking Initiatives That Prevent Terrorism." *The Council of Societies for the Study of Religion Bulletin* 31, no. 3 (September 2002): 59–65.

————. "The Unity, Realism, and Obligatoriness of Just Peacemaking Theory." *Journal of the Society of Christian Ethics* 23, no. 1 (2003): 171–94.

Stassen, Glen H., Diane M. Yeager, John Howard Yoder, and H Niebuhr, Richard. *Authentic Transformation: A New Vision of Christ and Culture*. Nashville: Abingdon Press, 1996.

Steinfels, Peter, Robert E. White, Bruce Martin Russett, and Jean Porter. "What Kind of War?" *Commonweal* 128, no. 16 (September 28, 2001): 8–10.

Stewart, Frances. "Root Causes of Violent Conflicts in Developing Countries." *British Medical Journal* 324 (February 9, 2002): 342–45.

Stuart, Barry. "Circle Sentencing: Turning Swords Into Ploughshares." In *Restorative Justice: International Perspectives*, edited by Burt Galaway and Joe Hudson, 193–206. Monsey, NY: Criminal Justice Press, 1996.

————. "Guiding Principles for Peacemaking Circles." In *Restorative Community Justice: Repairing Harm and Transforming Communities*, edited by S. Gordon Bazemore and Mara Schiff, 219–41. Cincinnati, OH: Anderson Pub., 2001.

Thiel, John E. *Senses of Tradition: Continuity and Development in Catholic Faith*. Oxford: Oxford University Press, 2000.

Thistlethwaite, Susan Brooks. "New Wars, Old Wineskins." In *Strike Terror no More: Theology, Ethics, and the New War*, edited by Jon L. Berquist. St. Louis, MO: Chalice Press, 2002.

Toews, Paul. *Mennonites in American Society, 1930–1970: Modernity and the Persistence of Religious Community*. The Mennonite Experience in America, vol. 4. Scottdale, PA: Herald Press, 1996.

Tomlinson, John. *Cultural Imperialism: A Critical Introduction*. London: Pinter Publishers, 1991.

Troeltsch, Ernst. *The Social Teaching of the Christian Churches*. Translated by Olive Wyon, with an introduction by Richard Niebuhr. 1981. New York: Macmillan, 1931.

Trojanowicz, Robert C., and Bonnie Bucqueroux. *Community Policing: A Contemporary Perspective*. 3rd ed. Cincinnati, Ohio: Anderson Pub. Co., 2002.

————. *Community Policing: How to Get Started*. Cincinnati, OH: Anderson Pub. Co., 1994.

Tutu, Desmond. *No Future Without Forgiveness*. New York: Doubleday, 1999.

The United Methodist Council of Bishops. *In Defense of Creation: The Nuclear Crisis and a Just Peace*. Foundation Document. Nashville: Graded Press, 1986.

United Nations Commission on the Truth. *From Madness to Hope: The 12-Year War in El Salvador: Report of the Commission on the Truth for El Salvador*. [New York]: United Nations, Security Council, 1993.

United Nations Development Programme. *Millennium Development Goals: A Compact Among Nations to End Human Poverty*. Human Development Report 2003. New York: UNDP, 2003.

United States Conference of Catholic Bishops (USCCB). *The Challenge of Peace: God's Promise and Our Response*. Washington DC: United States Catholic Conference, 1983.

————. *The Harvest of Justice is Sown in Peace*. Washington DC: United States Catholic Conference, 1993. Available December 12, 2006. www.usccb.org/sdwp/harvest.htm.

————. "Living with Faith and Hope After September 11." Pastoral message, November 14, 2001. *Origins* 31, no. 25 (November 29, 2001): 413–20.

————. "Statement on Iraq." *Origins* 32, no. 24 (November 21, 2002): 406–8.

Vatican Council, Second. *Gaudium et spes*. [Pastoral constitution on the Church in the modern world], 1965. In *The Basic Sixteen Documents Vatican Council II Constitutions Decrees Declarations*. A Completely Revised Translation in Inclusive Language. Edited by Austin Flannery, O.P. Northport, NY: Costello Publishing Company, 1996.

————. *Lumen gentium*. [Dogmatic constitution on the Church], 1964. In *The Basic Sixteen Documents Vatican Council II Constitutions Decrees Declarations*. A Completely Revised Translation in Inclusive Language. Edited by Austin Flannery, O.P. Northport, NY: Costello Publishing Company, 1996.

Wadman, Robert C. *Community Wellness: A New Theory of Policing*. A PERF Discussion Paper. Washington, DC: Police Executive Research Forum, 1990.

Walker, R.B.J. "After the Future: Enclosures, Connections, Politics." In *Reframing the International: Law, Culture, Politics*, eds. Richard A. Falk, Lester Edwin J. Ruiz, and R.B.J. Walker, 3–25. New York: Routledge, 2002.

Walker, Samuel. *Popular Justice: A History of American Criminal Justice*. New York: Oxford University Press, 1980.

Wallis, Jim. *God's Politics: Why the Right Gets It Wrong and the Left Doesn't Get It*. [San Francisco]: HarperSanFrancisco, 2005.

————. "Hard Questions for Peacemakers." *Sojourners*, January–February 2002, 29–33.

————. "An Interview with John Paul Lederach." *Sojo.Net: The Online Voice of Sojourners Magazine*, January–February 2002. Http://www.sojo.net/index.cfm?action=news. display_archives&mode=current_opinion&article=CO_010702l.

————. "Interview with Stanley Hauerwas." *Sojo.Net: The Online Voice of Sojourners Magazine*, January–February 2002. Http://sojo.net/index.cfm?action=news. display_archives&mode=current_opinion&article=CO_010702h.

Waltz, Kenneth Neal. *Man, the State, and War: A Theoretical Analysis*. New York: Columbia University Press, 1959.

————. *Theory of International Politics*. Addison-Wesley Series in Political Science. Reading, MA: Addison-Wesley Pub. Co., 1979.

Walzer, Michael. *Just and Unjust Wars: A Moral Argument with Historical Illustrations*. New York: Basic, 1977.

Wapner, Paul Kevin, and Lester Edwin J. Ruiz, eds. *Principled World: Politics the Challenge of Normative International Relations*. Lanham, MD: Rowman & Littlefield, 2000.

"War Leaders Will be 'Called to Account,' Says Dr. Williams." *The Tablet* (October 18, 2003): 30–31.

Weigel, George. "Moral Clarity in a Time of War." *First Things* 128 (January 2003): 20–27.

————. *Tranquillitas Ordinis: The Present Failure and Future Promise of American Catholic Thought on War and Peace*. Oxford: Oxford University Press, 1987.

Wendt, Alexander. *Social Theory of International Politics*. Cambridge Studies in International Relations, vol. 67. Cambridge, UK: Cambridge University Press, 1999.

West, Maya Harris, principle author. *Community-Based Policing: A Force for Change.* A Report by PolicyLink in partnership with the Advancement Project. Oakland, CA: PolicyLink, 2001. Http://www.policylink.org/Research/Police/.

Wheelis, Mark, Malcolm Dando, and Catherine Auer. "Back to Bioweapons?" *Bulletin of the Atomic Scientists* 59, no. 1 (January–February 2003): 40–47.

Williams, Rowan, and George Weigel. "War and Statecraft: An Exchange." *First Things* (March 2004): 14–21.

Winfree, L. Thomas, Jr. "Peacemaking and Community Harmony: Lessons (and Admonitions) from the Navajo Peacemaking Courts." In *Restorative Justice: Theoretical Foundations*, edited by Elmar G. M. Weitekamp and Hans-Jürgen Kerner, 285–307. Cullompton: Willan Publishing, 2002.

Winright, Tobias. "The Challenge of Policing: An Analysis in Christian Social Ethics." Ph.D. dissertation. University of Notre Dame, 2002.

———. "From Police Officers to Peace Officers." In *The Wisdom of the Cross: Essays in Honor of John Howard Yoder*, edited by Stanley Hauerwas, et al., 84–114. Grand Rapids, MI: Wm. B. Eerdmans Publishing Co., 1999.

———. "The Perpetrator as Person: Theological Reflections on the Just War Tradition and the Use of Force by Police." *Criminal Justice Ethics* 14, no. 2 (Summer/Fall 1995): 37–56.

———. "Two Rival Versions of Just War Theory and the Presumption Against Harm in Policing." *Annual of the Society of Christian Ethics* 18 (1998): 221–39.

Woodman, Peter. "Stay Away from Istanbul, Britons Told." *The Press Association Limited*, 20 November 2003.

World Council of Churches. *Vulnerable Populations at Risk: Statement on the Responsibility to Protect.* Approved by the 9th assembly, 14–23 February 2006. document no. PIC 02–2. Porto Alegre, Brazil.

Yoder, John Howard, ed. and trans. *The Schleitheim Confession.* With an introduction by Leonard Gross. Scottdale, PA: Herald Press, 1973.

———. "The Biblical Mandate for Evangelical Social Action." In *For the Nations: Essays Public and Evangelical*, 180–98. Grand Rapids, MI: Wm. B. Eerdmans, 1997.

———. "Binding and Loosing." In *The Royal Priesthood: Essays Ecclesiological and Ecumenical*, edited by Michael G. Cartwright, 323–58. Grand Rapids, MI: Wm. B. Eerdmans, 1994.

———. *Christian Attitudes to War, Peace, and Revolution a Companion to Bainton.* Elkhart, IN: Dist. by Co-op Bookstore, 1983.

———. *The Christian Witness to the State.* Institute of Mennonite Studies Series, no. 3. Newton, KS: Faith and Life Press, 1964.

———. *For the Nations: Essays Public and Evangelical.* Grand Rapids, MI: Wm. B. Eerdmans Publishing Co., 1997.

———. "How H. Richard Niebuhr Reasoned: A Critique of *Christ and Culture.*" In *Authentic Transformation: A New Vision of Christ and Culture*, edited by Glen H. Stassen, Diane M. Yeager, and John Howard Yoder, 31–89. Nashville: Abingdon Press, 1996.

———. "The Kingdom as Social Ethic." In *The Priestly Kingdom: Social Ethics as Gospel*, 80–101. Notre Dame, IN: University of Notre Dame Press, 1984.

———. *The Original Revolution: Essays on Christian Pacifism.* Christian Peace Shelf. Scottdale, PA: Herald Press, 1971.

———. "Peace Without Eschatology?" In *The Royal Priesthood: Essays Ecclesiological and Ecumenical,* edited by Michael G. Cartwright, 143–67. Grand Rapids, MI: Wm. B. Eerdmans, 1994.

———. *The Politics of Jesus.* 2nd ed. 1972. Grand Rapids, MI: Wm. B. Eerdmans, 1994.

———. *The Priestly Kingdom: Social Ethics as Gospel.* Notre Dame, IN: University of Notre Dame Press, 1984.

———. *The Royal Priesthood: Essays Ecclesiological and Ecumenical.* Edited with an introduction by Michael G. Cartwright. With a foreword by Richard J. Mouw. Grand Rapids, MI: Wm. B. Eerdmans, 1994.

———. "Surrender: A Moral Imperative." *The Review of Politics* 48 (Fall 1986): 576–95.

———. *When War is Unjust: Being Honest in Just-War Thinking.* Rev. ed. With a foreword by Charles P. Lutz, with an afterword by Drew Christiansen. Maryknoll, NY: Orbis Books, 1996.

Yoder, Perry B. *Shalom: The Bible's Word for Salvation, Justice, and Peace.* Newton, KS: Faith and Life Press, 1987.

Zakaria, Fareed. "The Arrogant Empire." *Newsweek* (March 24, 2003): 19–33.

———. "Suicide Bombers Can be Stopped." *Newsweek* (August 25, 2003): 57.

Zehr, Howard. *Changing Lenses: A New Focus for Crime and Justice.* Christian Peace Shelf Selection. Scottdale, PA: Herald Press, 1990.

———. "Journey to Belonging." In *Restorative Justice: Theoretical Foundations,* edited by Elmar G. M. Weitekamp and Hans-Jürgen Kerner, 21–31. Cullompton: Willan Publishing, 2002.

Zehr, Howard. *The Little Book of Restorative Justice.* Intercourse, PA: Good Books, 2002.

Biographical Sketch
of Contributors

Gerald W. Schlabach is Associate Professor of Theology at the University of St. Thomas, in St. Paul, Minnesota, where he teaches courses in social ethics and Christian morality. He has written books and journal articles on topics ranging widely from peace, social justice, and nonviolence in Latin America, to the thought of St. Augustine, Benedictine spirituality, and the Eucharist. Schlabach serves on the MCC Peace Committee and is Executive Director of Bridgefolk, a grassroots movement of Mennonites and Catholics seeking to exchange the gifts of one another's traditions. With Duane K. Friesen he co-edited *At Peace and Unafraid: Public Order, Security and the Wisdom of the Cross* (Herald Press, 2005). Schlabach is a member of St. Peter Claver Catholic Church in St. Paul, and an associate member of Faith Mennonite Church in Minneapolis.

Drew Christiansen, S.J., is editor-in-chief of the national Jesuit weekly *America.* From 1991 to 1998, he headed the United States Conference of Catholic Bishops' Office of International Justice and Peace, and from 1998–2004 he continued to serve the USCCB as counselor for international with special responsibility for the Middle East. From 2000–2004, he was a consultant to the International Catholic-Mennonite Dialogue. He is co-author of *Forgiveness in Conflict Resolution* (USCCB, 2004).

Ivan J. Kauffman is an independent writer, whose work over the past forty-five years has included poetry, history, and journalism. In the 1980s he wrote a syndicated weekly column for the Catholic diocesan newspapers in the United States entitled "Making Peace." He is one of the founding members of Bridgefolk, the grassroots North American Mennonite Catholic dialogue. He was an advisor to Bishop Joseph Martino, the

Catholic co-chair of the International Mennonite Catholic Dialogue, from 1994–2002. Raised and educated as a Mennonite, he became a Catholic in 1968.

John Paul Lederach is Professor of International Peacebuilding at the Joan B. Kroc Institute for International Peace Studies, University of Notre Dame. Widely known for his pioneering work on conflict transformation, Lederach is involved in conciliation work in Colombia, the Philippines, Nepal, and Tajikistan, plus countries in East and West Africa. He is the author of *The Moral Imagination: The Art and Soul of Building Peace* (Oxford University Press, 2005) and *The Journey Toward Reconciliation* (Herald Press, 1999).

Reina Neufeldt has a Ph.D. in International Relations from the School of International Service, American University (Washington, DC). She currently works for Catholic Relief Services (CRS) as a Regional Technical Advisor for Peacebuilding in Southeast Asia, and is based in Manila, Philippines. Neufeldt previously worked as a Peacebuilding Technical Advisor at CRS' headquarters, and has co-directed the Catholic Relief Services' Summer Institute on Peacebuilding—a partnership venture with the Joan B. Kroc Institute for International Peace, University of Notre Dame.

Margaret R. Pfeil is an Assistant Professor of Moral Theology at the University of Notre Dame. Her articles have appeared in *Louvain Studies*, *Josephinum Journal of Theology*, *The Journal for Peace & Justice Studies*, and the *Mennonite Quarterly Review*. She is currently finishing a book, *Social Sin: Social Reconciliation?*, and with Margaret Eletta Guider, O.S.F. she is co-editing a volume, *White Privilege: Implications for the Church, the Catholic University, and Theology*. She is a founder and resident of St. Peter Claver Catholic Worker House in South Bend.

Glen H. Stassen is Lewis B. Smedes Professor of Christian Ethics at Fuller Theological Seminary in Pasadena, California. His research, writing, and teaching interests are in social justice, peacemaking, recovering the Sermon on the Mount for Christian ethics, narrative ethics that take biblical justice seriously, and churches that practice what they preach. He is editor of *Just Peacemaking: Ten Practices for Abolishing War* (Pilgrim Press, 1998, 2004).

Tobias Winright is a Roman Catholic moral theologian and an Assistant Professor in the Department of Theological Studies at Saint Louis

University. With several years of experience in law enforcement, in both corrections and policing, he has written widely on ethics and police use of force, just war theory, capital punishment, and nonviolence for *Sojourners Magazine, The Cresset, Journal of the Society of Christian Ethics, National Catholic Reporter, Criminal Justice Ethics, FBI Law Enforcement Bulletin,* and others.

Index